WILLIAMS-SONOMA

Holiday Favorites

The Best of the Williams-Sonoma Kitchen Library

Holiday Favorites

GENERAL EDITOR
CHUCK WILLIAMS

RECIPE PHOTOGRAPHY
ALLAN ROSENBERG

Oxmoor House®

Contents

Introduction

Holidays are the busiest times of the year, and their celebratory meals, whether a big Thanksgiving Day feast, a small Christmas Day lunch, or an outdoor Fourth-of-July barbecue, are always much-anticipated events. Many hosts, busy year-round with work and family, worry that they won't be able to prepare a memorable meal during these hectic days.

In the next several pages, you will find everything you need to know to make your holiday meals easy and enjoyable for everyone. First, there is sound advice on planning every aspect of the the meal, from deciding on a menu and making the shopping list to decorating the dining room and picking out wines. Next, various holiday customs are explored, with an emphasis on dishes traditionally found on seasonal tables. Also included are sample menus and party-favor ideas to make every celebration extra special.

The recipe chapters are packed with holiday favorites, such as roast turkey for Thanksgiving, herring salad for Hanukkah, and hot-cross buns for Easter. A final chapter includes ideas for delicious gifts that you can make in your own kitchen for giving to friends and family as mementos of a holiday spent together. With this book in hand, you will be able to serve a holiday meal to remember for years to come.

HOLIDAY ENTERTAINING TIPS

The most enjoyable holiday gatherings are the result of careful planning. The successful host makes a dozen decisions—from the size of the budget to the length of the menu to the selection of the tableware—long before the first guest rings the doorbell.

Begin by determining the number of guests and then establishing a budget that keeps in mind both the celebratory nature of the occasion and the need to keep costs affordable. Next, create the menu. Most holidays have traditional dishes, which you will probably want to include. When selecting other recipes, consider both seasonal ingredients and your guests' tastes. Remember, too, to plan some foods that lend themselves to advance preparation, to lighten your workload on the day of the party. Be realistic about how much you can do; it is always better to serve a handful of truly exceptional dishes than a tableful of forgettable ones.

With the menu set, put together a master shopping list, including the beverages you will need. Indicate which items can be purchased in advance and which must be picked up at the last minute. At the same time, check to see that you have all of the necessary cooking equipment and serving plates, bowls, platters, and utensils. Write them down, so that nothing will be forgotten in the flurry of final preparations.

Select the tableware, linens, glassware, and silverware, making them appropriate both to the menu and to the spirit of the celebration. Count the pieces to make sure you have enough on hand for the number of guests who will be attending. If there are gaps, borrow or purchase what you need to fill them.

Survey the dining space, and decide on the best way to decorate it. Include a centerpiece for the table, candles for lighting and ambiance, and bouquets of flowers and/or swags of seasonal greenery for placing around the room. Prepare a list of all that you will need to carry off your decorating scheme. Check the list against the supplies that you already have.

Finally, when the day of the gathering arrives, don't worry if everything does not go according to plan. Little flaws that trouble the host will almost always go unnoticed by the guests.

HOLIDAY ENTERTAINING TRADITIONS

Every holiday has its customs, whether it's decorating a tree for Christmas, lighting the menorah during Hanukkah, or hiding painted eggs for the big hunt on Easter morning. Holidays also mean special meals, with family and friends eagerly looking forward to tables laden with familiar and traditional foods.

Thanksgiving dinner is one of most anticipated meals of the year. The Thanksgiving menu, which dates back to America's colonial harvest, is tradition bound. This much-loved late-autumn feast brings family and friends together in an expression of thanks for all the good things that have happened during the year. A plump roast turkey, stuffing, cranberry sauce, sweet potatoes, and at least two kinds of pie are the nearly inevitable accompaniments.

While the Christmas menu varies from household to household, some type of roast meat or poultry is the traditional main course. A crisp-skinned roast capon or a beautifully glazed baked ham graces many tables, but an English-inspired menu featuring roast prime rib of beef with Yorkshire pudding is popular, too.

The Hanukkah table is customarily laid with cold-weather favorites, such as braised brisket or roast chicken or goose. Only latkes, fried vegetable pancakes usually made from potatoes, appear on every Hanukkah menu. They symbolize the miracle of the oil, the central theme of the holiday.

Easter has a religious significance, but it is also a celebration of the start of spring. Roast lamb is at the heart of the traditional Easter meal, which is often served midday after the children have filled their Easter baskets. Seasonal vegetables—asparagus, English peas, artichokes, new potatoes—and a butter-and-egg-rich layer cake often round out the meal.

Indeed, virtually every holiday has some food traditions that are bound by many cultures, from the Champagne and oysters that begin the classic romantic Valentine's Day dinner for two to the barbecued ribs, corn on the cob, and blueberry pie that fuel a hungry crowd waiting to watch the fireworks on the Fourth of July.

SELECTING A GOOD WINE

Some hosts are intimidated at the thought of pairing wines with food for the holiday table. Convention calls for white wines with fish and shellfish and red wines with meats and poultry, but nowadays these rules are regularly broken. You can successfully pour a young Beaujolais with poultry or a rich, meaty shellfish, or a full-flavored Chardonnay with veal or pork.

Always think about what your guests may prefer, too. Some people drink only whites—or reds—so it is wise to have a seletion of both on hand. And do not forget your own preferences: for example, if you prefer Italian wines over Californian, try a red Brunello di Montalcino or a white Verdicchio. Also, carry a copy of your menu along with you to the wine store and ask the merchant for advice on what will best complement your dinner. As you shop, keep in mind that a good wine does not need to be the most expensive vintage on the shelf.

IDEAL PARTY FAVORS AND GIFTS

Handmade party favors are a much-appreciated addition to holiday gatherings. You can make simple place cards for your Christmas dinner by lashing together tiny bouquets of evergreen sprigs with lengths of florist's wire, covering the wires with red ribbons, and then gluing name cards onto the ribbons. Or simply decorate your mantel with a legion of two-inch pots of blooming narcissus, and then send each guest home with a pot to put on his or her own mantel.

Dozens of other wonderful yet simple gifts can be attractively packed up and presented to departing guests as souvenirs of the special occasion. You can piece together spice sachets for making hot spiced cider for Christmas, jars of cranberry chutney or spiced nuts for Thanksgiving, bottles of lemon-and-bay-infused olive oil for Hanukkah, or small canisters of amaretti, shortbread, or toffee for Easter. On the Fourth of July, present each arriving guest a red-white-and-blue paper fan to help keep them nice and cool in the heat of the day.

Holiday Menus

Here are six menus that illustrate the many combinations you can create using the recipes in this book. Some include traditional offerings, while others bring a new twist to the holiday table.

Valentine's Day

Carrot and Mint Soup

Filet Mignon with Wine Sauce

*Roasted New Potatoes
with Garlic and Thyme*

*Sauté of Julienned
Garden Vegetables*

Sweetheart Raspberry Tart

serves 4

New Year's Day

Smoked Salmon Toasts

*Garden Salad with Pears,
Pecans, and Gorgonzola*

*Bacon-Wrapped
Cornish Hens*

Scalloped Potatoes

Eggnog Tart

serves 8

Thanksgiving

*Butternut Squash Soup
with Marsala and Thyme*

*Cider-Glazed Turkey
with Cider-Shallot Gravy*

*Dried Fruit, Nut,
and Apple Stuffing*

Rum-Glazed Candied Yams

Broccoli with Sliced Almonds

Pumpkin-Orange Tart

serves 8

Hanukkah

Millie's Herring Salad

Sweet-and-Sour Brisket

Festive Challah

Potato Latkes with Applesauce

Dora Apter's Mandlebread

Dried Fruit Compote

serves 8

Holiday Buffet

*Smoked Salmon on Potatoes
with Dill Sauce*

Red, White, and Green Toasts

*Green Bean, Radicchio,
and Fennel Salad*

Holiday Ham Platter

*Wild Rice, Orange,
and Asparagus Salad*

Miniature Truffle Tartlets

serves 24

Christmas

*Pear, Walnut,
and Goat Cheese Salad*

Roast Leg of Lamb

*Mashed Potatoes
with Basil and Chives*

*Green Beans with Pearl Onions
and Tarragon Vinaigrette*

Onion-Herb Rolls

Pear Upside-Down Spice Cake

serves 8

Starters, Soups & Salads

Belgian Endive Spears with Caviar

This simple but elegant first course is both festive and light. For the freshest flavor and the most attractive presentation, fill the leaves just before serving. Replace the sour cream with Crème Fraîche (page 326) for added tanginess.

2 large heads Belgian endive (chicory/witloof)

½ cup (4 oz/125 g) sour cream

2 oz (60 g) caviar, salmon roe, or golden caviar, or a combination

2 tablespoons finely chopped fresh chives

Remove the outer leaves of the endives and discard or reserve them for another use. Separate from the heart the tenderest leaves that are large enough for filling. Discard the smallest leaves or reserve for another use. There should be 6–8 leaves from each endive that can be used for filling. Wrap the leaves in a clean, damp kitchen towel. Place in the refrigerator for up to 6 hours to chill and crisp.

Just before serving, spoon a dollop of sour cream onto the pointed end of each endive leaf. Using a 2-teaspoon measure, top the sour cream with the caviar. Sprinkle lightly with the chives, arrange on a platter, and serve immediately.

Serves 6

Smoked Salmon on Potatoes with Dill Sauce

The components for this elegant finger food can be prepared ahead of time.
Reheat about one-fourth of the potato slices at a time, then top them, arrange
them on a platter, and set out on the buffet. Refill the platter as needed.

In a small bowl, stir together the sour cream, minced dill, mustard, and brown sugar until well blended. Cover and refrigerate until well chilled.

Preheat the oven to 400°F (200°C).

In a large bowl, combine the potato slices, olive oil, and lemon zest. Season generously with salt and pepper. Using a rubber spatula or your hands, turn the potato slices to coat them evenly with the oil and seasonings. Arrange the slices in a single layer on large baking sheets. Bake, turning once, until golden brown on both sides and tender when pierced with the tip of a knife, about 15 minutes per side. (The potatoes can be prepared up to this point 4 hours in advance. Let cool completely, cover, and store at room temperature. Just before serving, reheat, uncovered, in a 375°F/190°C oven for 5 minutes.)

Place a dollop of the dill sauce atop each hot potato slice. Top each with a salmon piece and garnish with a dill sprig. Arrange on a warmed platter and serve at once.

Makes about 100 pieces; serves 24

2 cups (16 oz/500 g) sour cream

1 cup (1½ oz/45 g) minced fresh dill, plus tiny sprigs for garnish

¼ cup (2 oz/60 g) Dijon mustard

¼ cup (2 oz/60 g) firmly packed golden brown sugar

3 lb (1.5 kg) small red or white new potatoes, unpeeled and cut into slices ½ inch (12 mm) thick

6 tablespoons (3 fl oz/90 ml) olive oil

2 tablespoons finely grated lemon zest

Salt and freshly ground pepper

1 lb (500 g) thinly sliced smoked salmon, cut into 1-inch (2.5-cm) squares

Filo Pizza with Feta, Sun-Dried Tomatoes, and Olives

This pizza can be fully assembled a day in advance, stored in the refrigerator, and baked when needed. Filo dough can be purchased in the frozen section of most well-stocked markets.

20 sheets filo dough, each about 14 by 10 inches (35 by 25 cm), thawed in the refrigerator if frozen

2 tablespoons unsalted butter

3 tablespoons olive oil

1/2 lb (250 g) mozzarella cheese, shredded (about 2 cups)

1/4 lb (125 g) feta cheese, finely crumbled

1/2 cup (2 1/2 oz/75 g) oil-cured black olives, pitted and chopped

1/2 cup (2 1/2 oz/75 g) drained oil-packed sun-dried tomatoes, chopped

4 green (spring) onions, including tender green tops, thinly sliced

2 tablespoons chopped fresh mint

If necessary, trim the filo sheets to measure 14 by 10 inches (35 by 25 cm). Cover the filo with a damp kitchen towel to prevent it from drying out.

In a small saucepan over medium-low heat, melt the butter with the olive oil. Remove from the heat; set alongside the work surface.

Place about 3/4 cup (3 oz/90 g) of the mozzarella in a bowl. Add the feta, olives, sun-dried tomatoes, green onions, and mint and stir to mix well.

Position a rack in the upper third of the oven and preheat to 400°F (200°C). Using a pastry brush, lightly coat a 12-by-15-inch (30-by-38-cm) baking sheet with some of the butter-oil mixture. Place 1 filo sheet on the baking sheet and brush it lightly with the butter-oil mixture. Cover it with a second filo sheet, brush lightly with the butter-oil mixture, and sprinkle evenly with about 1/4 cup (1 oz/30 g) of the cheese mixture. Continue stacking in the same manner, brushing each filo sheet with the butter-oil mixture and sprinkling every other sheet with some of the filling, until all of the filo and filling have been used. Brush the top layer with the butter-oil mixture. Sprinkle the remaining 1 1/4 cups (5 oz/160 g) mozzarella cheese evenly over the top of the pizza.

Bake until the cheese melts and the filo is golden and crisp on the edges, about 25–35 minutes. Transfer to a cutting board and cut into 2-inch (5-cm) squares. Arrange on a platter and serve hot or warm.

Makes 35 pieces; serves 12

Smoked Salmon Toasts

These toasts are the perfect start to any holiday celebration. Serve them with a bottle of sparkling wine or Champagne. For an equally tasty variation, replace the tarragon with arugula (rocket).

Preheat the oven to 375°F (190°C).

In a small bowl, whisk together the olive oil and lime juice. Set aside.

Arrange the bread slices on a baking sheet. Bake until lightly browned, about 5 minutes. Turn the slices over and bake until lightly browned on the second side, about 5 minutes longer. Remove from the oven and brush with olive oil. Sprinkle with pepper to taste.

Top the toasts with the salmon, dividing it evenly. Brush the salmon with the oil and lime juice mixture. Sprinkle with the tarragon. Cut each toast into 4 pieces and arrange on a platter. Garnish with lime slices and zest strips, if desired, and serve.

Serves 8–10

1½ tablespoons olive oil, plus extra for brushing

1½ tablespoons fresh lime juice

8–10 slices coarse country bread, each 3 by 5 inches (7.5 by 13 cm) and ¼ inch (6 mm) thick, or 1 baguette cut into ¼-inch (6-mm) slices

Freshly ground pepper

1 lb (500 g) smoked salmon, thinly sliced

3 tablespoons chopped fresh tarragon

Lime slices and lime zest strips (optional)

Rosemary and Spice Nuts

The combination of fresh rosemary, cumin, and cayenne pepper lends an irresistible depth of flavor to this nibble. The recipe calls for using mixed nuts; try pecans, walnuts, and peanuts, or your own favorites.

2¹/₂ cups (10 oz/315 g) mixed raw nuts

2 tablespoons olive oil

1¹/₂ tablespoons chopped fresh rosemary

1 tablespoon sugar

1¹/₂ teaspoons ground cumin

Salt and freshly ground black pepper

Cayenne pepper

Preheat the oven to 300°F (150°C).

Place the nuts in a bowl. In a small, heavy saucepan, warm the olive oil over medium-low heat. Add the rosemary and stir until aromatic, 1 minute. Pour the oil over the nuts. Add the sugar, cumin, 1 teaspoon salt, 1 teaspoon black pepper, and ¹/₄ teaspoon cayenne and stir to coat the nuts evenly. Transfer the nuts to a baking pan.

Bake, stirring occasionally, until the nuts are toasted, about 20 minutes. Transfer to a plate and let cool completely. Store in an airtight container at room temperature for up to 4 days.

Makes about 2¹/₂ cups (10 oz/315 g)

Red, White, and Green Toasts

Prepare the vegetables up to 2 days in advance, then assemble these festive holiday appetizers right before your guests arrive, baking about one-fourth of them at a time. Use any good-quality blue cheese; Stilton or Gorgonzola are nice choices.

In a large, heavy frying pan over medium-high heat, warm the olive oil. Add the yellow onions and sauté until translucent, about 10 minutes. Add the bell peppers and chopped rosemary and sauté until the onions are soft, about 10 minutes longer. Add the sugar and vinegar and stir for 2 minutes. Remove from the heat. Season to taste with salt and pepper. (The recipe can be prepared up to this point 2 days in advance. Let cool completely, cover, and refrigerate.)

Preheat the oven to 375°F (190°C). Arrange the bread slices in a single layer on large baking sheets. Bake until golden brown on top, about 5 minutes. Remove from the oven. (The slices can be toasted up to 1 day in advance. Let cool completely, wrap tightly, and store at room temperature; then return them to the baking sheets, browned side up, before continuing.)

Brush the browned tops with olive oil and sprinkle with pepper. Spoon the onion mixture atop the bread slices, dividing it evenly. Sprinkle the cheese evenly over the tops. (The recipe can be prepared up to this point 2 hours in advance. Cover and let stand at room temperature.)

Reduce the oven temperature to 350°F (180°C). Bake until the onion mixture is hot and the cheese is melted, about 5 minutes. Sprinkle the green onions atop the toasts. Transfer to a warmed platter, garnish with the rosemary sprigs, and serve.

Makes about 72 toasts; serves 24

3 tablespoons olive oil, plus extra for brushing

4 yellow onions, halved and sliced

2 large red bell peppers (capsicums), seeded, deribbed, thinly sliced lengthwise, and slices cut crosswise into pieces 1 inch (2.5 cm) long

1 tablespoon plus 1 teaspoon chopped fresh rosemary, plus sprigs for garnish

1 teaspoon sugar

1 tablespoon sherry wine vinegar

Salt and freshly ground pepper

3–4 baguettes, cut into slices ½ inch (12 mm) thick

10 oz (315 g) blue cheese, crumbled

12 green (spring) onions, including tender green tops, thinly sliced

Oyster Chowder

Oysters were no doubt plentiful at the Pilgrims' first Thanksgiving dinner. This simple, quick soup shows them off in a robust yet elegant fashion. For a lighter version, omit the bacon and substitute half-and-half (half cream) or milk for the cream.

2 tablespoons unsalted butter

4 slices bacon, coarsely chopped

1 small yellow onion, finely diced

1 celery stalk, thinly sliced

1 small carrot, peeled and finely diced

1/2 red bell pepper (capsicum), seeded, deribbed, and finely diced

3 cups (24 fl oz/750 ml) heavy (double) cream

1 cup (8 fl oz/250 ml) dry white wine

Salt and freshly ground pepper

36 small bottled shucked oysters with their liquor

2 tablespoons finely chopped fresh flat-leaf (Italian) parsley

2 teaspoons finely chopped fresh tarragon

In a soup pot over medium heat, melt the butter. Add the bacon and sauté just until it begins to brown, 2–3 minutes. Using a slotted spoon, transfer to paper towels to drain. Set aside.

Pour off about half of the fat from the pot and return the pot to medium heat. Add the onion, celery, carrot, and bell pepper. Cover, reduce the heat to low, and cook, stirring occasionally, until the vegetables are soft, about 12 minutes.

Add the cream, wine, and salt and pepper to taste. Raise the heat to medium. Heat just until bubbles appear around the edges of the pot. Reduce the heat to low, add the oysters and their liquor and the reserved bacon, and simmer very gently until the oysters are cooked, 1–2 minutes; they should be slightly firm to the touch. Do not allow to boil. Stir in the parsley and tarragon.

Ladle into warmed bowls and serve immediately.

Serves 6–8

Butternut Squash Soup
with Marsala and Thyme

With its earthy colors and flavors, this delicious soup is an ideal first course for any autumn meal. The soup can be prepared up to 1 day in advance and then reheated over medium heat just before serving. Garnish with thyme leaves, if desired.

1 butternut squash, about 3 lb (1.5 kg), halved length-wise, fibers and seeds removed

6 slices bacon, chopped

2 large yellow onions, chopped

1½ tablespoons chopped fresh thyme or 1½ teaspoons dried thyme

5¼ cups (42 fl oz/1.3 l) Chicken Stock (page 314), or as needed

⅓ cup (3 fl oz/80 ml) heavy (double) cream or half-and-half (half cream)

3 tablespoons dry Marsala wine or dry sherry

Pinch of cayenne pepper

Salt and freshly ground black pepper

Fresh thyme leaves (optional)

Preheat the oven to 375°F (190°C).

In a baking pan, place the squash cut sides down. Add water to the pan to a depth of ¼ inch (6 mm). Bake until the squash is tender, about 50 minutes. Let cool, then use a spoon to scrape the flesh from the skin. You will need 3¾ cups (30 oz/940 g) for this soup; reserve any remaining squash for another use.

In a large, heavy saucepan over medium heat, sauté the bacon until the fat is rendered, about 3 minutes. Add the onions and thyme and sauté until tender, about 8 minutes. Remove from the heat.

Transfer the onion mixture to a blender or food processor. Working in batches, add the squash and purée until smooth. Return the purée to the saucepan. Place over medium-low heat and stir in the 5¼ cups (42 fl oz/1.3 l) of the stock. Simmer, uncovered, stirring occasionally, for 20 minutes to blend the flavors. Stir in the cream and Marsala. Add the cayenne and season to taste with salt and black pepper. If the soup is too thick, thin it out with additional stock to the desired consistency.

Ladle into warmed bowls. Serve hot.

Serves 8–10

Brandied Chestnut Soup

To save time, use 4½ cups (22 oz/690 g) vacuum-packed steamed chestnuts in place of the fresh chestnuts. A dry red wine such as Zinfandel or Petite Syrah would work well in the soup, and the remainder can be served with dinner.

In a large saucepan over medium heat, melt the butter with the olive oil. Add the celery, onion, and bay leaves and sauté, stirring occasionally, until the onion is tender, about 10 minutes. Add the flour and cook, stirring constantly, for 2 minutes. Gradually stir in the stock, then add the chestnuts. Bring to a boil, reduce the heat to medium-low, cover partially, and simmer until the chestnuts are very tender, about 45 minutes.

Remove the bay leaves and discard. Working in batches, purée the soup in a blender or food processor. Return the purée to the saucepan and place over medium-high heat. Add the wine and ½ teaspoon nutmeg and bring to a boil. Season to taste with salt and pepper. Reduce the heat to low and keep hot.

To make the croutons, in a large, heavy frying pan over high heat, melt the butter. Add the bread cubes and sauté until golden brown on all sides, about 3 minutes.

Just before serving, stir the brandy into the soup. Taste and add the remaining ¼ teaspoon nutmeg, if desired. Ladle into warmed bowls, top with the croutons, and serve immediately.

Serves 8–10

3 tablespoons unsalted butter

3 tablespoons olive oil

3 celery stalks with leaves, chopped

1 large yellow onion, chopped

2 bay leaves

⅓ cup (2 oz/60 g) all-purpose (plain) flour

3 qt (3 l) Chicken Stock (page 314)

2¼ lb (1.1 kg) fresh chestnuts, boiled and peeled (page 325), then halved

1½ cups (12 fl oz/375 ml) dry red wine

½–¾ teaspoon ground nutmeg

Salt and freshly ground pepper

⅓ cup (3 fl oz/80 ml) brandy

FOR THE CROUTONS:

2 tablespoons unsalted butter

3 cups (6 oz/185 g) cubed crustless French bread (½-inch/12-mm cubes)

Curried Leek and Apple Soup

This fragrant, savory soup makes excellent cold-weather fare and is the perfect start to any holiday meal. It is also just as tasty when served chilled. Reserve 4–6 thin slices of the tender green portion of the leeks for garnish, if desired.

1 tablespoon unsalted butter

3 large apples such as Golden Delicious, pippin, or Granny Smith, peeled, cored, and cut into 1/2-inch (12-mm) dice

2 stalks celery, thinly sliced

2 teaspoons curry powder

4 large leeks, white part and 2 inches (5 cm) of the green, halved lengthwise, carefully rinsed, and sliced crosswise

4 cups (32 fl oz/1 l) Roasted Vegetable Stock (page 314)

1 small baking potato, peeled and cut into 1/2-inch (12-mm) dice

1/2 cup (4 fl oz/125 ml) reduced-fat (2%) milk

Salt and freshly ground pepper

In a large saucepan over medium-low heat, melt the butter. Add the apples, celery, curry powder, and leeks and stir well. Cook, stirring occasionally, until the leeks soften, about 5 minutes. Cover the pan and cook for 5 minutes longer, stirring once. Add the stock and potato and bring to a boil over medium-high heat. Reduce the heat to low, cover, and simmer until the apples and potato are tender when pierced with the tip of a knife, about 20 minutes.

Working in batches, purée the soup in a blender or food processor until smooth. Alternatively, pass the soup through a food mill.

If serving the soup hot, return it to the pan and stir in the milk. Season to taste with salt and pepper. Reheat over low heat without boiling, then ladle into warmed bowls. Serve at once.

If serving the soup cold, transfer to a bowl or other container, stir in the milk, and season to taste with salt and pepper. Cover and refrigerate, stirring every hour or so, until thoroughly chilled, about 4–6 hours. When ready to serve, taste and adjust the seasonings, then ladle into chilled bowls and serve at once.

Serves 6

Carrot and Mint Soup

This soup can be made up to 24 hours in advance, through the step of puréeing the vegetables; combine the purée and cooking liquid, then cover and refrigerate. Any leftover soup can be stored in a covered bowl in the refrigerator for 1 day.

In a large saucepan over medium heat, melt the butter. Add the onions and sauté until translucent, 2–3 minutes. Add the carrots, stock, and mint sprigs. Reduce the heat to low, cover, and simmer until the carrots are tender, 25–30 minutes. Remove the mint sprigs and discard.

Set a colander over a bowl and pour the contents of the pan into the colander. Reserve the cooking liquid. Transfer the vegetables to a food processor and purée until smooth. Return the purée and the reserved liquid to the pan. Over medium-low heat, stir in the milk and cream. Season to taste with salt and a little paprika and heat almost to a boil, but do not allow the soup to boil.

Ladle into warmed bowls and top with a dollop of sour cream and a sprinkling of chopped mint.

Serves 6–8

2 tablespoons unsalted butter

2 yellow onions, diced

10–12 carrots, peeled and sliced (about 4 cups/1 lb/500 g)

4 cups (32 fl oz/1 l) Chicken Stock (page 314)

3 large fresh mint sprigs

2 cups (16 fl oz/500 ml) milk

1 cup (8 fl oz/250 ml) heavy (double) cream

Salt

Paprika

1/4 cup (2 oz/60 g) sour cream

2 tablespoons chopped fresh mint

Blood Oranges and Celery Root with Mustard Vinaigrette

Blood oranges and celery root are available during the cool months, making this dish an ideal first course for a Christmas meal. You may also use regular oranges and fresh fennel in their place. If you use fennel, chop the bulbs coarsely.

3 blood oranges

1 tablespoon fruit-flavored vinegar such as peach or raspberry, or mild white wine vinegar

Salt and freshly ground pepper

2 teaspoons Dijon mustard

2 teaspoons honey

1/3 cup (3 fl oz/80 ml) extra-virgin olive oil

1 celery root (celeriac), about 1 lb (500 g)

8–10 oz (250–315 g) mixed salad greens or a mixture of romaine (cos) lettuce, butter (Boston) lettuce, and chicory (curly endive)

Using a sharp knife, cut a slice from the bottom and top of each orange to expose the flesh. Stand the fruit upright on a cutting board and slice off the peel in wide strips, removing all the pith and membrane to expose the flesh. Working over a bowl, carefully cut along both sides of each segment to free it from the membrane, then let the segments drop into the bowl. Discard any seeds. Set aside.

In a small bowl, combine the vinegar, 1/8 teaspoon salt, and pepper to taste. Using a small whisk, stir until the salt dissolves. Add the mustard and honey and whisk until blended. Add the olive oil, a little at a time, and whisk until well blended. Taste and adjust the seasonings. Pour half of the vinaigrette into a medium bowl.

Using a sharp knife, carefully peel the celery root and shred on the medium holes of a handheld grater. Place in the bowl holding the mustard vinaigrette and mix well. (This step can be done up to 1 hour in advance of serving.)

Rinse the lettuces and dry well. If necessary, tear into bite-sized pieces. Place in a large salad bowl. Add the remaining mustard vinaigrette and toss until well coated.

Divide the lettuces among 6 salad plates, arranging them in a ring on each. Divide the shredded celery root among the plates, placing it in the center. Arrange the orange segments on the lettuces and serve at once.

Serves 6

Pear, Walnut, and Goat Cheese Salad

Comice pears work best for this salad, but Anjou or Bartlett (Williams') are good choices, too. Be sure the pears are ripe but still firm to the touch. A good-quality, natural goat's or sheep's milk feta cheese has the best flavor and crumbles well.

Wash and trim the watercress, removing and discarding the tough stems and old leaves. Drain, dry well, and wrap in a clean, damp kitchen towel. Place in the refrigerator for at least 1 hour to chill and crisp.

Peel, quarter, and core the pears. Cut each quarter into 3 lengthwise slices and place in a bowl with the juice of 1 lemon. Toss carefully and thoroughly to keep the flesh from turning brown.

Squeeze 3 tablespoons of juice from 1 or 2 lemons into a small bowl. Add $1/2$ teaspoon salt and stir to dissolve. Whisk in the honey and then the olive oil and a little pepper. Taste and adjust the seasoning.

Arrange the watercress on individual salad plates and top with the pear slices. Scatter the walnut pieces and crumbled cheese over the top. Whisk the dressing again and drizzle over the salad, or pass it separately in a bowl.

Serves 8–10

3–4 large bunches watercress

4–5 ripe but firm pears

2–3 lemons

Salt and freshly ground pepper

3 tablespoons honey, preferably thyme honey

$1/2$ cup (4 fl oz/125 ml) mild extra-virgin olive oil

$1^1/2$ cups (6 oz/185 g) walnut halves, broken into small pieces

$1/2$ lb (250 g) feta cheese, crumbled

Green Bean, Radicchio, and Fennel Salad

This is a zesty and crisp salad that is perfect for a large group, as it holds up well on a buffet. You can prepare the vegetables a day ahead and refrigerate them; dress the salad just before serving.

3 lb (1.5 kg) green beans, trimmed

Salt

2³/4 lb (1.4 kg) fennel bulbs

2 heads radicchio, 1¹/2 lb (750 g) total weight, halved, cored, and sliced lengthwise

1 cup (8 fl oz/250 ml) plus 2 tablespoons extra-virgin olive oil

6 tablespoons (3 fl oz/90 ml) balsamic vinegar

3¹/2 cups (14 oz/435 g) coarsely grated Parmesan cheese

Freshly ground pepper

Bring a large pot three-fourths full of water to a boil. Add the green beans and salt to taste and cook just until tender-crisp, about 8 minutes. Drain and rinse under cold water to cool. Drain well. Transfer to a large bowl.

Trim off the tops from the fennel bulbs. Cut away any bruised areas on the bulbs and then cut into quarters lengthwise. Cut away the cores and slice the quarters lengthwise. Add the fennel and radicchio to the beans. (The salad can be prepared up to this point 1 day in advance. Cover and refrigerate.)

Pour the olive oil over the vegetables and toss to coat. Add the vinegar and toss to coat again. Add 3 cups (12 oz/375 g) of the Parmesan cheese and salt and pepper to taste and mix well.

Transfer to a serving bowl. Sprinkle with the remaining ¹/2 cup (2 oz/60 g) Parmesan cheese and serve.

Serves 24

Wild Rice, Orange, and Asparagus Salad

Mix up this flavorful salad the night before a gathering, then add the oranges, pecans, and green (spring) onions just before serving. If asparagus is unavailable, broccoli florets can be used instead.

Place the wild rice in a large saucepan and add 3 qt (3 l) water and salt to taste. Bring to a boil. Reduce the heat to low, cover, and simmer until the rice is tender, about 40 minutes. Drain the rice well and transfer to a large bowl.

Meanwhile, using a sharp knife, cut off the tough ends of the asparagus and discard. Cut off the tips and reserve. Cut the stalks crosswise into slices $1/2$ inch (12 mm) long. Bring a large saucepan three-fourths full of water to a boil. Add the asparagus tips and stalks and salt to taste and cook until tender-crisp, about 8 minutes. Drain and rinse under cold water to cool. Drain well. Add to the rice.

In a bowl, combine the orange juice and vinegar. Mix in the olive oil, orange zest, and tarragon. Add to the rice and mix well. Season to taste with salt and pepper.

Peel the oranges, cutting away all of the white pith. Cut the oranges in half through their stem ends and remove any white membrane on the cut surfaces, then chop the pulp. Add the oranges, green onions, and pecans to the salad and mix well.

Line a large serving bowl with the romaine leaves. Spoon the salad into the center of the bowl and serve.

Serves 24

2¹/₂ cups (1 lb/500 g) wild rice, well rinsed

Salt and freshly ground pepper

4 lb (2 kg) thin asparagus spears

²/₃ cup (5 fl oz/160 ml) fresh orange juice

¹/₄ cup (2 fl oz/60 ml) sherry or red wine vinegar

²/₃ cup (5 fl oz/160 ml) extra-virgin olive oil

3 tablespoons grated orange zest

¹/₃ cup (¹/₂ oz/15 g) chopped fresh tarragon

4 navel oranges

8 green (spring) onions, chopped

2 cups (8 oz/250 g) coarsely chopped pecans

2 heads romaine (cos) lettuce, cored and separated into leaves

Black and White Bean Salad with Fennel and Red Pepper

The variety of ingredients in this salad adds color to any buffet table. If you prefer, use all white or all black beans. Serve the salad in a large, pretty bowl and garnish with big, leafy sprigs of flat-leaf (Italian) parsley.

Pick over the white beans and discard any stones or misshapen beans. Rinse the beans and put in a bowl. Add water to cover generously and let soak for about 3 hours. Repeat with the black beans in a separate bowl.

Drain the beans and put them in separate saucepans. Add water to cover by 2 inches (5 cm) to each pan and bring to a boil over high heat. Reduce the heat to low and simmer, uncovered, until tender. The white beans will take 35–45 minutes, and the black beans will take 45–60 minutes. Drain the beans and set them aside. (The beans can be cooked up to 1 day in advance, then drained, covered, and refrigerated.)

In a large bowl, whisk together the vinegar, olive oil, garlic, and salt and pepper to taste. Add the black and white beans and toss to mix well. Cover and refrigerate until completely cool, about 1 hour.

Meanwhile, trim the stalks and feathery fronds from the fennel bulbs and reserve. Cut away the cores and any bruised areas on the bulbs and then cut the bulbs into 1/4-inch (6-mm) dice. Chop the reserved tops. Add the chopped fennel tops and diced fennel, red onion, green onions, bell pepper, and parsley to the beans and toss to mix well. Season to taste with salt and pepper and serve at room temperature.

Serves 12

3/4 cup (51/2 oz/170 g) dried small white (navy) beans

3/4 cup (51/2 oz/170 g) dried black beans

1/2 cup (4 fl oz/125 ml) red wine vinegar

2/3 cup (5 fl oz/160 ml) extra-virgin olive oil

5 cloves garlic, minced

Salt and freshly ground pepper

3 fennel bulbs with stalks and feathery fronds attached, 11/4 –11/2 lb (625–750 g) total weight

1 small red onion, cut into 1/4-inch (6-mm) dice

8 green (spring) onions, including tender green tops, cut into slices 1/4 inch (6 mm) thick

1 large red bell pepper (capsicum), seeded, deribbed, and cut into 1/4-inch (6-mm) dice

1/3 cup (1/2 oz/15 g) chopped fresh flat-leaf (Italian) parsley

Garden Salad with Pears, Pecans, and Gorgonzola

This is a perfect salad for winter. Pears are in season, and the flavors of the fruit, pecans, and Gorgonzola are wonderfully complementary. Be sure not to toss the salad with the dressing too early; toss just before serving.

3/4 lb (375 g) mixed salad greens, carefully washed and well dried

3 tablespoons sherry vinegar

2 tablespoons red wine vinegar

2 tablespoons walnut oil or other flavorful nut oil (optional)

3/4 cup (6 fl oz/180 ml) extra-virgin olive oil

Salt and freshly ground pepper

3 ripe but firm pears such as Bosc or Comice

2/3 cup (2 1/2 oz/75 g) pecan halves, toasted (page 328)

1/2 lb (250 g) Gorgonzola cheese

Wrap the greens in a clean, damp kitchen towel. Place in the refrigerator at least 1 hour and for up to 24 hours to chill and crisp.

In a bowl, whisk together the sherry vinegar, red wine vinegar, walnut oil (if using), and olive oil until blended. Season to taste with salt and pepper.

Peel, quarter, and core the pears. Thinly slice the quarters lengthwise. In a large bowl, combine the greens, pecans, and pears. Drizzle with the dressing and toss well to coat. Taste and adjust the seasonings. Crumble the cheese on top and serve.

Serves 12

Spiced Apple, Cranberry, and Pecan Salad

Caramelized pecans and dried cranberries, along with cumin and cayenne pepper, add new twists to the classic Waldorf salad. The light yogurt-based dressing lends a refreshing finish.

1¹⁄₂ teaspoons ground cumin

¹⁄₄ teaspoon cayenne pepper

1 tablespoon extra-virgin olive oil

1 cup (4 oz/125 g) pecan halves

3 tablespoons sugar

¹⁄₂ cup (4 oz/125 g) plain yogurt

¹⁄₂ cup (4 fl oz/125 ml) mayonnaise

2 tablespoons honey

1 teaspoon sherry vinegar or balsamic vinegar

5 large sweet apples such as Gala, Golden Delicious, or Fuji

3 large celery stalks, thinly sliced

¹⁄₂ cup (2 oz/60 g) dried cranberries

8–10 red-leaf lettuce leaves

In a bowl, combine ³⁄₄ teaspoon of the cumin and ¹⁄₈ teaspoon of the cayenne. In a small saucepan, warm the olive oil over medium heat. Add the pecans and stir until the nuts are lightly browned, about 5 minutes. Sprinkle with the sugar and cook, stirring constantly, until the sugar melts and begins to brown, about 3 minutes longer. Add the hot nut mixture to the bowl containing the spices and stir to coat. Let cool completely. Chop the nuts coarsely. Set aside.

In a small bowl, stir together the yogurt, mayonnaise, honey, and vinegar. Add the remaining ³⁄₄ teaspoon cumin and ¹⁄₈ teaspoon cayenne pepper.

Quarter each apple through the stem end and cut away the core. Cut each quarter in half crosswise, then slice. In a large bowl, combine the apples, celery, and dried cranberries. Add the yogurt dressing and toss to coat.

Line individual plates with lettuce leaves. Mound an equal amount of the salad in the center of each plate. Sprinkle with the nuts and serve.

Serves 8–10

Frisée, Pear, and Prosciutto Salad

Luscious fall pears are the perfect counterpoint to crisp frisée and mildly salty prosciutto. If frisée is unavailable, substitute chicory (curly endive). For easy serving, make the dressing early in the day.

In a small bowl, whisk together the vinegar, shallot, mustard, honey, and thyme. Gradually whisk in the olive oil until well blended.

Peel, quarter, and core the pears. Slice the quarters lengthwise and cut each slice in half crosswise.

In a large bowl, combine the pears, frisée, and prosciutto. Drizzle with the dressing and toss well to coat. Season to taste with salt and pepper and serve.

Serves 8–10

3 tablespoons cider vinegar

1 shallot, minced

1½ teaspoons Dijon mustard

1½ teaspoons honey

2 teaspoons chopped fresh thyme or ¾ teaspoon dried thyme

6 tablespoons (3 fl oz/90 ml) extra-virgin olive oil

2 ripe but firm pears such as Bosc or Anjou

10 cups (10 oz/315 g) frisée (see note), separated into leaves

3 oz (90 g) thinly sliced prosciutto, cut crosswise into strips ¼ inch (6 mm) wide

Salt and freshly ground pepper

Shrimp and Grapefruit Cocktail

If you can't find cooked and peeled bay shrimp, use 2 lb (1 kg) small raw shrimp. Cook them in boiling salted water until pink and opaque throughout, about 3–5 minutes; then drain, cool, and peel.

Using a sharp knife, cut a thick slice from the bottom and top of each grapefruit to expose the flesh. Stand the fruit upright on a cutting board and thickly slice off the peel in wide strips, removing all the pith and membrane to expose the flesh. Working over a bowl, carefully cut along both sides of each segment to free it from the membrane, then cut in half crosswise and let the halves drop into the bowl. Cover and refrigerate.

Peel the cucumber and cut lengthwise into quarters. If the seeds are large, cut away the seed section and discard. Slice each quarter crosswise into pieces $1/8$ inch (3 mm) thick. Set aside.

In a small bowl, stir together the vinegar and $1/8$ teaspoon salt until the salt dissolves. Stir in the mustard and pepper to taste. Gradually add the olive oil, whisking constantly until a slightly thickened dressing forms. Stir in the green onions and the minced tarragon and parsley. Taste and adjust the seasonings. Set aside.

Discard any bits of shell from the shrimp and drain off any liquid. Place in a bowl, add the cucumber and the dressing, and stir well. Cover and refrigerate for about 30 minutes; stir occasionally.

To serve, line footed compotes or small, shallow bowls with the lettuce leaves. Divide the grapefruit evenly among the leaves. Stir the shrimp mixture and spoon over the grapefruit, dividing it evenly. Spoon any excess dressing over the top. Garnish with the tarragon and parsley sprigs.

Serves 8–10

3–4 grapefruits

1/2 English (hothouse) cucumber

2 tablespoons tarragon vinegar

Salt and freshly ground pepper

1 teaspoon Dijon mustard

1/2 cup (4 fl oz/125 ml) extra-virgin olive oil

2–3 green (spring) onions, including tender green tops, minced (about 3 tablespoons)

1 tablespoon minced fresh tarragon, plus sprigs for garnish

1 tablespoon minced fresh flat-leaf (Italian) parsley, plus sprigs for garnish

1 1/2 lb (750 g) cooked and peeled bay shrimp

8–10 small butter (Boston) lettuce leaves

Orange and Avocado Salad

All the components of this salad can be prepared up to 3 hours ahead and assembled at the last moment. If cutting the avocado in advance, sprinkle with lemon juice to prevent it from turning brown.

1/2–3/4 lb (250–375 g) baby spinach leaves, trimmed, washed, and well dried

2–3 ripe avocados

4–5 oranges, preferably seedless

3 tablespoons fresh lemon juice

Salt and freshly ground pepper

1/4 cup (3 oz/90 g) honey, preferably mild flavored

1/2 cup (4 fl oz/125 ml) mild extra-virgin olive oil

2 tablespoons minced sweet red onion or green (spring) onion

1 1/2 teaspoons minced fresh mint leaves or 1 teaspoon crushed dried mint

Wrap the spinach in a clean, damp kitchen towel. Place in the refrigerator for at least 2–3 hours to chill and crisp.

Cut each avocado in half lengthwise, remove the pit, and peel. Cut lengthwise into thin slices. Set aside.

Peel the oranges, remove any remaining white membrane covering them, and then cut crosswise into thin slices, discarding any seeds. Set aside.

In a small bowl, stir together the lemon juice and 1/2 teaspoon salt until the salt dissolves. Whisk in the honey and a little pepper, then whisk in the olive oil, onion, and mint. Taste and adjust the seasoning. Set aside.

To assemble, arrange the chilled spinach on individual plates. Top with avocado slices and orange slices. Whisk the dressing again and drizzle over the salad, or pass it separately in a bowl.

Serves 8–10

Millie's Herring Salad

Look for herring snacks (marinated herring pieces) in jars in the refrigerated case of well-stocked food stores and delicatessens. The salad can be made up to 3 days in advance, covered, and refrigerated.

1 jar (32 oz/1 kg) herring snacks

1 day-old roll or 1 slice day-old white bread

¼ cup (2 fl oz/60 ml) cider vinegar

1 yellow onion, cut into large chunks

1 large celery stalk, cut into 1-inch (2.5-cm) pieces

1 Granny Smith or other firm, tart apple, peeled, quartered, and cored

1 peeled hard-boiled egg, quartered

1 tablespoon sugar

Crackers or thinly sliced pumpernickel bread for serving

Place the herring into a sieve to drain; discard the liquid. Break the roll into several pieces, place in a small bowl, and sprinkle with the vinegar. Set aside.

In a food processor, combine the onion, celery, and apple. Using on-off pulses, process just until coarsely chopped. Add the egg and process for 5 seconds. Then add the herring, the roll and any unabsorbed vinegar, and the sugar. Using on-off pulses, process until the ingredients are incorporated but not puréed. The consistency should be coarse.

Transfer to a serving bowl and serve immediately with crackers or pumpernickel bread. If making the salad in advance, bring to room temperature before serving.

Serves 8

Mixed Greens
with Beets and Cucumbers

Toasted walnuts and rosy chopped beets contribute a wealth of texture to this pretty salad. The dressing is nicely balanced, combining rich balsamic and light lemon flavors with pungent and grainy mustard.

Bring a saucepan three-fourths full of water to a boil. Meanwhile, trim off all but $1/2$ inch (12 mm) of each beet stem. Do not cut off the root ends. Add the beets to the boiling water and cook until tender but still slightly resistant when pierced, 25–35 minutes, depending on their size.

To make the dressing, in a bowl, combine the shallot, mustard, lemon juice, and vinegar and whisk to mix. Slowly add the olive oil, whisking constantly until completely blended. Whisk in $1/2$ teaspoon salt, $1/4$ teaspoon pepper, and parsley. Taste and adjust the seasoning. Set aside.

Drain the beets and, when cool enough to handle, trim off the stems and roots. Peel the beets, then finely chop them and set aside. Cut the cucumber into slices $1/2$ inch (12 mm) thick and set aside. (The salad can be prepared up to this point 8 hours in advance. Cover and refrigerate the dressing, beets, greens, and cucumber separately. Bring the dressing to room temperature before serving.)

Core, separate into leaves, and tear into bite-sized pieces the butter lettuce and radicchio. Thinly slice the endive.

In a large bowl, combine the lettuce, radicchio, and endive. Drizzle half of the dressing over the greens and toss to coat. Divide the greens evenly among 6 plates and top each serving with the beets and cucumber. Sprinkle the toasted walnuts over the top. Pass the remaining dressing in a bowl.

Serves 6

2 beets

FOR THE DRESSING:

1 shallot, finely chopped

1 tablespoon whole-grain mustard

2 tablespoons lemon juice

2 tablespoons balsamic vinegar

3/4 cup (6 fl oz/180 ml) extra-virgin olive oil

Salt and freshly ground pepper

2 tablespoons finely chopped fresh flat-leaf (Italian) parsley

1 cucumber, peeled, halved lengthwise, and seeded

2 heads butter (Boston) lettuce

1 small head radicchio

2 heads Belgian endive (chicory/witloof)

1/3 cup (1 1/2 oz/45 g) walnuts, toasted (page 328) and chopped

Green Bean, Caramelized Onion, and Blue Cheese Salad

Here is a stylish way to begin a holiday dinner. The salad is equally good with fresh goat cheese. To make the party preparations easier, prepare the beans, dressing, and onions early in the day, then assemble the salad just before serving.

2¹/₂ lb (1.25 kg) green beans, trimmed

¹/₂ cup (4 fl oz/125 ml) plus 2 tablespoons extra-virgin olive oil, plus extra for greasing

3 tablespoons plus 2 teaspoons sherry vinegar

2 tablespoons chopped fresh thyme or 2 teaspoons dried thyme

2 teaspoons soy sauce

1 teaspoon sugar

Salt and freshly ground pepper

3 large red onions, cut through the stem ends into wedges ¹/₃–¹/₂ inch (9–12 mm) thick

5 oz (155 g) blue cheese, crumbled

Preheat the broiler (grill). Lightly grease a baking sheet.

Bring a large pot three-fourths full of lightly salted water to a boil over high heat. Add the beans and cook until tender-crisp, about 5 minutes. Drain, rinse with cold water, and drain well.

In a small bowl, whisk together the olive oil, vinegar, thyme, soy sauce, and sugar until well blended. Season to taste with salt and pepper.

Arrange the onion wedges on the prepared baking sheet. Brush with some of the dressing. Slip under the broiler about 3 inches (7.5 cm) from the heat source. Broil (grill) the onions, without turning, until deep brown, 8–12 minutes.

Place the beans in a large bowl. Add the remaining dressing and toss to coat. Divide the beans evenly among individual plates. Top with the onions, dividing evenly. Drizzle any dressing remaining at the bottom of the bowl over the onions. Sprinkle evenly with the cheese and serve.

Serves 8–10

New Potato and Roasted Pepper Salad

Canned whole Spanish Lodosa red peppers are an excellent substitute for the fresh bell peppers (capsicums) in this salad. If you can find them, use 4 or 5 canned peppers and omit the step of roasting and peeling.

Roast the bell peppers (page 324). Pull off the loosened skin and remove the stem, seeds, and ribs. Slice the peppers into long, thin strips and set aside.

Put the potatoes in a saucepan with water to cover and 1 tablespoon salt. Bring to a boil, reduce the heat slightly, cover partially, and cook gently until just tender, 25–30 minutes. Drain and set aside to cool.

In a small bowl, stir together the lemon juice and $1/2$ teaspoon salt until the salt dissolves. Add the olive oil, green onion, and pepper to taste and whisk together until well mixed.

To serve, divide the chicory among individual plates or place in a bowl. Cut the potatoes into thick slices and arrange atop the greens. Top with the red pepper strips. Whisk the dressing again, drizzle over the salad, and serve.

Serves 6–8

2 large red bell peppers (capsicums)

$1^1/2$ lb (750 g) small red new potatoes

Salt and freshly ground pepper

1 tablespoon fresh lemon juice

$1/2$ cup (4 fl oz/125 ml) extra-virgin olive oil

2 tablespoons chopped green (spring) onion

1 or 2 bunches chicory (curly endive) or frisée, cored, separated into leaves, and chilled

Main Dishes

Roasted Fall Vegetables
with Wild Rice Pilaf

A cornucopia of autumn's bountiful offerings surrounds a pilaf accented
with holiday spices to create a spectacular meatless main course. Acorn squash
is a common winter squash with a dark green skin and orange flesh.

2 tan-skinned sweet potatoes,
well scrubbed

4 parsnips, peeled

2 small acorn squashes

2 large red bell peppers
(capsicums)

1 lb (500 g) small white
boiling onions, 1–1½ inches
(2.5–4 cm) in diameter,
unpeeled

8 shallots, peeled and halved

4 tablespoons (2 fl oz/60 ml)
olive oil

6 tablespoons (3 oz/90 g)
unsalted butter

2 teaspoons ground cinnamon

2 teaspoons ground turmeric

Salt and freshly ground pepper

4 bay leaves

Wild Rice and Dried Cranberry
Pilaf (page 124)

Preheat the oven to 425°F (220°C).

Halve the sweet potatoes crosswise, then cut each half lengthwise into 8 wedges. Cut
the parsnips in half crosswise, then cut in half lengthwise. Cut the acorn squashes in
half crosswise and remove and discard the seeds and any fibers. Cut each half lengthwise into 8 wedges, then cut each wedge in half crosswise. Trim off the peel from
the squash pieces. Cut each bell pepper lengthwise into quarters. Remove and discard
the seeds and ribs and cut each quarter in half crosswise.

Bring a large pot three-fourths full of water to a boil. Add the onions and boil for
3 minutes to loosen the skins. Drain and rinse with cold water to cool; drain again.
Cut off the root and stem ends and slip off the skins.

Divide the sweet potatoes, parsnips, squashes, bell peppers, onions, and shallots
evenly between 2 large baking pans. Drizzle 2 tablespoons of the olive oil and dot
3 tablespoons of the butter evenly over the contents of each pan. Sprinkle each
with 1 teaspoon cinnamon, 1 teaspoon turmeric, and salt and pepper to taste. Add
2 bay leaves to each pan. Stir to coat the vegetables.

Roast, stirring occasionally, until the vegetables are golden brown and tender when
pierced with a fork, about 1 hour.

Meanwhile, make the pilaf and mound in the center of a large warmed platter.
Surround with the vegetables and serve.

Serves 8

Roast Fish with Almond and Bread Crumb Stuffing

A whole roasted fish makes a delicious and dramatic main course for a holiday meal. The stuffing is enriched with nuts for a pleasing crunch. You can substitute fresh fennel for the celery; if you do, use tarragon or dill rather than marjoram.

Preheat the oven to 425°F (220°C). Grease a baking dish large enough to hold the fish flat.

In a frying pan over medium heat, melt the butter. Add the onion and sauté for 5 minutes. Add the celery and sauté, stirring, for 3 minutes. Remove from the heat. Add the bread crumbs, parsley, marjoram, lemon zest, and almonds. Season to taste with salt and pepper. Stuff the mixture into the fish cavity and skewer closed. Place the fish in the prepared baking dish.

Bake the fish, basting occasionally with the melted butter, until it tests done, 8–10 minutes per inch (2.5 cm) of thickness or about 40 minutes' total cooking time. To test, open a slit near the bone with a knife to see if the fish is cooked through and flaky. Alternatively, insert a metal skewer into the thickest part of the fish to the bone; if it feels hot on the tongue, the fish is done.

Carefully transfer to a warmed platter and serve immediately.

Serves 4

Olive oil for greasing

2 tablespoons unsalted butter

½ yellow onion, diced

1 celery stalk, diced

2 cups (4 oz/125 g) fresh bread crumbs

¼ cup (⅓ oz/10 g) chopped fresh flat-leaf (Italian) parsley

1 tablespoon chopped fresh marjoram

2 teaspoons grated lemon zest

½ cup (2½ oz/75 g) chopped almonds, toasted (page 328)

Salt and freshly ground pepper

1 sea bass or snapper, 4–5 lb (2–2.5 kg), cleaned

½ cup (4 fl oz/125 ml) melted unsalted butter or olive oil

Roast Fish with Saffron Rice Stuffing

Serve with spinach and carrots seasoned with cinnamon and dill.
For a nice addition to the stuffing, add ¼ cup (1 oz/30 g) golden raisins
(sultanas), plumped in hot water for 20–30 minutes and well drained.

3 tablespoons unsalted butter, plus melted butter or olive oil for basting

½ yellow onion, diced

2 green (spring) onions, including tender green tops, minced

1 cup (7 oz/220 g) long-grain white rice

2 cups (16 fl oz/500 ml) hot water

½ teaspoon saffron threads, steeped in 2 tablespoons dry white wine

Olive oil for greasing

1 snapper, salmon, or rock cod, 5–6 lb (2.5–3 kg), cleaned

½ teaspoon ground cinnamon

Grated zest of 1 large orange

2 teaspoons chopped fresh thyme or dill

Salt and freshly ground pepper

In a sauté pan over medium heat, melt the 3 tablespoons butter. Add the yellow onion and sauté until tender, about 10 minutes. Add the green onion and sauté for 2 minutes. Add the rice, hot water, and saffron with wine, stir well, and bring to a boil. Reduce the heat to low, cover, and cook until the liquid is absorbed, 15–20 minutes.

Meanwhile, preheat the oven to 400°F (200°C). Lightly grease a baking dish large enough to hold the fish flat. Bring the fish to room temperature.

Remove the rice from the heat. Fold in the cinnamon, orange zest, and thyme. Season to taste with salt and pepper. Let cool completely.

Spoon the rice into the fish cavity and skewer closed. Place the fish in the prepared dish. Bake, basting occasionally with melted butter or olive oil, until the fish tests done, about 8–10 minutes per inch (2.5 cm) of thickness or about 40 minutes total cooking time. To test, open a slit near the bone with a knife to see if the fish is cooked through and flaky.

Transfer the fish to a warmed platter and serve at once.

Serves 4

Cracked Crab with Two Sauces

If you are short of time, you can buy fresh cooked and cracked crab at your local fishmonger. Blue or stone crabs can be used if Dungeness crabs are unavailable; adjust cooking time as necessary.

To make the tangerine butter, in a small saucepan over medium heat, melt the butter. Stir in the tangerine juice and zest, mustard, and salt and pepper to taste. Immediately remove from the heat and let stand for 1 hour.

To make the dill vinaigrette, in a small bowl, whisk together the lemon juice, garlic, olive oil, and salt and pepper to taste. Stir in the dill and green onion, and mix until well blended. Set aside.

In a stockpot, bring 4 qt (4 l) water to a boil, then add 2 tablespoons salt. Add the crabs, immersing completely, and boil until cooked, about 12 minutes. Using tongs, transfer to a plate to cool slightly.

Working with 1 crab at a time, place the crab on its back. Pull off the tail section and discard; the intestinal vein will pull free at the same time. Then turn the crab over and, grasping the large top shell firmly, lift it, snap it off, and discard. Remove the white spongy gills and any other organs from the body and discard. Using a large, heavy knife, cut the body in half from head to tail. Cut each half crosswise into thirds. Using a mallet, crack the claws and legs. If the crabs have cooled, warm them on a steamer rack over boiling water for 5–7 minutes.

To serve, reheat the tangerine butter over medium heat, whisking constantly. Pour into a small bowl. Arrange the crab on a platter. Serve immediately with the sauces.

Serves 6

FOR THE TANGERINE BUTTER:

3/4 cup (6 oz/185 g) unsalted butter

3 tablespoons fresh tangerine juice

1/2 teaspoon grated tangerine zest

1 tablespoon Dijon mustard

Salt and freshly ground pepper

FOR THE DILL VINAIGRETTE:

3–4 tablespoons lemon juice

1 clove garlic, minced

1/2 cup (4 fl oz/125 ml) extra-virgin olive oil

Salt and freshly ground pepper

2 tablespoons chopped dill

2 green (spring) onions, including tender green tops, thinly sliced

Salt

3 live Dungeness crabs, 2–2 1/2 lb (1–1.25 kg) each

Citrus-Scented Roast Turkey with Cranberry Sauce

Vegetable oil for greasing

1 turkey, 10–12 lb (5–6 kg)

Salt and freshly ground pepper

2 celery stalks, cut into 2-inch (5-cm) lengths

1 yellow onion, quartered

1 orange, quartered

1 lemon, quartered

1 bay leaf

3 fresh parsley sprigs

1/4 cup (2 oz/60 g) unsalted butter, at room temperature

1 cup (8 fl oz/250 ml) Chicken Stock (page 314)

FOR THE CRANBERRY SAUCE:

3 cups (12 oz/375 g) fresh cranberries

1 cup (8 oz/250 g) sugar

Finely grated zest and juice of 1 orange

1 cinnamon stick, about 3 inches (7.5 cm) long, broken in half

1/4 teaspoon ground cloves

1 cup (4 oz/125 g) coarsely chopped walnuts, toasted (page 328) (optional)

Position a rack in the lower third of the oven and preheat to 425°F (220°C). Lightly grease a V-shaped rack in a roasting pan. When the turkey reaches room temperature, remove the neck, gizzard, and heart from the turkey and discard or reserve for another use. Rinse the turkey inside and out and pat dry with paper towels. Season the cavity with salt and pepper and place the celery, onion, orange, lemon, bay leaf, and parsley inside. Truss the turkey, if desired (page 320). Rub the outside of the bird with the butter and sprinkle with salt and pepper.

Place the turkey on the rack in the pan, breast side down. Roast for 40 minutes, basting with the pan juices after 20 minutes. Add the stock to the pan. Reduce the heat to 325°F (165°C). Turn breast side up, and continue to roast, basting every 15–20 minutes with the pan juices. Roast until golden and cooked through. After about 2 hours, start testing for doneness by inserting an instant-read thermometer into the thickest part of the breast away from the bone; it should register 165°F (74°C). The turkey should roast for a total of 2 1/2–3 1/4 hours.

As soon as the turkey is in the oven, begin to make the cranberry sauce. Sort through the cranberries, discarding any soft ones. In a saucepan over medium-high heat, stir together the cranberries, sugar, orange zest and juice, cinnamon stick, cloves, and 1 cup (8 fl oz/250 ml) water. Bring to a boil, reduce the heat to low, and cover partially. Simmer gently, stirring occasionally, until the sauce thickens, 10–15 minutes. Transfer to a bowl and let cool, then cover and refrigerate until serving. Stir in the toasted walnuts, if using, just before serving.

Transfer the turkey to a warmed platter, cover loosely with aluminum foil, and let rest for 20–30 minutes before carving. Serve with the cranberry sauce.

Serves 6–8

Cider-Glazed Turkey with Cider-Shallot Gravy

In a saucepan over high heat, bring the cider to a boil; boil until reduced to 1 cup (8 fl oz/250 ml), about 30 minutes. Set aside ½ cup (4 fl oz/125 ml) for the gravy. Mix the butter and thyme into the remaining ½ cup cider; refrigerate until cold.

Position a rack in the lower third of the oven and preheat to 325°F (165°C). Rinse the turkey inside and out and pat dry with paper towels. Discard any pieces of fat from the cavities. Place the turkey on a rack in a large roasting pan. Spread the cider butter inside and over the outside of the turkey. Sprinkle with salt and pepper. Tie the legs together. Tuck the wing tips under the body.

Roast for 45 minutes, then baste with the pan juices. Continue to roast, basting every 20 minutes and covering with aluminum foil when dark brown, until an instant-read thermometer inserted into the thickest part of the thigh away from the bone registers 180°F (82°C), about 2½ hours longer. Transfer to a platter, cover loosely with aluminum foil, and let stand for 20 minutes. Pour the pan juices into a large measuring pitcher and skim off and discard the fat.

To make the gravy, in a saucepan over medium-high heat, melt the butter. Add the shallots and thyme and sauté until the shallots are golden brown, about 8 minutes. Add the flour and cook, stirring frequently, until browned, about 5 minutes. Add enough stock to the pan juices to measure 5 cups (40 fl oz/1.25 l). Gradually whisk the stock mixture into the butter mixture. Bring to a boil, whisking frequently. Mix in the reserved reduced cider and boil until thickened, about 10 minutes. Mix in the Calvados and return to a boil. Season to taste with salt and pepper.

Garnish the turkey with thyme sprigs, if desired, and carve at the table (page 321). Serve with the gravy.

Serves 8–10

3 cups (24 fl oz/750 ml) apple cider or apple juice

¾ cup (6 oz/185 g) butter, at room temperature

2 tablespoons chopped fresh thyme or 2 teaspoons dried thyme

1 turkey, 14–16 lb (7–8 kg), neck and giblets reserved for making stock

Salt and freshly ground pepper

FOR THE GRAVY:

6 tablespoons (3 oz/90 g) butter

3 oz (90 g) shallots, sliced

2 tablespoons chopped fresh thyme or 2 teaspoons dried thyme

6 tablespoons (2 oz/60 g) all-purpose (plain) flour

About 4½ cups (36 fl oz/1.1 l) Turkey Stock (page 314)

3 tablespoons Calvados, applejack, or brandy

Salt and freshly ground pepper

Fresh thyme sprigs for garnish (optional)

Stuffed Turkey Breast

Add a new twist to Thanksgiving by serving a turkey breast. A boned and butterflied breast cooks quickly and is easier to carve than a conventional turkey. Ask your butcher to butterfly it for you.

1/2 cup (4 oz/125 g) unsalted butter

1 celery stalk, finely chopped

1/2 yellow onion, finely chopped

3 cups (6 oz/185 g) fresh white bread crumbs

1 teaspoon dried thyme

1 teaspoon dried sage

1/3 cup (1 1/2 oz/60 g) raisins

1/3 cup (1 1/2 oz/45 g) chopped walnuts

Salt and freshly ground pepper

1/4 cup (2 fl oz/60 ml) Chicken Stock or Turkey Stock (page 314), if needed

1 turkey breast, 6–8 lb (3–4 kg), boned and butterflied, with skin intact

Vegetable oil for greasing

In a frying pan, melt the butter. Add the celery and onion and cook until soft, about 5 minutes. Transfer to a large bowl. Add the bread crumbs, thyme, sage, raisins, and walnuts and mix well. Season to taste with salt and pepper. The mixture should be moist but not wet. If too dry, add the stock.

Soak 3 handfuls (about 5 oz/155 g) hickory chips or oak chips in water to cover for about 1 hour. Place the turkey breast, skin side down, on a work surface; you will have two large flaps of meat. Sprinkle with salt and pepper. Spread the stuffing over one flap of meat and down the center of the breast, then fold the other flap over it. With heavy kitchen string, tie the breast together in 4 or 5 places to make a tight, cylindrical roll. Coat with oil and sprinkle with salt and pepper.

Lightly grease a grill rack and prepare a fire for indirect-heat cooking in a covered grill (page 327). Position the grill rack 4–6 inches (10–15 cm) above the fire. Drop half of the wood chips on the fire. Place the rolled breast in the center of the rack, cover the grill, and open the vents halfway. Cook for about 1 hour, turning twice. Sprinkle the remaining chips on the fire and add more coals if necessary. Cook for 45–60 minutes longer. It is done when a meat thermometer registers 170°F (80°C). Remove from the grill. Cover loosely with aluminum foil and let stand for about 10 minutes. Remove the strings, cut into slices, and serve.

Serves 8–10

Bacon-Wrapped Cornish Hens

Cornish hens tend to dry out during cooking, but a couple of slices of blanched bacon tied around each bird helps to keep them moist and succulent. Removing the kitchen string before serving also makes a nice presentation.

Prepare a fire for indirect-heat cooking in a covered grill (page 327). Position the grill rack 4–6 inches (10–15 cm) above the fire.

Bring a large saucepan two-thirds full of water to a boil over high heat. Add the bacon and blanch for 3 minutes. Drain, then rinse the bacon with cold water and pat dry with paper towels. Set aside.

Pat the hens dry with paper towels. Sprinkle them inside and out with salt and pepper to taste. Tuck a sprig or two of parsley and thyme into each body cavity. Crisscross 2 slices of bacon across the breast of each hen. Using kitchen string, tie the bacon securely to the birds.

Place the hens, breast side up, in the center of the grill rack. Cover the grill and open the vents halfway. Cook for 30 minutes, then turn breast side down. Continue cooking in the covered grill until the birds are well browned, opaque throughout, and the juices run clear, or until an instant-read thermometer inserted into the thickest part of a breast registers 170°F (77°C) or inserted into the thickest part of a thigh registers 185°F (85°C), 20–25 minutes longer.

To serve, snip the strings, if desired, and arrange the birds on a warmed platter or individual plates with the bacon alongside.

Serves 4

8 slices bacon

4 Cornish hens, about 1¼ lb (625 g) each

Salt and freshly ground pepper

4–8 fresh parsley sprigs

4–8 fresh thyme sprigs

Roast Whole Turkey Breast with Fennel and Bay Leaves

Seek out a fresh rather than frozen turkey breasts. Be sure the neck and back bones have been removed, so the breast lies flat. Remove the breast from the refrigerator about 45 minutes before roasting.

Vegetable oil for greasing

1 bone-in whole turkey breast, 6–7 lb (3–3.5 kg), at room temperature

1 yellow onion, cut into large chunks

1 lemon, quartered

2–3 bay leaves

1 small fennel bulb, preferably with stalk intact, sliced

Salt and freshly ground pepper

¼ cup (2 oz/60 g) unsalted butter, melted

Position a rack in the lower third of the oven and preheat to 350°F (180°C). Lightly grease a flat rack in a roasting pan.

Rinse the turkey breast in cold water and pat dry with paper towels. Place skin side down on a flat surface. Place the onion, lemon, bay leaves, and fennel in the breast cavity. Sprinkle with salt and pepper. Place the oiled rack, upside down, over the turkey cavity and, holding the rack tightly against the cavity, turn the breast over and place in the roasting pan, skin side up. Brush with some of the melted butter and cover loosely with aluminum foil.

Roast for 50 minutes, basting a couple of times with the butter. Remove the foil and reserve it. Continue to roast, basting several times with the pan juices, until the breast is golden and cooked through, 50–60 minutes longer. Test for doneness by inserting an instant-read thermometer into the thickest part of the breast away from the bone. It should register 165°–170°F (74°–77°C), but not more than 170°F or the meat will be dry.

Transfer the turkey breast to a warmed platter, cover loosely with the reserved foil, and let stand for about 20 minutes. Meanwhile, use the pan juices to make gravy (page 315). To carve the turkey breast, start near the breastbone, carve thin slices vertically, cutting parallel to the rib cage, and end each slice at the base cut. Serve with the gravy.

Serves 6–8

Roast Chicken
with Parsley-Lemon Stuffing

Cooked whole in the intense, dry heat of the oven, a chicken develops a crisp, golden brown skin that conceals tender, juicy meat. Serve with minted cranberry sauce (page 317).

Preheat the oven to 150°F (65°C). Slice the bread; discard the crusts. Tear into pieces and place in a food processor. Process to form coarse crumbs. Spread the crumbs on baking sheets and dry in the oven, 1 1/2–2 hours; do not allow to color. Let cool. Raise the heat to 325°F (165°C). Position a rack in the lower third of the oven. Lightly grease a V-shaped rack in a roasting pan. Rinse the chicken in cold water and pat dry with paper towels. Trim off all fat.

In a bowl, toss the bread crumbs, parsley, thyme, and lemon zest. In another bowl, combine the eggs, lemon juice, 1/4 cup (2 oz/60 g) of the butter, 1 teaspoon salt, and a little pepper. Mix well. Add the egg-butter mixture; toss to mix. Spoon into the chicken cavity. Skewer closed and truss (see page 320). Brush with some of the butter and sprinkle with salt and pepper. Lay the bird on its side. Grease the shiny side of a piece of foil and place, buttered side down, over the chicken. Roast for 50 minutes. Turn the chicken onto its other side, brush with more butter, replace the foil, and roast for 50 minutes longer. Remove the foil and reserve it. Turn the chicken breast side up and brush with the butter. Roast until golden brown, 20–30 minutes longer. Test for doneness by inserting an instant-read thermometer in the thickest part of the thigh away from the bone; it should register 180°F (82°C).

Transfer the chicken to a warmed platter, cover loosely with the reserved foil, and let stand for 10 minutes. Meanwhile, use the pan juices to make gravy (page 315). Carve the chicken (page 321) and serve with the stuffing and gravy.

Serves 6–8

1 small loaf French bread, about 1 lb (500 g)

Vegetable oil for greasing

1 roasting chicken, 7–8 lb (3.5–4 kg), at room temperature

1/3 cup (1/2 oz/15 g) finely chopped fresh flat-leaf (Italian) parsley

1 teaspoon dried lemon thyme or regular thyme

Finely grated zest of 1 lemon

2 eggs, lightly beaten

3 tablespoons fresh lemon juice

1/2 cup (4 oz/125 g) unsalted butter, at room temperature, plus extra for greasing

Salt and freshly ground pepper

Maple-Glazed Turkey
with Gingersnap Gravy

Position a rack in the lower third of the oven and preheat to 325°F (165°C).

Rinse the turkey inside and out and pat dry with paper towels. Discard any pieces of fat from the cavities. Place the turkey on a rack in a large roasting pan. Brush with half of the melted butter. Sprinkle with the sage and thyme. Season with salt and pepper. Tie the legs together. Tuck the wing tips under the body. Pour the chicken stock into the roasting pan.

Roast the turkey, basting with the pan juices every 30 minutes, for 2 3/4 hours. Stir the maple syrup into the remaining melted butter. Brush the glaze over the turkey. Continue to roast until an instant-read thermometer inserted into the thickest part of the thigh away from the bone registers 180°F (82°C), about 30 minutes longer. Transfer to a platter, cover loosely with aluminum foil, and let stand for 20 minutes. Pour the pan juices into a large measuring pitcher and skim off and discard the fat. Reserve the pan juices.

To make the gravy, in a large saucepan over medium heat, melt the butter. Add the shallots and sauté until tender, about 3 minutes. Add the sage, thyme, and ginger and stir for 1 minute to blend the flavors. Add the turkey stock and bring to a boil. Boil until reduced to 3 cups (24 fl oz/750 ml), about 20 minutes. Add the reserved pan juices and the gingersnaps and boil, whisking frequently, until mixture forms a thin gravy, about 10 minutes. Season to taste with salt and pepper.

Garnish the turkey with sage and thyme sprigs, if desired, and carve at the table (page 321). Serve with the gravy.

Serves 8–10

1 turkey, 14–16 lb (7–8 kg), neck and giblets reserved for making stock

1/4 cup (2 oz/60 g) unsalted butter, melted

1 tablespoon chopped sage

1 tablespoon chopped thyme

Salt and freshly ground pepper

2 cups (16 fl oz/500 ml) Chicken Stock (page 314)

1 tablespoon pure maple syrup

FOR THE GRAVY:

3 tablespoons unsalted butter

5 shallots, chopped

1 1/2 tablespoons chopped fresh sage or 3/4 teaspoon dried sage

1 1/2 tablespoons chopped fresh thyme or 3/4 teaspoon dried thyme

3/4 teaspoon ground ginger

4 1/2 cups (36 fl oz/1.1 l) Turkey Stock (page 314)

9 gingersnap cookies, crumbled

Salt and freshly ground pepper

Fresh sage and thyme sprigs for garnish (optional)

Herbed Roast Turkey

Vegetable oil for greasing

1 turkey, 12–14 lb (6–7 kg), at room temperature

1 yellow onion, quartered

2 celery stalks, cut into 2-inch (5-cm) lengths

3–4 fresh parsley sprigs

1 bay leaf

1 tablespoon dried sage

2 teaspoons dried thyme

2 teaspoons dried marjoram

Salt and freshly ground pepper

6 tablespoons (3 oz/90 g) unsalted butter, melted

Position a rack in the lower third of the oven and preheat to 425°F (220°C). Lightly grease a V-shaped rack in a roasting pan.

Remove the neck, gizzard, and heart from the turkey, if included, and reserve for another use. Rinse the bird in cold water and pat dry with paper towels. Place the onion, celery, parsley, and bay leaf in the cavity. In a small bowl, mix together the sage, thyme, and marjoram. Place 2 teaspoons of the mixture in the cavity, then sprinkle with salt and pepper. Truss the turkey if desired (page 320). Brush with some of the butter and lightly sprinkle, especially the breast and thighs, with the remaining herb mixture and salt and pepper.

Place the turkey on the rack in the pan, breast side down. Roast for 40 minutes, basting with butter after 20 minutes. Reduce the heat to 325°F (165°C). Turn breast side up and continue to roast, basting with the remaining butter until used up and then with the pan juices every 15–20 minutes. Roast until golden and cooked through. After about 2 1/2 hours, start testing for doneness by inserting an instant-read thermometer into the thickest part of the breast away from the bone; it should register 165°F (74°C). Alternatively, insert it into the thickest part of the thigh; it should register 180°F (82°C). The turkey should roast a total of about 3–4 hours or 15–17 minutes per pound (500 g).

Transfer to a warmed platter, cover loosely with aluminum foil, and let rest for about 20 minutes. Meanwhile, use the pan juices to make the gravy (page 315). Carve the turkey (page 321) and serve with the gravy.

Serves 8–10

Hickory-Smoked Fresh Ham

A fresh ham is often called leg of pork, and it is large enough to feed a crowd. Have your butcher trim the ham of excess fat and tie it for roasting. Serve the ham garnished with fresh herbs, accompanied with scalloped or mashed potatoes.

Soak 3 handfuls (about 5 oz/155 g) of hickory chips in water to cover for 1 hour.

Prepare a fire for indirect-heat cooking in a covered grill (page 327). Position the grill rack 4–6 inches (10–15 cm) above the fire.

In a small bowl, stir together 2 tablespoons salt, 2 teaspoons pepper, the thyme, sage, garlic, and allspice. Pat the pork dry with paper towels. Rub the entire surface of the meat with the oil, then rub the meat with the herb mixture.

Scoop half of the soaked wood chips out of the water and drop them onto the fire. Place the pork on the center of the rack, cover the grill, and open the vents halfway. Cook for about 1 hour. Turn the roast over and add a few more coals to the fire if necessary to maintain a constant temperature. Scoop the remaining wood chips from the water and drop them onto the fire. Continue to cook until the pork is well browned all over and the herb rub has formed a dry, crispy crust or until an instant-read thermometer inserted into the thickest part of the pork away from the bone registers 160°F (71°C), about 2 hours longer. Add a few more coals to the fire as necessary to maintain a constant temperature.

Remove the pork from the grill and transfer to a cutting board. Cover loosely with aluminum foil and let rest for 15 minutes. To serve, snip the strings, carve the meat across the grain into slices about 1/4 inch (6 mm) thick, and arrange on a platter.

Serves 10–14

Coarse or kosher salt and freshly ground pepper

2 teaspoons dried thyme

2 teaspoons dried sage

3 cloves garlic, minced

1/2 teaspoon ground allspice or ground cloves

1 shank-end partial leg of pork, about 10 1/2 lb (5.25 kg), trimmed of excess fat and tied for roasting (see note)

2 tablespoons vegetable oil or olive oil

Crown Roast of Pork
with Sausage and Herb Stuffing

This dramatic presentation is actually quite simple to prepare, as the butcher does the hard part. Be sure to check periodically and cover the rib ends with aluminum foil if they start to brown before the meat is done.

1 crown roast of pork with 16 chops, about 6 lb (3 kg)

Salt and freshly ground pepper

FOR THE STUFFING:

1/4 cup (2 oz/60 g) unsalted butter

1 large yellow onion, minced

1 large celery stalk, cut into 1/4-inch (6-mm) dice

2 cloves garlic, minced

1/2 lb (250 g) bulk sweet pork sausage, crumbled

2 1/2 cups (5 oz/155 g) fresh Herbed Bread Crumbs (page 315)

1 egg, well beaten

About 1/4 cup (2 fl oz/60 ml) Chicken Stock (page 314)

Salt and freshly ground pepper

Position a rack in the middle of the oven and preheat to 400°F (200°C). Set the pork on a rack in a roasting pan. Season to taste with salt and pepper. Roast, uncovered, for 30 minutes. Reduce the heat to 325°F (165°C) and, basting frequently with the pan juices, continue to roast for 45 minutes longer.

Meanwhile, to make the stuffing, in a large frying pan over medium-low heat, melt the butter. Add the onion and celery and sauté, stirring, until very soft, about 15 minutes. Add the garlic and sausage and cook, stirring, until the sausage is browned, about 10 minutes longer. Using a slotted spoon, transfer the sausage mixture to a bowl. Discard the fat from the pan.

Add the bread crumbs and egg to the sausage mixture. Add stock just to moisten the stuffing, then season to taste with salt and pepper. Mix well.

Mound the stuffing in the center of the crown roast and return the roast to the oven. Bake until an instant-read thermometer inserted into the center of the roast away from the bone registers 150°F (65°C) or a chop is pale pink when cut in the center, about 30 minutes longer. (Check periodically and cover the rib ends with aluminum foil if they brown before the meat is done.)

Remove the roast from the oven, cover with a large piece of aluminum foil, and let stand for 10 minutes before carving. To serve, cut the meat between the rib bones. Accompany each serving with a spoonful of stuffing.

Serves 6–8

Holiday Ham Platter

A purchased, fully baked ham stars in this festive but simple-to-assemble menu.
Look for a ham that is spiral cut (presliced) to make serving easier. Buy prepared
horseradish from a well-stocked grocery store, as it has a fresh, strong flavor.

FOR THE CRANBERRY-
HORSERADISH SAUCE:

6 cups (1¹/₂ lb/750 g) fresh
cranberries

2 cups (1 lb/500 g) sugar

1¹/₂ cups (12 fl oz/375 ml) fresh
orange juice

¹/₃ cup (2¹/₂ oz/75 g) prepared
horseradish

¹/₂ teaspoon ground cloves

FOR THE ARUGULA-MUSTARD
MAYONNAISE:

3 cups (24 fl oz/750 ml)
mayonnaise

3 cups (4¹/₂ oz/140 g) chopped
arugula (rocket)

¹/₄ cup (2 oz/60 g) Dijon
mustard

¹/₄ cup (2 fl oz/60 ml) fresh
lemon juice

Freshly ground pepper

8–10 leaves ornamental kale

1 fully baked ham, about
14 lb (7 kg)

Lady apples

Assorted breads and rolls

To make the sauce, sort through the cranberries and discard any soft ones. In a large, heavy saucepan over medium-high heat, combine the sugar and orange juice. Bring to a boil, stirring until the sugar dissolves. Add the cranberries and return to a boil. Reduce the heat to medium and simmer, stirring occasionally, until the cranberries begin to burst, about 8 minutes. Remove from the heat and let cool completely. Stir in the horseradish and cloves and transfer to a bowl. Cover and refrigerate until well chilled. You should have about 4¹/₂ cups (36 fl oz/1.1 l).

To make the mayonnaise, in a food processor, combine the mayonnaise, arugula, mustard, lemon juice, and 1¹/₂ teaspoons pepper. Process until the arugula is finely chopped and the mixture is well blended. Transfer to a bowl, cover, and refrigerate until needed. You should have about 4¹/₂ cups (36 fl oz/1.1 l).

Line a platter with the kale. Top with the ham and garnish with the apples. Set bowls of the cranberry-horseradish sauce and arugula-mustard mayonnaise and baskets of breads and rolls alongside the platter.

Serves 24

Glazed Ham with Poached Orange Slices

A partially cooked ham from a specialty meat market or the meat department of a large, quality food market with a butcher in attendance is the best choice. It is superior in flavor and texture to hams that are tenderized and fully baked.

Position a rack in the lower third of the oven and preheat to 350°F (180°C).

Pat the ham dry with paper towels. Trim off any skin and excess fat. Place on a flat rack in a roasting pan, fat side down. Bake for about 1½ hours, basting frequently with some of the wine, until the internal temperature registers 130°F (55°C). To test, insert an instant-read thermometer into the thickest part of the ham away from the bone. Remove the ham from the oven and turn it fat side up. In a small bowl, stir together the brown sugar and enough wine to form a thick paste. Spread evenly on top of the ham.

Return to the oven. Bake, continuing to baste 2 or 3 times with wine or with the pan juices if the wine is used up, until the internal temperature registers 160°F (70°C), 30–45 minutes longer. The ham should be a rich burgundy color.

Transfer the ham to a warmed platter, cover loosely with aluminum foil, and let rest for at least 10–15 minutes before carving.

Garnish the ham with the orange slices and then carve. Include an orange slice with each serving.

Serves 8–10

1 bone-in ham, 10–12 lb (5–6 kg), preferably only partially cooked, at room temperature

2–3 cups (16–24 fl oz/ 500–750 ml) Madeira wine

3/4 cup (6 oz/185 g) firmly packed light or dark brown sugar

Poached Orange Slices made from 2 oranges (page 319)

Roast Pork Loin and Onions

Olive oil for greasing

1¹/₂ lb (750 g) small white boiling onions, about 1 inch (2.5 cm) in diameter (about 30)

1 center-cut boneless pork loin, 2¹/₂–3 lb (1.25–1.5 kg), trimmed of excess fat and tied in several places

2 teaspoons chopped fresh thyme, plus 6 sprigs

Salt and freshly ground pepper

¹/₂ cup (4 fl oz/125 ml) dry white wine, plus extra for basting

1 teaspoon cornstarch (cornflour) mixed with 1 tablespoon water

Position a rack in the lower third of the oven and preheat to 425°F (220°C). Lightly grease a heavy roasting pan with olive oil.

Trim the onions, then peel and cut a shallow X in the root end. Bring a saucepan three-fourths full of water to a boil. Add the onions, return the water to a boil, and boil for 2 minutes. Drain the onions and set aside.

Pat the pork loin dry with paper towels. Coat the pork with olive oil. Sprinkle with the chopped thyme and season lightly with salt and pepper. Place the pork loin, fat side up, in the roasting pan (without a rack) and add the ¹/₂ cup (4 fl oz/125 ml) wine. Surround the meat with the onions.

Roast, stirring the onions occasionally and basting the pork and onions a few times with the extra wine or the pan juices, until the pork and onions are lightly golden and the juices run clear when the pork is pierced with a knife, 50–70 minutes. To test for doneness, insert an instant-read thermometer into the center of the pork loin; it should read 160°–165°F (71°–74°C).

Transfer the roast to a warmed platter; cover loosely with aluminum foil and set aside. Using a slotted spoon, transfer the onions to a bowl and cover to keep warm. Pour the juices from the pan into a medium saucepan. Skim off the fat with a large spoon and discard. Stir the cornstarch mixture into the juices, set over medium-low heat, and bring to a boil, stirring constantly. When the mixture thickens, season with salt and pepper. If it thickens too much, add a little water to thin. Return the onions to the sauce and coat well.

To serve, cut the pork into slices ¹/₂ inch (12 mm) thick and layer them on the platter. Surround the pork with the onions and their sauce. Garnish with the thyme sprigs, if desired.

Serves 6

Filet Mignon with Wine Sauce

There are two secrets to successful panfrying: the meat must be at room temperature to start, and the frying pan must be a thick and heavy one as the steaks will stick and scorch in a thin-bottomed pan.

4 filet mignon steaks, each about 6 oz (185 g) and 1 inch (2.5 cm) thick

1 tablespoon olive oil

Salt and freshly ground pepper

1/2 cup (4 fl oz/125 ml) dry red wine

2 tablespoons unsalted butter, at room temperature, cut into pieces

1 small bunch watercress, trimmed, carefully washed, and well dried

Trim off excess fat from the steaks. Pat the steaks dry with paper towels.

Place a heavy frying pan over medium-high heat. When the pan is hot, add the olive oil and heat until hot but not smoking. Add the steaks and cook, turning as needed, until evenly browned, 6–8 minutes total. When small beads of red juice appear on the surface, the meat is medium-rare; an instant-read thermometer inserted into the thickest part will read 130°–135°F (54°–57°C). Transfer the steaks to a warmed plate, season to taste with salt and pepper, and cover with aluminum foil to keep warm. They will continue to cook for a few seconds longer and the juices will settle.

Add the wine to the frying pan over high heat, stirring to deglaze the pan. Bring to a boil and boil until reduced to about 1/4 cup (2 fl oz/60 ml). Remove from the heat and whisk in the butter. Taste and adjust the seasonings.

Place the steaks on warmed individual plates and pour the sauce over the top. Garnish with the watercress and serve at once.

Serves 4

Braised Rolled Leg of Veal

This dish is a little bit of work, but well worth the effort. Ask your butcher to bone and butterfly the leg for you. Serve with noodles or Mashed Potatoes with Parsnips (page 139).

In a small bowl, whisk together the eggs, parsley, thyme, and salt and pepper to taste. Warm 2 tablespoons of the oil in a wide frying pan over high heat. Pour in the eggs in a thin sheet; cook until set. Slip onto a plate; set aside.

Put the spinach in a frying pan with only the water clinging to the leaves. Cover and cook over medium heat until wilted, about 3 minutes. Drain and press out moisture. Chop finely and season with salt, pepper, and 1/2 teaspoon of the nutmeg.

Trim the gristle, tendons, and excess fat from the veal leg. Place between sheets of plastic wrap and pound gently to an even thickness. Sprinkle with salt, pepper, and the remaining 1/2 teaspoon nutmeg. Cover the leg completely with the pancetta. Top with the omelet and spinach. Roll up and tie with kitchen string. Poke in several places with a knife and insert the garlic slivers into the slits. Sprinkle with salt and pepper. Warm 2 tablespoons of the oil in a frying pan over high heat. Add the veal and brown on all sides, about 10 minutes.

Warm the remaining 2 tablespoons oil in a large, heavy pot over medium heat. Add the onions, carrot, and celery and sauté until soft, 10–15 minutes. Add the veal, wine, and stock and bring to a boil. Reduce the heat to low, cover, and simmer on the stove top or in the oven preheated to 325°F (165°C) until the veal is tender or an instant-read thermometer registers 140°F (60°C), about 1 1/2 hours.

Transfer to a platter and let rest for 10 minutes. Discard the string and cut into slices 1/3 inch (9 mm) thick. Season with salt and pepper and serve.

Serves 6

2 eggs

3 tablespoons chopped fresh flat-leaf (Italian) parsley

1 teaspoon chopped fresh thyme

Salt and freshly ground pepper

6 tablespoons (3 fl oz/90 ml) olive oil

2 small bunches spinach, trimmed and carefully washed (about 4 cups/4 oz/125 g leaves)

1 teaspoon ground nutmeg

1 leg of veal, boned and butterflied, about 4 lb (2 kg)

6 slices pancetta or prosciutto

2 cloves garlic, cut into slivers

3 yellow onions, diced

1 large carrot, peeled and diced

1 celery stalk, diced

1 1/2 cups (12 fl oz/375 ml) dry white wine

2 cups (16 fl oz/500 ml) Chicken or Beef Stock (page 314)

Sweet-and-Sour Brisket

This mouthwatering dish can be simmered on top of the stove or cooked in a slow cooker. It can be made 3 days in advance and refrigerated, or frozen for up to 6 months (slice it before wrapping for freezing).

In a Dutch oven or other heavy pot over medium heat, sear the meat, fat side down, for 5–10 minutes. Turn and brown the other side, 5–10 minutes longer. Remove the brisket from the pot. Using a large spoon, skim off any fat from the drippings and discard, but leave the drippings in the pot.

Add the onions, celery, chili sauce, garlic, bay leaves, brown sugar, mustard, soy sauce, vinegar, molasses, and 1/4 cup (2 fl oz/60 ml) water to the pot and stir to mix well. Return the brisket to the pot, cover, and cook over medium-low heat for 3 hours. Add the beer, paprika, and potatoes. Re-cover and continue to cook for 1 hour longer. Add water, if necessary, to keep the mixture moist.

Allow the brisket to cool in the liquid for 30 minutes, then transfer it to a dish. Pour the cooking liquid and potatoes into a bowl. Discard the bay leaves. Let the liquid and meat cool for at least 2 hours, then skim off the fat from the liquid. Return the liquid and potatoes to a heavy pot with a lid.

Cut the meat across the grain into slices 1/4 inch (6 mm) thick and add it to the liquid. Cover and reheat the meat and potatoes over low heat. Season to taste with salt and pepper.

To serve, arrange the slices on a large warmed platter. Surround or top with the cooking liquid and potatoes.

Serves 8

1 beef brisket, 5–6 lb (2.5–3 kg)

2 large yellow onions, cut into slices 1/2 inch (12 mm) thick

4 large celery stalks, including leaves, cut into slices 1/2 inch (12 mm) thick

1 cup (8 fl oz/250 ml) chili sauce or spicy tomato ketchup

4 large cloves garlic, chopped

2 bay leaves

1/2 cup (3 1/2 oz/105 g) firmly packed dark brown sugar

1/3 cup (2 1/2 oz/75 g) Dijon mustard

1/4 cup (2 fl oz/60 ml) soy sauce

1/4 cup (2 fl oz/60 ml) red wine vinegar

3 tablespoons molasses

1 1/2 cups (12 fl oz/375 ml) beer

1/2 teaspoon paprika

4 large baking potatoes, peeled and cut into slices 1 inch (2.5 cm) thick

Salt and freshly ground pepper

Beer-Basted Prime Rib with Horseradish Cream

Basting with beer gives meat a slightly smoky taste, and deglazing the pan with beef stock and beer provides a rich sauce for this dish. Serve with glazed carrots and baked potatoes topped with horseradish cream.

1 standing rib roast, about 8 lb (4 kg)

4–6 cloves garlic, cut into slivers

$1/4$ cup (2 fl oz/60 ml) soy sauce

Freshly ground pepper

$1/2$ teaspoon ground allspice

About 3 cups (24 fl oz/750 ml) dark beer or stout

1 cup (8 fl oz/250 ml) Beef Stock (page 314)

FOR THE HORSERADISH CREAM:

$1/2$ cup (4 oz/125 g) thinly sliced, peeled fresh horseradish

3–4 tablespoons (about 2 fl oz/ 60 ml) distilled white vinegar

3 tablespoons finely minced white onion

$1 1/2$ cups (12 fl oz/125 ml) sour cream

$1/2$ cup (4 fl oz/125 ml) heavy (double) cream

1 teaspoon salt

$1/2$ teaspoon freshly ground pepper

Using the tip of a sharp knife, make slits 1 inch (2.5 cm) deep at regular intervals over the entire surface of the roast. Insert the garlic slivers into the slits. Place in a roasting pan. Brush the outside of the roast with the soy sauce. Sprinkle with 1 tablespoon pepper and the allspice. Let the roast stand at room temperature for about 1 hour.

Preheat the oven to 350°F (180°C). Roast the beef for about $1 3/4$ hours, or until an instant-read thermometer reads 120°F (49°C) for rare, basting every 10 minutes with the beer.

Transfer to a warmed platter and let rest for 15 minutes before carving.

Skim the fat from the roasting pan and discard. Place the pan on the stove top over medium-high heat. Pour in the stock (or more beer). Deglaze the pan by stirring to dislodge any browned bits. Simmer for a few minutes, then taste and adjust the seasoning. Carve the roast (page 322) and spoon some of the sauce over the meat.

To make the horseradish cream, you may use 5 tablespoons (3 oz/90 g) prepared horseradish for making this sauce, but the fresh root is hotter and more flavorful. If you use prepared horseradish, you may not need as much vinegar or salt.

Place the horseradish and 3 tablespoons of the vinegar in a blender or food processor and purée until smooth. Transfer to a bowl. Stir in the remaining ingredients until mixed, adding another tablespoon vinegar if needed for tartness and flavor balance.

Serves 6–8

Roast Prime Rib of Beef

A prime rib roast is a good choice for Christmas dinner. The beef must be chosen with care; its flavor is of utmost importance. Seek out a butcher who carries high-quality, dry-aged beef. Ask the butcher to tie the roast.

1 prime rib roast with
3–4 bones, 7–8 lb (3.5–4 kg)
trimmed weight, at room
temperature

Salt and freshly ground
pepper

Position a rack in the lower third of the oven and preheat to 500°F (260°C). In a roasting pan without a rack, place the roast rib side down (fat side up). Sprinkle with pepper, if desired. If you wish to salt the roast, do so toward the end of roasting. Roast for 15 minutes. Reduce the heat to 325°F (165°C) and continue roasting.

After 1 1/2 hours of roasting, start testing for doneness by inserting an instant-read thermometer into the thickest part of the meat away from the bone; it should register 130°F (55°C) for medium-rare. It should reach this point 2–2 1/2 hours after you turned down the heat.

Transfer the roast to a warmed platter. Cover loosely with aluminum foil and let rest for 15–20 minutes. Meanwhile, pour off just the fat from the pan and heat the remaining juices over medium heat. Add 1/2 cup (4 fl oz/125 ml) water and deglaze the pan by stirring to dislodge any browned bits stuck to the bottom. Bring to a boil and season with salt and pepper. Add more water for desired consistency and taste.

Carve the roast (page 322) and serve with the pan juices in a bowl on the side.

Serves 8–10

Roast Rack of Lamb with Herbed Crust

This variation on rack of lamb uses a Provençal-style mixture of herbs. Don't worry if the coating falls off when you carve the lamb; simply spoon it onto the individual plates with the lamb chops.

Preheat the oven to 450°F (230°C). Trim any excess fat from the lamb racks. Using a small, sharp knife, scrape off any meat from the top 1 1/2 inches (4 cm) of each bone.

Place the lamb racks in a roasting pan, bone side down, and roast for 18–25 minutes for medium-rare. The timing will depend on their size. To test for doneness, insert an instant-read meat thermometer into the thickest part of the lamb away from the bone; it should register 135°F (57°C).

While the lamb is roasting, in a small bowl, combine the bread crumbs, shallots, basil, chopped thyme, parsley, olive oil, stock, 1/4 teaspoon salt, and 1/8 teaspoon pepper and mix well. (You can prepare this mixture up to 2 hours in advance of when the lamb is ready; set aside at room temperature.)

Preheat the broiler (grill). When the lamb is done roasting, spread the bread crumb mixture evenly over the meat side of the racks. Place the lamb under the broiler about 3 inches (7.5 cm) from the heat source and broil (grill) until lightly browned, 2–3 minutes. Be careful not to let the coating burn.

Transfer the racks to a warmed serving platter. Separate the chops by cutting between the bones. Serve 2 or 3 chops per person, garnishing the plates with the thyme sprigs. Serve immediately.

Serves 6

2 racks of lamb, 8 chops or about 2 1/2 lb (1.25 kg) each

1 cup (2 oz/60 g) fresh bread crumbs

2 shallots, finely chopped

1 tablespoon finely chopped fresh basil

1 tablespoon finely chopped fresh thyme, plus thyme sprigs for garnish

2 tablespoons finely chopped fresh flat-leaf (Italian) parsley

3 tablespoons olive oil

2 tablespoons Chicken Stock (page 314)

Salt and freshly ground pepper

Butterflied Leg of Lamb with Mint Sauce

A butterflied leg of lamb is a large, flat, boneless piece of meat weighing about 4 lb (2 kg); ask your butcher to prepare it for you. The tart mint sauce accompanying the lamb here bears no resemblance to the sweet mint jelly often served with lamb.

To make the mint sauce, combine the vinegar and sugar in a small saucepan and bring to a boil, stirring just until the sugar dissolves. Remove from the heat and add the mint and salt to taste. Set aside to allow the flavors to mellow.

Place the lamb in a glass or porcelain baking dish or enameled baking pan large enough for it to lie flat. In a bowl, stir together the wine, olive oil, shallot, rosemary, garlic, 1 teaspoon salt, and $^1/_2$ teaspoon pepper. Pour over the lamb and marinate for at least 2 hours, or all day if you wish, turning occasionally.

Lightly grease a grill rack and prepare a fire in a grill. Position the grill rack 4–6 inches (10–15 cm) above the fire. Remove the lamb from the marinade and pat it dry with paper towels; reserve the marinade. Place the lamb on the rack. Grill for 35–45 minutes, turning frequently and brushing occasionally with the reserved marinade. The meat should remain pink inside; make a small cut in the thickest part to check for doneness; an instant-read thermometer will register 125°F (52°C) for rare, 130°F (55°C) for medium-rare.

Remove the lamb from the grill and let rest for 5 minutes, covered loosely with aluminum foil. Carve across the grain into thin slices. Serve with the mint sauce.

Serves 6

FOR THE MINT SAUCE:

$^1/_2$ cup (4 fl oz/125 ml) cider vinegar

$^1/_3$ cup (3 oz/90 g) sugar

$^2/_3$ cup (1 oz/30 g) chopped fresh mint leaves

Salt

1 leg of lamb, 6–7 lb (3–3.5 kg), boned, butterflied, and trimmed of excess fat

$^2/_3$ cup (5 fl oz/160 ml) dry red wine

$^1/_3$ cup (3 fl oz/80 ml) olive oil

1 shallot, chopped

1 tablespoon chopped fresh rosemary or 1 teaspoon dried rosemary

2 cloves garlic, minced

Salt and freshly ground pepper

Vegetable oil for greasing

Roast Leg of Lamb

1 leg of lamb, 6–7 lb
(3–3.5 kg), at room
temperature

2 tablespoons dry mustard

2 tablespoons olive oil or
vegetable oil

1 tablespoon chopped fresh
rosemary or 1 teaspoon
dried rosemary

Salt and freshly ground pepper

Apple-Mint Chutney (page 316)
for serving

Position a rack in the lower third of the oven and preheat to 350°F (180°C).

Remove the papery film and excess fat from the leg of lamb, if not done by the butcher. Wipe the lamb with a damp cloth.

In a small bowl, stir together the mustard, oil, and rosemary to form a paste. Spread over the surface of the lamb. Sprinkle with salt and pepper and place on a flat rack in a roasting pan, fat side up. Roast until browned and done as desired. Check for doneness by inserting an instant-read thermometer into the thickest part of the leg away from the bone. It should register 135°F (57°C) for pink. It will reach this point after about 1 1/2 hours.

Transfer to a warmed platter. Cover loosely with aluminum foil and let rest for 10–15 minutes. Meanwhile, prepare the pan juices. Pour off just the fat from the roasting pan, leaving the pan juices. Heat the pan juices over medium heat. Add 1/2 cup (4 fl oz/125 ml) water and deglaze the pan by stirring to dislodge any browned bits stuck to the bottom. Bring to a boil and season to taste with salt and pepper. Add more water if needed to reach the desired consistency.

Carve the lamb (page 322) and serve with the apple-mint chutney. Serve the pan juices in a bowl on the side.

Serves 6–8

Breads & Stuffings

Buckwheat-Fennel Crisp Bread

Crisp bread is a Christmas tradition in Scandinavia. There, a hobnailed rolling pin is used to roll out the dough, but poking the dough with fork tines works well, too. Serve the bread plain, or with smoked salmon or gravlax and watercress, if you like.

Preheat the oven to 350°F (180°C). Grease 2 baking sheets.

Pour the warm water into a large bowl. Sprinkle the yeast over the top. Stir in the sugar and let stand until the mixture is bubbly, about 5 minutes. Add the milk, melted butter, salt, and baking soda to the yeast mixture and stir until well mixed. Add the buckwheat flour and, using a wooden spoon, beat until smooth, about 2 minutes. Beat in about $2^{1}/4$ cups ($11^{1}/2$ oz/360 g) of the all-purpose flour to make a dough that is semisoft but no longer sticky.

Transfer the dough to a lightly floured work surface and knead, adding flour as needed to prevent sticking, until smooth, about 5 minutes. Divide the dough in half. Roll out each half into a 9-by-11-inch (23-by-28-cm) rectangle about $^{1}/8$ inch (3 mm) thick. Pierce each rectangle all over with a fork.

Carefully transfer a dough rectangle to each baking sheet. Sprinkle half of the fennel seeds evenly over each rectangle and then gently press the seeds into the dough. Using a pastry wheel or sharp knife, cut each rectangle into 24 rectangular pieces.

Bake until the breads are crisp and golden brown, about 25 minutes. Transfer the baking sheets to racks and let cool completely. Break the rectangles apart into crackers. Store in an airtight container at room temperature for up to 1 week.

Makes 48 crackers

Unsalted butter for greasing

$^{1}/4$ cup (2 fl oz/60 ml) warm water (105°–115°F/40°–46°C)

1 tablespoon active dry yeast

1 teaspoon sugar

$^{3}/4$ cup (6 fl oz/180 ml) milk

$^{1}/2$ cup (4 oz/125 g) unsalted butter, melted and cooled

$^{1}/2$ teaspoon salt

$^{1}/2$ teaspoon baking soda (bicarbonate of soda)

$^{1}/2$ cup ($2^{1}/2$ oz/75 g) buckwheat flour

About $2^{1}/2$ cups ($12^{1}/2$ oz/ 390 g) all-purpose (plain) flour

1 tablespoon fennel seeds

Festive Challah

Challah is the traditional Jewish egg bread served on the Sabbath. Although it can be shaped in many different ways, braiding is the most common. Here, the addition of fragrant saffron gives it a deep golden hue.

About 5 cups (25 oz/780 g) all-purpose (plain) flour

1/4 cup (2 oz/60 g) sugar

1 tablespoon active dry yeast

1 teaspoon salt

1/8 teaspoon powdered saffron

1 1/4 cups (10 fl oz/315 ml) warm water (105°–115°F/40°–46°C)

6 tablespoons (3 oz/90 g) unsalted butter, at room temperature, plus extra for greasing

3 eggs

1 tablespoon milk

1 tablespoon sesame seeds

In the bowl of a heavy-duty mixer fitted with the dough hook, combine 1 1/2 cups (7 1/2 oz/235 g) of the flour, the sugar, yeast, salt, and saffron. Add the warm water and beat on medium-high speed until well mixed. Beat in the butter and 2 of the eggs. Then beat in about 3 cups (15 oz/470 g) more flour to make a dough that is semisoft but no longer sticky.

Transfer the dough to a floured work surface and knead, adding more flour as needed to prevent sticking, until smooth and elastic, about 5 minutes. Gather the dough into a ball, place in a large greased bowl, turn to coat with butter, and cover the bowl with a clean kitchen towel. Place in a warm, draft-free area and let rise until doubled in bulk, about 1 1/2 hours.

Punch down the dough and transfer to a lightly floured work surface. Knead until smooth, about 3 minutes. Divide the dough into 3 equal pieces. Using your palms, roll each piece into a rope 20 inches (50 cm) long. Grease a baking sheet. Braid the ropes together and transfer the braid to the baking sheet, tucking the ends under. Cover with the kitchen towel and let rise in a warm, draft-free area until doubled in bulk, about 1 hour.

Meanwhile, preheat the oven to 350°F (180°C). In a small bowl, beat the remaining egg with the milk until blended. Brush evenly over the braid. Sprinkle with the sesame seeds. Bake until the bread is golden brown and sounds hollow when thumped on the bottom, about 55 minutes. Let cool on a wire rack.

Makes 1 large loaf

Chive Cream Biscuits

Serve these delicious biscuits with your Thanksgiving turkey or holiday ham. For an extra burst of chive flavor, stir minced chives into softened butter for spreading on these light biscuits.

Position a rack in the upper third of the oven and preheat to 425°F (220°C).

In a large bowl, combine the flour, chives, baking powder, salt, and 1 teaspoon pepper. Using a wooden spoon, mix well. Gradually stir in enough cream to form a dough that comes together into a ball.

Transfer the dough to a floured work surface and knead gently, adding flour as needed to prevent sticking, until smooth, about 10 turns. Roll out the dough 1/2 inch (12 mm) thick. Using a round or heart-shaped biscuit cutter 2 1/2 inches (6 cm) in diameter, cut out biscuits. Transfer the biscuits to an ungreased baking sheet, spacing them 1 inch (2.5 cm) apart. Gather together the scraps and roll out 1/2 inch (12 mm) thick. Cut out additional biscuits and transfer them to the baking sheet as well.

Brush the biscuits with the melted butter and sprinkle with pepper to taste. Bake until light brown, about 15 minutes. Remove from the oven and serve hot, or transfer to a wire rack to cool and serve warm.

Makes about 12 biscuits

2 cups (10 oz/315 g) all-purpose (plain) flour, plus extra for kneading

1/4 cup (1/3 oz/10 g) minced fresh chives or 1/4 cup (3/4 oz/20 g) minced green (spring) onion, including tender green tops

1 tablespoon baking powder

1/2 teaspoon salt

1 teaspoon freshly ground pepper, plus extra for sprinkling

About 1 1/3 cups (11 fl oz/ 340 ml) heavy (double) cream

2 tablespoons butter, melted

Hot Cross Buns

¼ cup (2 fl oz/60 ml) warm water (105°–115°F/40°–46°C)

1 tablespoon active dry yeast

½ cup (4 fl oz/125 ml) milk, warmed

6 tablespoons (3 oz/90 g) unsalted butter, melted and cooled, plus extra butter at room temperature for greasing

¼ cup (2 oz/60 g) sugar

1 whole egg, plus 1 egg yolk

2 teaspoons grated lemon zest

1 teaspoon ground nutmeg

½ teaspoon salt

About 3½ cups (17½ oz/545 g) all-purpose (plain) flour

1 cup (6 oz/185 g) raisins, chopped

½ cup (4 fl oz/125 ml) White Icing (page 319)

Pour the warm water into a large bowl. Sprinkle the yeast over the top and let stand until dissolved, about 1 minute. Stir in the milk, 4 tablespoons (2 fl oz/60 ml) of the melted butter, and the sugar. Whisk in the whole egg and egg yolk until blended. Add the lemon zest, nutmeg, and salt and stir well. Stir in 1½ cups (7½ oz/235 g) of the flour and the raisins. Using a wooden spoon, beat in about 1 cup (5 oz/155 g) more flour to make a dough that is semisoft but no longer sticky.

Transfer the dough to a lightly floured work surface and knead, adding flour as needed to prevent sticking, until smooth and elastic, about 5 minutes. Gather the dough into a ball, place in a large greased bowl, turn to coat with butter, and cover the bowl with a clean kitchen towel. Place in a warm, draft-free area and let rise until the dough doubles in bulk, about 1½ hours.

Punch down the dough and transfer to a lightly floured work surface. Knead until smooth, about 3 minutes. Divide the dough into 12 equal pieces and form each piece into a ball. Grease a baking sheet and place the balls well apart on the sheet. Cover with the kitchen towel and let rise in a warm, draft-free area until doubled in bulk, about 45 minutes.

Meanwhile, preheat the oven to 375°F (190°C). Using a sharp knife, cut an X about ½ inch (12 mm) deep in the top of each bun. Brush the remaining 2 tablespoons melted butter evenly over the tops. Bake until the buns are golden brown and sound hollow when thumped on the bottoms, about 25 minutes. Let cool completely on a wire rack, then, using a spoon, fill each X with the icing.

Makes 12 buns

Popovers

Have the ingredients measured and ready for quick assembly, as popovers need to be baked just before serving time. Popovers can be baked in muffin tins as well as popover pans. The muffin size is particularly nice for a holiday dinner.

Grease 12 standard-sized muffin cups or a popover pan.

In a large bowl, combine the eggs and salt. Using a whisk, beat lightly. Stir in the milk and melted butter and then beat in the flour just until blended. Be careful to not overbeat.

Fill each cup about half full and place in the cold oven. Set the oven temperature to 425°F (220°C) and bake for 20 minutes. Reduce the oven temperature to 375°F (190°C) and bake until the popovers are golden, 10–15 minutes longer. They should be crisp on the outside.

Quickly pierce each popover with a thin metal skewer or the tip of a small knife to release the steam. Leave in the oven a couple of minutes longer for further crisping, then remove and serve at once.

Makes 12 popovers

Unsalted butter for greasing

2 eggs

1/4 teaspoon salt

1 cup (8 fl oz/250 ml) milk

2 tablespoons unsalted butter, melted

1 cup (5 oz/155 g) all-purpose (plain) flour

Spoonbread

This recipe from Chuck Williams for spoonbread, a tradition in the Southern United States, has the characteristics of a soufflé because the egg whites are beaten separately and then folded into the cornmeal mixture.

4¹/₂ cups (36 fl oz/1.1 l) milk

1¹/₂ cups (7¹/₂ oz/235 g) yellow cornmeal, preferably stone-ground

1¹/₂ teaspoons salt

¹/₈ teaspoon ground nutmeg

3 tablespoons unsalted butter, cut into small cubes, plus extra for greasing

6 eggs, separated

2 teaspoons baking powder

¹/₂ cup (2 oz/60 g) grated Parmesan cheese

Preheat the oven to 400°F (200°C). Grease a 3-qt (3-l) baking dish with sides 2–2¹/₂ inches (5–6 mm) deep.

Pour 4 cups (32 fl oz/1 l) of the milk into a saucepan, place over medium heat, and heat until small bubbles appear along the edges of the pan. Remove from the heat and, using a whisk, stir vigorously while slowly pouring in the cornmeal. Continue to whisk until the mixture is smooth. Return to medium heat and stir until thickened, 1–2 minutes.

Remove from the heat and stir in the remaining ¹/₂ cup (4 fl oz/125 ml) milk and the salt, nutmeg, and butter, stirring continuously until the butter melts. Add the egg yolks one at a time, stirring well after each addition. Stir in the baking powder and Parmesan cheese.

In a bowl, using a whisk or an electric mixer set on medium speed, beat the egg whites until soft peaks form. Using a rubber spatula, stir about one-fourth of the beaten egg whites into the cornmeal mixture to lighten it, then carefully fold in the remaining whites just until no whites remain. Immediately spoon the batter into the prepared baking dish.

Bake until puffed and golden and a toothpick inserted into the center comes out clean, 45–50 minutes. Remove from the oven and serve at once.

Serves 10–12

Onion-Herb Rolls

1/3 cup (3 fl oz/80 ml) olive oil, plus extra for greasing

1 large yellow onion, finely chopped

2 cloves garlic, finely chopped

1 teaspoon minced fresh sage

1 teaspoon minced fresh rosemary

1 teaspoon minced fresh thyme

1 cup (8 fl oz/250 ml) warm water (105°–115°F/40°–46°C)

1 tablespoon active dry yeast

3 tablespoons wheat bran

Scant 1 1/2 teaspoons salt

1/4 teaspoon freshly ground pepper

About 3 cups (15 oz/470 g) all-purpose (plain) flour

In a heavy frying pan over medium heat, warm the olive oil. Add the onion and garlic and sauté until tender, about 8 minutes. Stir in the sage, rosemary, and thyme and sauté until the flavors have blended, about 2 minutes. Remove from the heat and let cool.

Pour the warm water into a large bowl. Sprinkle the yeast over the top and let stand until dissolved, about 1 minute. Stir in the bran, salt, and pepper, then mix in the onion mixture. Using a wooden spoon, gradually beat in about 2 1/2 cups (12 1/2 oz/390 g) flour to make a semisoft dough.

Transfer the dough to a floured work surface and knead, adding flour as needed to prevent sticking, until just smooth and elastic. Grease a large, clean bowl with olive oil. Gather the dough into a ball, place in the bowl, and turn to coat with oil. Cover the bowl with a clean kitchen towel. Place in a warm, draft-free area and let rise until the dough is doubled in bulk, about 1 hour.

Punch down the dough and transfer to a lightly floured work surface. Knead until smooth, about 2 minutes. Divide the dough into 12 equal pieces and form each piece into a strip about 7 inches (18 cm) long and 2 inches (5 cm) wide. Beginning at a narrow end, roll up each strip to form a roll. Grease a baking sheet with olive oil and place the rolls seam side down and well apart. Cover with the kitchen towel and let rise in a warm, draft-free area until doubled in bulk, about 35 minutes.

Meanwhile, preheat the oven to 400°F (200°C). Bake until the rolls are golden brown and sound hollow when thumped on the bottoms, 15–18 minutes. Serve warm.

Makes 12 rolls

Whole-Kernel Corn Bread

If stone-ground cornmeal is available, buy it for this recipe. It makes a nicely textured, well-flavored bread. If there is any bread left over, slice it and toast it in the oven. It is excellent served for breakfast with almost any fruit jam.

Preheat the oven to 425°F (220°C). Lightly grease an 8–9 inch (20–23 cm) square baking pan that is 1 1/2 inches (4 cm) deep.

Bring a large saucepan three-fourths full of water to a boil. Add the corn and cook for 5 minutes. Drain and immediately plunge into cold water to cool. Using a sharp knife and holding each ear of corn upright on a cutting surface, cut the kernels from the cobs. You should have 1 1/2–2 cups (9–12 oz/280–375 g) kernels. Set aside.

In a bowl, stir together the cornmeal, flour, sugar, salt, baking powder, and cayenne. Stir in the eggs and milk, then the corn kernels and butter.

Pour the batter into the prepared pan. Bake until golden, 25–30 minutes. Remove from the oven and let cool slightly on a wire rack for 2–3 minutes. Cut into squares and serve warm.

Serves 8–10

3 large ears of yellow corn, husks and silk removed

1 1/4 cups (8 oz/250 g) yellow cornmeal, preferably stone-ground

3/4 cup (4 oz/125 g) all-purpose (plain) flour

2 teaspoons sugar

1 1/4 teaspoons salt

1 tablespoon baking powder

1/8 teaspoon cayenne pepper

2 eggs, lightly beaten

1 cup (8 fl oz/250 ml) milk

1/4 cup (2 oz/60 g) unsalted butter, melted, plus extra butter at room temperature for greasing

Parsley Biscuits

American biscuits are a tradition as well as an excellent accompaniment to any holiday dinner, and they are quite easy to prepare. To save time, have your ingredients measured and pans ready before you begin to mix the dough.

Unsalted butter for greasing

2 cups (10 oz/315 g)
all-purpose (plain) flour

1/2 teaspoon salt

1 tablespoon baking powder

Finely shredded zest of
1 lemon

3 tablespoons finely chopped
fresh flat-leaf (Italian) parsley

1/2 cup (4 oz/125 g) vegetable
shortening

1/2 cup (4 fl oz/125 ml) milk

1/4 cup (2 fl oz/60 ml)
heavy (double) cream

Preheat an oven to 425°F (220°C). Grease 1 or 2 baking sheets or pans and set aside.

In a large bowl, stir together the flour, salt, baking powder, lemon zest, and parsley. Add the shortening and, using a pastry blender, your fingertips, or 2 knives, mix together until the mixture resembles oatmeal. Add the milk and cream and, using a fork, mix together until the mixture forms a mass and holds together.

Gather up the dough into a ball, place on a floured board and knead a few times. Flatten the dough with your hands (or roll it out with a rolling pin) until it is 3/8–1/2 inch (9–12 mm) thick. Using a round cutter or glass 2–2 1/2 inches (5–6 cm) in diameter, cut out as many biscuits as possible. Place on the prepared pan about 1/4 inch (6 mm) apart. Gather up the scraps of dough and press together to make more biscuits.

Place in the oven and bake until golden and light, about 15 minutes. Remove from the oven and serve at once.

Makes 20–24 biscuits

Corn Bread and Dried Fruit Dressing

1 cup (5 oz/155 g) each yellow cornmeal and all-purpose (plain) flour

2 tablespoons sugar

1 tablespoon baking powder

½ teaspoon salt

2 eggs, lightly beaten

1 cup (8 fl oz/250 ml) nonfat milk

¼ cup (2 fl oz/60 ml) vegetable oil

½ cup (3 oz/90 g) each raisins and dried apricots, chopped

1 cup (8 fl oz/250 ml) dry white wine

¼ cup (2 oz/60 g) unsalted butter, plus extra for greasing

1 yellow onion, diced

1 clove garlic, minced

2 celery stalks, diced

1 small tart green apple, cored and diced

1 tablespoon dried sage

2 cups (16 fl oz/500 ml) Chicken Stock (page 314)

¼ cup (⅓ oz/10 g) chopped parsley

1 cup (4½ oz/140 g) slivered almonds, toasted (page 328)

Salt and freshly ground pepper

The day before, make the corn bread: Preheat the oven to 400°F (200°C). Lightly grease an 8-inch (20-cm) square baking pan.

In a large bowl, stir together the cornmeal, flour, sugar, baking powder, and salt. In another bowl, stir together the eggs, milk, and oil until well blended. Pour the egg mixture into the cornmeal mixture and stir just until smooth. Pour into the prepared baking pan. Bake until golden brown and a toothpick inserted into the center comes out clean, about 30 minutes. Let cool in the pan on a wire rack for 10 minutes, then turn out and let cool to room temperature. Cut the bread in half horizontally, then cut into ½–1-inch (12-mm–2.5-cm) cubes. Spread on 2 baking sheets and let dry overnight at room temperature.

The next day, make the dressing: Put the raisins and dried apricots in a bowl, pour in the wine, and let soak for about 30 minutes. Grease a 3-qt (3-l) baking dish.

In a large frying pan over medium heat, melt the butter. Add the onion and garlic and sauté until translucent, about 2–3 minutes. Add the celery, apple, and sage and mix well. Sauté for 2 minutes. Remove from the heat and set aside. Put the corn-bread cubes in a large bowl. Gradually add the stock, tossing to moisten evenly. Drain the soaked fruits and add to the bowl. Add the sautéed mixture, parsley, almonds, and salt and pepper to taste. Mix until blended. Spoon the dressing into the prepared dish.

To bake the dressing alongside a turkey in a 325°F (165°C) oven, place the dressing on a rack in the lower third of the oven about 30 minutes before the turkey is done roasting. When the turkey has been removed, raise the oven temperature to 375°F (190°C) and continue baking until golden, 20–30 minutes longer. Serve immediately.

Serves 6–8

Sausage, Apple, and Chestnut Stuffing

A Thanksgiving tradition, this stuffing is the perfect accompaniment to a roast turkey. For the fresh chestnuts, you may substitute 2 cups (about 10 oz/315 g) vacuum-packed steamed chestnuts, which have already been peeled.

Preheat the oven to 400°F (200°C). Place the bread cubes in a large baking pan. Bake, stirring often, until lightly golden, 12 minutes. Transfer the bread to a large bowl. In a large frying pan over medium-high heat, cook the sausage, crumbling with a fork, until browned, about 10 minutes. Transfer to the bowl with the bread. Add the butter to the drippings in the pan, reduce the heat to medium, and melt the butter. Add the onion and celery and sauté until tender, about 8 minutes. Add the apples and thyme and sauté for 1 1/2 minutes. Add to the bread. Add the stock to the frying pan and bring to a boil, scraping up any browned bits. Add to the bread. Mix in the chestnuts and parsley, and season with salt and pepper to taste. Mix in the eggs.

To bake the stuffing in a turkey, fill the cavities with the stuffing and truss (page 320); increase the roasting time of the turkey by 30 minutes. Butter a baking dish large enough to hold the remaining stuffing and spoon the stuffing into it; cover with aluminum foil. Bake alongside the turkey for 30 minutes. Uncover and bake until the top is crisp, about 30 minutes longer.

To bake all the stuffing in a baking dish, preheat the oven to 325°F (165°C). Grease a 13-by-9-by-2-inch (33-by-23-by-5-cm) baking dish and spoon the stuffing into it; cover with foil. Bake for 30 minutes. Uncover and bake until the top is crisp, about 30 minutes longer.

Makes about 12 cups (5 lb/2.5 kg) stuffing, enough for a 16-lb (8-kg) turkey; serves 8–10

1 lb (500 g) sourdough bread or coarse country white bread, crusts trimmed, cut into 1/2-inch (12-mm) cubes

3/4 lb (375 g) bulk pork sausage

1/4 cup (2 oz/60 g) butter, plus extra for greasing

1 large yellow onion, chopped

3 large celery stalks, chopped

2 large tart apples such as pippin or Granny Smith, peeled, quartered, cored, and chopped

3 tablespoons chopped fresh thyme or 1 tablespoon dried thyme

3/4 cup (6 fl oz/180 ml) Chicken Stock (page 314)

1 lb (500 g) fresh chestnuts, roasted and peeled (page 325), then coarsely chopped

1/2 cup (3/4 oz/20 g) chopped fresh flat-leaf (Italian) parsley

Salt and freshly ground pepper

2 eggs, well beaten

Wild Rice and Dried Cranberry Pilaf

This dish combining pine nuts, dried cranberries, and golden raisins (sultanas) with wild and long-grain rice makes a delicious addition to a Thanksgiving dinner featuring turkey or ham.

9 cups (72 fl oz/2.25 l) low-sodium vegetable broth or 4¹/₂ cups (36 fl oz/1.1 l) each broth and water

1¹/₃ cups (8 oz/250 g) wild rice, well rinsed

4 tablespoons (2 oz/60 g) butter

3 large yellow onions, chopped

³/₄ teaspoon ground cardamom

1 teaspoon ground allspice

2 bay leaves

1 cup (4 oz/125 g) dried cranberries

1 cup (6 oz/185 g) golden raisins (sultanas)

2 teaspoons grated orange zest

Salt and freshly ground pepper

1¹/₂ cups (10¹/₂ oz/330 g) long-grain white rice

¹/₂ cup (2¹/₂ oz/75 g) pine nuts, toasted (page 328)

¹/₂ cup (³/₄ oz/20 g) chopped fresh flat-leaf (Italian) parsley

In a saucepan over high heat, bring 6 cups (48 fl oz/1.5 l) of the vegetable broth or 3 cups (24 fl oz/750 ml) *each* broth and water to a boil. Add the wild rice and return to a boil. Reduce the heat to medium and simmer, uncovered, stirring occasionally, until the wild rice is tender but still slightly firm to the bite, about 40 minutes.

Meanwhile, in a large, heavy saucepan over medium-high heat, melt the butter. Add the onions and sauté, stirring occasionally, until tender, about 12 minutes. Add the cardamom and allspice and stir for about 20 seconds until aromatic. Add the remaining 3 cups (24 fl oz/750 ml) broth or 1¹/₂ cups (12 fl oz/375 ml) *each* broth and water, the bay leaves, dried cranberries, raisins, and grated orange zest. Season to taste with salt and pepper. Bring to a boil. Add the white rice, reduce the heat to low, cover, and cook until the liquid is absorbed and the rice is tender, about 20 minutes.

Drain the wild rice well. Remove the bay leaves from the white rice mixture and discard. Gently mix the wild rice into the white rice. Stir in the pine nuts and chopped parsley. Taste and adjust the seasoning. Transfer to a warmed serving bowl. Garnish with parsley sprigs and zest strips, if desired, and serve at once.

Serves 8–10

Dried Fruit, Nut, and Apple Stuffing

This stuffing can be baked inside a turkey as well as on its own. Use tart green apples such as pippin or Granny Smith. It's best to prepare the bread cubes the night before so they can dry overnight.

Preheat the oven to 400°F (200°C). Cut the bread into ¹/₂-inch (12 mm) cubes. Place the cubes in a single layer in a large baking pan (see note). Bake, stirring often, until golden brown, 10 minutes. Remove from the oven and transfer to a bowl. Let cool, then crumble slightly with your fingers. Coarsely chop the walnuts and almonds and add to the bread. Add the figs, dried cranberries, raisins, and prunes.

In a large, heavy frying pan over medium heat, melt the butter. Chop the celery stalks and leaves. Add the onions, apples, and celery and sauté, stirring frequently, until the onions and celery are tender, about 15 minutes. Add to the bread mixture. Mix in the parsley and marjoram. Add the stock to the same frying pan and place over high heat. Bring to a boil, scraping up any browned bits. Add to the bread mixture and mix well. Season to taste with salt and pepper. Mix in the eggs.

To bake the stuffing in a turkey, fill the cavities with the stuffing and truss (page 320); increase the roasting time of the turkey by 30 minutes. Grease a baking dish large enough to hold the remaining stuffing and spoon the stuffing into it; cover with aluminum foil. Bake alongside the turkey for 45 minutes. Uncover and bake until the top is brown, about 15 minutes longer.

To bake all the stuffing, preheat the oven to 325°F (165°C). Grease a 13-by-9-by-2-inch (33-by-23-by-5-cm) baking dish and fill with the stuffing; cover with foil. Bake for 45 minutes. Uncover and bake until the top is brown, about 15 minutes longer.

Makes about 12 cups (5 lb/2.5 kg) stuffing, enough for a 16-lb (8-kg) turkey; serves 8–10

1 loaf sliced whole-wheat (wholemeal) bread, 1 lb (500 g)

1 cup (4 oz/125 g) walnuts, toasted (page 328)

1 cup (5¹/₂ oz/170 g) whole almonds, toasted (page 328)

1 cup (6 oz/185 g) chopped dried figs

1 cup (4 oz/125 g) dried cranberries

¹/₂ cup (3 oz/90 g) *each* golden raisins (sultanas) and chopped pitted prunes

4 tablespoons (2 oz/60 g) butter, plus extra for greasing

2 large yellow onions, chopped

2 tart green apples quartered, cored, and chopped

3 celery stalks with leaves

¹/₂ cup (³/₄ oz/20 g) chopped fresh flat-leaf (Italian) parsley

1¹/₂ tablespoons dried marjoram

³/₄ cup (6 fl oz/180 ml) Chicken Stock (page 314)

Salt and freshly ground pepper

2 eggs, well beaten

Herbed Corn Bread and Red Pepper Stuffing

Preheat the oven to 375°F (190°C). Spread the corn bread cubes in a large jelly-roll pan. Bake, stirring occasionally, until slightly dry and toasted, about 30 minutes. Transfer the cubes to a large bowl.

In a large, heavy frying pan over high heat, melt the butter. Add the bell peppers, onions, celery, sage, and marjoram and sauté, stirring often, until the vegetables are tender, about 20 minutes. Add to the bread cubes. Mix in the chili powder. Season to taste with salt and pepper. Mix in the eggs.

To bake the stuffing in a turkey, stir ½ cup (4 fl oz/125 ml) of the stock into the stuffing. Fill the cavities with the stuffing and truss (page 320); increase the roasting time of the turkey by 30 minutes. Mix enough of the remaining stock into the remaining stuffing to moisten slightly (½–1 cup/4–8 fl oz/125–250 ml, depending on the amount of remaining stuffing). Grease a baking dish large enough to hold the stuffing and spoon the stuffing into it; cover with aluminum foil. Bake alongside the turkey for 30 minutes. Uncover and bake until the top begins to brown, about 15 minutes longer.

To bake all the stuffing in a baking dish, preheat the oven to 325°F (165°C). Grease a 13-by-9-by-2-inch (33-by-23-by-5-cm) baking dish. Mix 1½ cups (12 fl oz/375 ml) stock into the stuffing. Transfer to the dish; cover with foil. Bake until the stuffing is firm and heated through, about 45 minutes. Uncover and bake longer until the top begins to brown, about 15 minutes longer.

Makes about 12 cups (4½ lb/2.25 kg) stuffing, enough for a 16-lb (8-kg) turkey; serves 8–10

1 recipe Whole-Kernel Corn Bread (page 117), cut into ½-inch (12-mm) cubes

4 tablespoons (2 oz/60 g) unsalted butter, plus extra for greasing

2 large red bell peppers (capsicums), seeded, deribbed, and chopped

2 large yellow onions, chopped

3 celery stalks, chopped

2 teaspoons dried sage

2 teaspoons dried marjoram

1 tablespoon chili powder

Salt and freshly ground pepper

4 eggs, well beaten

1½ cups (12 fl oz/375 ml) Chicken Stock (page 314)

Baked Chestnut and Ham Dressing

This dressing has better texture when baked separately in a dish. Start the dressing in the 325°F (165°C) oven with the turkey. When the turkey is removed, increase the oven temperature to 375°F (190°C) to finish baking the dressing.

1 large loaf French or Italian bread, about 1¼ lb (625 g)

2 tablespoons unsalted butter, plus extra for greasing

2 yellow onions, diced

½ lb (250 g) cooked ham, trimmed of excess fat and coarsely chopped

3 celery stalks, diced

1 red bell pepper (capsicum), diced

2 teaspoons dried sage

2 cups (16 fl oz/500 ml) Chicken Stock or Turkey Stock, (page 314)

1 lb (500 g) fresh chestnuts, boiled and peeled (page 325), then chopped

3–4 tablespoons chopped fresh flat-leaf (Italian) parsley

Salt and freshly ground pepper

The night before, slice or tear the bread, including the crusts, into small pieces. Place in a food processor and process to form coarse crumbs. (You should have about 12 cups/1½ lb/750 g.) Spread out the crumbs on large baking sheets or newspapers to dry overnight.

Preheat the oven to 375°F (190°C). Grease a 3-qt (3-l) baking dish. In a large frying pan over medium heat, melt the butter. Add the onion and cook gently, stirring occasionally, until translucent, 2–3 minutes. Add the ham, celery, bell pepper, and sage. Mix well and cook for 2 minutes. Set aside.

Place the bread crumbs in a large bowl. While rapidly tossing and stirring the crumbs, gradually add the stock; the crumbs should be evenly moistened. Add the sautéed mixture, the chestnuts, parsley, and salt and pepper to taste. (Remember the stock may have been seasoned and ham is salty.) Mix and toss until blended.

Spoon the dressing loosely into the prepared baking dish. Bake until golden on top, 40–50 minutes.

Serves 8–10

Baked Pork and Grape Dressing

This dressing is a nice accompaniment to roast turkey and gravy. If possible, prepare the bread crumbs well ahead of time, even the night before, so that they dry out. If using fresh sage, garnish the dish with sage leaves.

Preheat the oven to 150°F (65°C). Slice or tear the bread, including the crusts, into small pieces. Place in a food processor and pulse to form coarse crumbs. Spread the crumbs on baking sheets and dry fully in the oven, about 2 hours. The crumbs should not color. Let cool.

Raise the oven temperature to 350°F (180°C). Grease a 2- or 2½-qt (2- or 2.5-l) baking dish.

In a large frying pan over medium heat, melt the 2 tablespoons butter. Add the pork and stir, breaking it up with a fork until crumbly, about 8 minutes (cook the pork in 2 batches if the pan is not big enough to spread out the meat). Add the sage, 1 teaspoon salt, ¼ teaspoon black pepper, and the cayenne. Continue stirring and tossing until lightly browned, 4–5 minutes longer. Using a slotted spoon, transfer the meat to a plate, leaving the drippings in the pan.

Add the onion and celery to the pan, adding more butter if needed, and sauté until translucent, 1–2 minutes. Add the chopped apple and grapes. Stir and toss over medium heat for 2 minutes. Set aside.

Put the bread crumbs into a large bowl. In a separate bowl, stir together the stock and eggs. While rapidly tossing the crumbs, gradually add the stock-egg mixture; the crumbs should be evenly moistened.

Mix in the reserved meat and the apple-grape mixture. Taste and adjust the seasoning. Spoon loosely into the prepared baking dish. Bake until golden, 40–50 minutes.

Serves 6–8

1 loaf French bread, about 1 lb (500 g)

2 tablespoons unsalted butter, or as needed, plus extra for greasing

1 lb (500 g) ground (minced) pork

4 teaspoons chopped fresh sage or 2 teaspoons dried sage

Salt and freshly ground black pepper

Pinch of cayenne pepper

½ yellow onion, diced

1 celery stalk, diced

1 small tart apple, peeled, cored, and chopped

1 cup (6 oz/185 g) seedless green grapes, stemmed

½ cup (4 fl oz/125 ml) Chicken Stock (page 314)

3 eggs, lightly beaten

Brown Rice Pilaf with Pecans

This dish can be prepared ahead up to the point when the pecans are added to the cooked rice. Keep the rice warm over a pan of hot water for up to 1 hour. When ready to serve, mix in the pecans and parsley.

2 tablespoons unsalted butter

1 yellow onion, diced

1 celery stalk, diced

1^1/$_2$ cups (10^1/$_2$ oz/330 g) long-grain brown rice

1 teaspoon ground cumin

1 lemon

3 cups (24 fl oz/750 ml) Chicken Stock (page 314)

Salt and freshly ground pepper

1^1/$_2$ cups (6 oz/185 g) pecan pieces, toasted (page 328)

2 tablespoons chopped fresh flat-leaf (Italian) parsley

In a large saucepan over medium-low heat, melt the butter. Add the onion and sauté, stirring occasionally, until translucent, 5–6 minutes. Add the celery, rice, and cumin, raise the heat to medium, and continue to sauté until the onion and celery are tender and the rice is golden, 3–4 minutes. Remove from the heat.

Using a zester or a small shredder and holding the lemon over the pan of rice, shred the zest of the lemon directly onto the rice. Add the stock, ^{1}/$_2$ teaspoon salt, and pepper to taste. Return the pan to medium-high heat and bring to a boil. Reduce the heat to low, cover, and simmer until all of the liquid has been absorbed and the rice is tender, 45–60 minutes.

Remove the pan from the heat and let stand, tightly covered, for 10 minutes.

To serve, chop the pecans coarsely. Fluff the rice with a fork and gently stir the pecans into the rice. Taste and adjust the seasonings. Transfer to a warmed serving dish and sprinkle with the parsley.

Serves 6

Vegetables

Rum-Glazed Candied Yams

Rum adds a slightly exotic touch to this holiday favorite. Choose one of two methods for finishing the dish, depending upon whether you are short of oven or stove-top space. You can use 2 teaspoons pumpkin pie spice in place of the assorted spices.

4 yams, about 1/2 lb (250 g) each, unpeeled and well scrubbed

Unsalted butter for greasing

FOR THE RUM GLAZE:

3/4 cup (6 oz/185 g) firmly packed dark brown sugar

6 tablespoons (3 fl oz/90 ml) light rum

4 tablespoons (2 oz/60 g) unsalted butter

1/8 teaspoon ground cinnamon

1/8 teaspoon ground allspice

1/8 teaspoon ground nutmeg

1/8 teaspoon ground ginger

Fresh mint leaves

Bring a large pot three-fourths full of water to a boil. Add the yams and simmer until tender but slightly resistant when pierced with a fork, 35–45 minutes. Drain and let cool. Peel the yams and slice off the ends. Cut crosswise into slices about 2 inches (5 cm) thick.

If baking the yams, preheat the oven to 400°F (200°C). Grease a large 9-inch (23-cm) baking dish and arrange the yams, cut sides down, in it. To make the glaze, in a saucepan over medium heat, combine the brown sugar, rum, butter, and ground spices. Simmer, stirring, until the sugar dissolves and the syrup is slightly thickened, about 3 minutes. Pour evenly over the yams. Bake, basting about every 5 minutes, until a glaze forms on top, about 15 minutes. Garnish with mint leaves and serve immediately, directly from the dish.

Alternatively, if cooking on the stove top, combine the glaze ingredients in a large, heavy pot over medium heat. Simmer, stirring, until the sugar dissolves and the syrup is slightly thickened, about 3 minutes. Add the yams and simmer gently, basting frequently, until the potatoes are nicely glazed, 10–15 minutes. Arrange on a warmed platter or place in a warmed bowl and garnish with mint leaves.

Serves 6–8

Mashed Potatoes with Parsnips

Parsnips give this dish a sweet flavor and smooth texture. It is important to mash the vegetables by hand with a potato masher or push them through a ricer. Do not use a food processor, as it will make the potatoes gluey.

Put the potatoes and parsnips into a large saucepan and add water to cover. Add 1 tablespoon salt, cover partially, and bring to a boil over high heat. Reduce the heat to medium-low and boil gently until tender when pierced with a fork, 20–25 minutes. Drain well.

Mash the potatoes and parsnips together with a potato masher, or pass them through a ricer, until free of all lumps. Gradually add the warm milk, beating with a wooden spoon until smooth and fluffy. Add only as much of the milk as needed to achieve the desired consistency.

Season with salt and pepper. Heat over medium heat until very hot. Spoon into a warmed serving dish with a pat of butter. Garnish with chopped parsley, if desired.

Serves 8–10

8 russet or Yukon gold potatoes, about 4 lb (2 kg) total weight, peeled and cut into 1 1/2-inch (4-cm) chunks

4 parsnips, about 1 lb (500 g) total weight, peeled and cut into 1-inch (2.5-cm) chunks

Salt and freshly ground pepper

1/2–3/4 cup (4–6 fl oz/ 125–180 ml) milk, warmed

2 tablespoons chopped fresh flat-leaf (Italian) parsley (optional)

Mixed Roasted Root Vegetables

Oven-roasted carrots and parsnips are worthy companions to traditional roasted potatoes. The vegetables can be left unpeeled, which gives them an appealing rustic look and a better, crustier surface when cooked.

Salt and freshly ground pepper

2 white-fleshed potatoes, well scrubbed and cut into 2-inch (5-cm) pieces

4 large carrots, well scrubbed and cut into 2-inch (5-cm) pieces

4 parsnips, well scrubbed and cut into 2-inch (5-cm) pieces

2 tablespoons unsalted butter, melted

2 tablespoons olive oil

2 tablespoons chopped fresh flat-leaf (Italian) parsley

Preheat the oven to 375°F (190°C).

Bring a large pot three-fourths full of water to a boil. Add 1 tablespoon salt, the potatoes, carrots, and parsnips. Return to a boil, reduce the heat slightly, cover partially, and cook for 5 minutes. Drain well.

In a baking dish large enough to hold all of the vegetables in a single layer, toss with the butter and olive oil. Season to taste with salt and pepper.

Roast the vegetables, on the middle rack, turning them several times, until tender and golden, 20–30 minutes.

Transfer to a serving dish, sprinkle with the parsley, and serve.

Serves 6–8

Potato-Mushroom Gratin

Prepare this dish 2 hours in advance and store at room temperature until ready to place under the broiler. When browning the top under the broiler, be sure to watch carefully, as the topping will burn easily.

1 tablespoon unsalted butter

1 tablespoon olive oil, plus extra for greasing

1¹/₂ lb (750 g) mixed fresh wild mushrooms such as chanterelle, porcini, and morel, brushed clean and thinly sliced

1 clove garlic, minced

4–5 waxy, white-fleshed potatoes, about 2¹/₂ lb (1.25 kg) total weight

1¹/₄ cups (10 fl oz/310 ml) milk

1 cup (8 fl oz/250 ml) heavy (double) cream

Salt and freshly ground pepper

1 cup (4 oz/125 g) shredded Gruyère cheese

3 tablespoons fine dried bread crumbs

In a large frying pan over medium heat, melt the butter with the olive oil. Add the mushrooms and sauté until softened, 5–7 minutes. Add the garlic and sauté for 1 minute longer. Remove from the heat and set aside.

Peel the potatoes, then cut them into uniform slices no more than ¹/₈ inch (3 mm) thick. Place the slices in a kitchen towel and wring tightly with your hands to remove excess moisture. Pour the milk into a large, deep, heavy saucepan over medium-high heat. Add the potatoes, separating the slices as you drop them into the pan, and bring to a boil. Cover, reduce the heat to low, and simmer for about 10 minutes. Stir with a wooden spoon often to prevent the potatoes from sticking. Uncover and continue to simmer until most of the milk has been absorbed, about 3 minutes longer.

Add the cream, 1 teaspoon salt, and 1 teaspoon pepper and return to a boil. Reduce the heat to low, cover, and simmer until there is still liquid left but the potatoes are very soft, about 10 minutes. Stir with a wooden spoon to prevent sticking. Uncover and continue to simmer until almost all of the cream has been absorbed, about 3 minutes longer. Taste and adjust the seasoning. Remove from the heat.

Grease a 9-inch (23-cm) flameproof baking dish with 2-inch (5-cm) sides. Transfer half of the potato mixture to the dish and top with the mushrooms. Cover with the remaining potatoes. Sprinkle with the cheese and then the crumbs.

Preheat the broiler (grill). Place the dish about 4 inches (10 cm) from the heat source and broil (grill) until browned on top, 8–10 minutes. Serve immediately.

Serves 6

Sweet Potatoes with Brown Butter and Parmesan Cheese

Here is a dish for people who do not like their sweet potatoes sweet. The chestnut-flavored, tan-skinned sweet potato variety is best for this recipe, or use acorn squash in its place. Garnish with fresh sage sprigs.

Place the sweet potatoes on a steamer rack and set over a pan of boiling water. Do not allow the rack to touch the water. Cover and steam until just tender when pierced with a fork, about 15 minutes. Remove from the steamer and let cool.

Preheat the oven to 400°F (200°C). Grease a 13-by-9-by-2-inch (33-by-23-by-5-cm) baking dish. Transfer the sweet potatoes to the dish.

In a heavy frying pan over medium-low heat, melt the butter and cook, swirling the pan occasionally, until the butter is golden brown, about 5 minutes. Add the chopped sage and season to taste with salt and pepper. Continue to cook until the butter is a deep golden brown, about 2 minutes longer. Pour the browned butter over the sweet potatoes. Sprinkle evenly with 3/4 cup (3 oz/90 g) of the Parmesan cheese. Stir to coat. Taste and adjust the seasoning. Cover the dish with aluminum foil.

Bake the sweet potatoes until heated through, about 20 minutes. Transfer to a warmed serving platter and sprinkle evenly with the remaining 1/2 cup (2 oz/60 g) Parmesan. Garnish with sage sprigs, if desired, and serve at once.

Serves 8–10

8 tan-skinned sweet potatoes, about 4 lb (2 kg) total weight, peeled and cut into 1-inch (2.5-cm) cubes

1/2 cup (4 oz/125 g) plus 2 tablespoons unsalted butter, plus extra for greasing

1/4 cup (1/3 oz/10 g) chopped fresh sage or 1 1/2 tablespoons dried sage

Salt and freshly ground pepper

1 1/4 cups (5 oz/150 g) grated Parmesan cheese

Roasted New Potatoes with Garlic and Thyme

Substitute rosemary for the thyme, if you like. If you have coarse salt, this recipe benefits from its use. Any leftover potatoes can be used to make a salad. A true new potato is freshly harvested, has a thin skin, and is low in starch, perfect for roasting.

Preheat the oven to 375°F (190°C).

Bring a large pot three-fourths full of water to a boil. Add 1 tablespoon salt and the potatoes. Return to a boil, reduce the heat slightly, cover partially, and cook for 5 minutes. Drain well.

Arrange the potatoes in a baking dish or baking pan, preferably in a single layer. Drizzle the olive oil over the top, then turn the potatoes over several times so they are well coated with the oil. Scatter the garlic over the potatoes. Sprinkle on the thyme and a little salt and pepper.

Bake, turning the potatoes over several times, until tender and golden, about 20–25 minutes.

Transfer to a serving dish, sprinkle with the parsley, and serve.

Serves 6–8

Salt and freshly ground pepper

2–2¹/₂ lb (1–1.25 kg) red new potatoes, 1¹/₂–2 inches (4–5 cm) in diameter, cut in half crosswise

¹/₄ cup (2 fl oz/60 ml) olive oil

4–5 cloves garlic, cut in half

1 tablespoon coarsely chopped fresh thyme or 2 teaspoons dried thyme

2 tablespoons chopped fresh flat-leaf (Italian) parsley

Mashed Yams with Brown Sugar and Spice

Prepare this dish a day ahead and cover and store in the refrigerator, then bring to room temperature and slip into the oven about 30 minutes before serving. For the best flavor, use the orange-fleshed sweet potatoes (marketed as yams).

6–10 yams (see note), about 6 lb (3 kg) total weight

1 cup (7 oz/220 g) firmly packed light or dark brown sugar

1/2 cup (4 fl oz/125 ml) heavy (double) cream or half-and-half (half cream)

6 tablespoons (3 oz/90 g) unsalted butter, at room temperature, plus extra for greasing

1 teaspoon ground cinnamon

1/2 teaspoon ground nutmeg

1/2 teaspoon ground allspice

1 tablespoon vanilla extract (essence)

Salt

1/2 cup (2 oz/60 g) coarsely chopped pecans

Preheat the oven to 325°F (165°C).

Place the yams on a baking sheet. Pierce in several places with a fork. Bake until very tender when pierced with a fork, about 1 hour. Remove from the oven and let cool slightly. Maintain the oven temperature.

Grease a 2- or 3-qt (2- or 3-l) baking dish. Halve the yams and, using a spoon, scrape the flesh from the skins into a large bowl. Add 3/4 cup (6 oz/180 g) of the brown sugar and the cream, butter, cinnamon, nutmeg, allspice, and vanilla. Using an electric mixer set on medium speed, a potato masher, or a wooden spoon, beat until smooth, about 2 minutes. Season to taste with salt. Spoon into the prepared baking dish, smoothing the top. Sprinkle the pecans and the remaining 1/4 cup (1 oz/30 g) brown sugar evenly over the top.

Bake until heated through, about 30 minutes. Serve immediately from the dish.

Serves 8–10

Glazed Carrots and Parsnips

These two vegetables complement each other nicely (see also Mixed Roasted Root Vegetables, page 140). They can be prepared in advance up to the point of glazing. Additional carrots may be substituted for the parsnips.

Peel the carrots and parsnips. Cut into 3-inch (7.5-cm) lengths. Slice each piece in half lengthwise and slice the thick upper portions into quarters lengthwise so the pieces are of equal size for cooking. Put them into a saucepan with 1 cup (8 fl oz/ 250 ml) water, $1/2$ teaspoon salt, and 2 tablespoons of the butter. Cover tightly and simmer gently over low heat until just tender, 10–15 minutes. Drain and set aside.

In a large frying pan over medium heat, melt the remaining 2 tablespoons butter. Add the brown sugar, wine, and ginger. Cook, stirring, until the sugar dissolves. Reduce the heat to medium-low and continue to cook until reduced and thickened, 2–3 minutes. Add the carrots and parsnips and toss until well coated. Cook until the vegetables are heated through, 2–3 minutes.

Transfer to a serving dish and garnish with the herbs.

Serves 8–10

6 large carrots

4 parsnips

Salt

4 tablespoons (2 oz/60 g) unsalted butter

$1/2$ cup ($3 1/2$ oz/105 g) firmly packed light or dark brown sugar

3 tablespoons Madeira wine

$1/2$ teaspoon peeled and finely grated fresh ginger

2 tablespoons chopped fresh mint, flat-leaf (Italian) parsley, or sage, or whole sprigs

Scalloped Potatoes

In this classic dish, potatoes bake in a flour-and-milk mixture that forms a creamy sauce. For maximum creaminess, use baking potatoes, such as russet, which take on a softer texture during cooking.

1 tablespoon unsalted butter, melted, plus 3 tablespoons unsalted butter, cut into small pieces, plus extra for greasing

1 clove garlic, minced

3 tablespoons all-purpose (plain) flour

Salt and freshly ground white pepper

6 yellow-fleshed or white-fleshed potatoes, about 3 lb (1.5 kg) total weight, peeled and sliced ¼ inch (6 mm) thick

1 small yellow onion, thinly sliced

3 cups (24 fl oz/750 ml) milk

2 tablespoons finely chopped fresh flat-leaf (Italian) parsley

Preheat the oven to 350°F (180°C). Brush a 9-by-13-inch (23-by-33-cm) baking dish with the melted butter.

In a small bowl, stir together the garlic, flour, 1½ teaspoons salt, and ⅛ teaspoon white pepper.

Arrange one-third of the potatoes in the bottom of the prepared dish and top with one-half of the onion slices. Sprinkle half of the flour mixture over the onion and dot with 1 tablespoon of the butter pieces. Repeat the vegetable layers, sprinkle the remaining half of the flour mixture over top, and dot again with 1 tablespoon of the butter pieces. Layer with the remaining potatoes and dot with the remaining butter pieces. Pour the milk evenly over the top. Butter a piece of foil on one side large enough to cover the dish. Place the foil over the dish, buttered side down.

Place the covered dish on a baking sheet and place in the middle of the oven. Bake for 50 minutes. Remove the foil and continue baking until the top is golden brown and the potatoes are tender, about 45 minutes longer.

Sprinkle with the parsley and serve immediately.

Serves 6–8

Creamed Turnips and Chard

Turnips and chard enveloped in a creamy sauce makes for a homey side dish that complements turkey as well as other vegetables, such as Sweet Potatoes with Brown Butter and Parmesan Cheese (page 143).

6 turnips, about 2 lb (1 kg) total weight, peeled and cut into 3/4-inch (2-cm) pieces

8 slices bacon, finely chopped

5 tablespoons (2 oz/60 g) all-purpose (plain) flour

2 3/4 cups (22 fl oz/680 ml) milk

1/2 cup (4 fl oz/125 ml) half-and-half (half cream)

1/2 teaspoon ground nutmeg

1 large bunch green Swiss chard, about 1 lb (500 g), stems removed and leaves thinly sliced crosswise

Salt and freshly ground pepper

Bring a large pot three-fourths full of lightly salted water to a boil over high heat. Add the turnips and boil until just tender when pierced with a fork, about 5 minutes. Drain well and set aside.

In a heavy saucepan over medium heat, cook the bacon, stirring frequently, until the fat is rendered and the bacon begins to brown, about 5 minutes. Add the flour and cook, stirring frequently, for 2 minutes. Gradually whisk in the milk. Bring to a simmer, stirring constantly. Reduce the heat to low and simmer, uncovered, until thickened to a medium-thick cream sauce, about 5 minutes.

Gradually stir in the half-and-half and nutmeg. Add the chard and simmer over medium-low heat, stirring frequently, until just tender, about 4 minutes. Add the turnips and stir until heated through, about 3 minutes.

Season to taste with salt and pepper. Transfer to a serving dish and serve at once.

Serves 8–10

Mashed Potatoes
with Basil and Chives

Updated with a generous amount of chopped fresh herbs, this holiday standard is terrific with roast chicken or roast beef, as well as turkey. The mashed potatoes can be made up to 2 hours ahead.

Bring a large pot three-fourths full of lightly salted water to a boil over high heat. Carefully add the potatoes and boil until tender when pierced with a fork, about 20 minutes. Drain well.

Immediately transfer the potatoes to a large bowl. Add the butter. Using an electric mixer set on medium speed, a potato masher, or a wooden spoon, beat until almost smooth. Add 1 cup (8 fl oz/250 ml) of the milk, the chopped basil, and the 1/3 cup (1/2 oz/15 g) chopped chives. Mash with the masher or wooden spoon until smooth. Add more milk as needed to achieve a creamy texture. Season with salt and pepper.

Transfer to a warmed bowl and garnish with basil sprigs and chives. Serve hot.

Serves 8–10

10 russet or Yukon gold potatoes, about 5 lb (2.5 kg) total weight, peeled and cut into 2-inch (5-cm) pieces

5 tablespoons (2 1/2 oz/75 g) unsalted butter, at room temperature

1–1 1/4 cups (8–10 fl oz/ 250–310 ml) milk, warmed

1/2 cup (3/4 oz/20 g) packed chopped fresh basil, plus sprigs for garnish

1/3 cup (1/2 oz/15 g) chopped fresh chives, plus long pieces for garnish

Salt and freshly ground pepper

Potato Latkes with Applesauce

You may peel the potatoes, but leaving the peel on imparts extra texture and flavor. The cooked latkes can be placed between layers of plastic wrap on a baking sheet and refrigerated for up to 1 day, or frozen in freezer bags for up to 3 months.

6 large russet or Yukon gold potatoes, about 2½–3 lb (1.25–1.5 kg) total weight, well scrubbed and cut into 2-inch (5-cm) pieces

2 yellow onions, quartered

2 extra-large eggs

½ cup (2½ oz/75 g) all-purpose (plain) flour

½ teaspoon baking soda (bicarbonate of soda)

Salt and freshly ground pepper

Vegetable oil for frying

Applesauce (page 316) for serving

Have ready a large metal bowl filled with ice water. In a food processor fitted with the coarse grating blade, grate the potatoes in 3 batches (or use a handheld grater). Transfer to the bowl of ice water. Refrigerate for 2–3 hours, changing the water twice during that time. Grate the onions and set aside.

Drain the potatoes in a large sieve or colander and, using your hands, press out as much water as possible. In a large bowl, combine the potatoes and onions and mix well. In a small bowl, beat the eggs until blended. In another small bowl, stir together the flour and baking soda. Stir the eggs and the flour mixture into the potatoes. Stir in 1 tablespoon salt and 2 teaspoons pepper.

Preheat the oven to 200°F (95°C).

In a large frying pan or griddle over high heat or an electric frying pan set at 400°F (200°C), pour in vegetable oil to a depth of ¼ inch (6 mm). When the oil is hot enough to make a drop of water sizzle, spoon mounds of batter about 2½ inches (6 cm) in diameter into the oil, being careful not to crowd the pan. Flatten the tops slightly with a spatula and fry until the undersides are golden brown and crisp, about 4 minutes. Gently turn the latkes and cook the second sides until brown, another 4 minutes longer. Using a slotted metal spatula, transfer the latkes to a baking sheet lined with paper towels to drain. Cover the baking sheet loosely with aluminum foil and keep warm in the oven until all the latkes have been cooked.

Arrange on a warmed platter and serve hot with applesauce.

Serves 8

Broccoli with Sliced Almonds

Broccoli is a good accompaniment to poultry. Be sure to crisp the broccoli in ice water before cooking. The ice water step is important because broccoli loses moisture after it is picked; the cold bath will ensure that it remains crisp during cooking.

2 large bunches broccoli, 2–3 lb (1–1.5 kg) total weight

1/3 cup (11/2 oz/45 g) sliced (flaked) almonds

4 tablespoons (2 oz/60 g) unsalted butter

Salt

Pinch of ground nutmeg

Using a paring knife, cut off the broccoli florets from the stems. Peel the thickest stems, removing all of the tough, stringy outer surface. Cut into pieces 1/2–1 inch (12 mm–2.5 cm) long, depending on the thickness of the stem. Place in a bowl with the florets and add ice water to cover. Set aside for 30 minutes.

Preheat the oven to 300°F (150°C). Spread the almonds on a baking sheet and toast in the oven until just beginning to color, 5–6 minutes. Let cool.

Melt the butter in a small saucepan and set aside.

Bring a large pot three-fourths full of water to a rapid boil and add 2 tablespoons salt. Drain the broccoli well and plunge it into the boiling water. Return to a boil and cook, uncovered, until the broccoli turns bright green and is tender-crisp, 3–5 minutes. Drain well.

Transfer the broccoli to a warmed serving dish. Add the toasted almonds and a little nutmeg to the melted butter. Spoon over the broccoli and serve.

Serves 6–8

Stir-Fried Brussels Sprouts with Mustard and Lemon

Mustard and lemon add sparkle and flare to Brussels sprouts. The Brussels sprouts can be parboiled several hours in advance, then covered and refrigerated. If you prefer, substitute Savoy cabbage, cut into strips 1 inch (2.5 cm) wide; omit the parboiling.

Bring a large saucepan three-fourths full of water to a boil. Add 1 teaspoon salt and the Brussels sprouts and cook until tender-crisp, 2–3 minutes. Drain the sprouts well and let cool to room temperature.

In a bowl, stir together the lemon juice and mustard. Set aside.

Just before serving, heat the olive oil in a wok or heavy frying pan over medium-high heat. Add the Brussels sprouts and stir and toss until their edges just begin to turn golden, 1–2 minutes. At the last moment, add the lemon juice–mustard mixture and stir briskly. Season to taste with salt and pepper.

Transfer to a warmed bowl and serve at once.

Serves 6–8

Salt and freshly ground pepper

1½ lb (750 g) Brussels sprouts, trimmed and halved lengthwise

3 tablespoons fresh lemon juice

1½ tablespoons whole-grain mustard

3 tablespoons extra-virgin olive oil

Green Beans and Pearl Onions with Tarragon Vinaigrette

Look for young, tender green beans. If they are limp, immerse them in ice water for 30 minutes before cooking. Use a high-quality tarragon-flavored vinegar. The best vinegars begin with good wine; Champagne vinegar from France is a good choice.

Roast the bell pepper (page 324). Pull off the loosened skin and remove the stem, seeds, and ribs. Cut the roasted pepper into long, thin strips. Set aside.

Bring a saucepan three-fourths full of water to a boil. Add the onions and 1 tablespoon salt and return to a boil. Reduce the heat slightly, cover partially, and cook for 2–3 minutes. Drain and plunge the onions into cold water. Cut off the root ends; trim the stems, if desired. Slip off the skins and set the onions aside.

Cut the green beans into 3-inch (7.5-cm) lengths. Bring a large saucepan of water to a boil. Add 2 tablespoons salt and the beans. Bring back to a rapid boil and cook, uncovered, until just tender-crisp, about 5 minutes. Drain immediately and plunge into ice water to stop the cooking and to cool. Drain again and set aside.

Just before serving, combine 1 tablespoon of the vinegar and a pinch of salt in a small bowl and stir to dissolve the salt. Add the olive oil and pepper to taste and whisk together. Pour into a saucepan and warm over medium heat. Add the roasted bell pepper, onions, and beans and toss until heated through, 1 minute. Taste for seasoning, adding more vinegar or salt if needed.

Serves 8–10

1 red bell pepper (capsicum)

12–14 oz (375–440 g) pearl onions, about 3/4 inch (2 cm) in diameter, unpeeled

Salt and freshly ground pepper

2 lb (1 kg) green beans, preferably Blue Lake, trimmed

1–2 tablespoons tarragon white wine vinegar

5 tablespoons (3 fl oz/80 ml) extra-virgin olive oil

Sauté of Julienned Garden Vegetables

Colorful and garden fresh, these mixed vegetables will add sparkle to your holiday table. If haricots verts are unavailable, Blue Lake beans will also work. Blanching the vegetables first softens their texture, setting up a perfect tender-crisp sauté.

4 carrots

4 celery stalks

3/4 lb (375 g) young, slender green beans such as haricots verts

1 tablespoon unsalted butter

1 tablespoon extra-virgin olive oil

1 red onion, thinly sliced

Salt and freshly ground pepper

1 tablespoon finely chopped fresh flat-leaf (Italian) parsley

Peel the carrots. Trim away the tough ends and any strings from the celery stalks. Cut the carrots and celery stalks into 2-by-$^1/_4$-by-$^1/_4$-inch (5-cm-by-6-mm-by-6-mm) julienne strips, keeping them separate. Trim off the stem ends from the green beans and, if the beans are large and more than 2 inches (5 cm) long, cut them into julienne strips to match the carrots and celery.

Bring a saucepan three-fourths full of water to a boil. Add the carrots and boil for 1 minute. Using a slotted spoon, scoop out the carrots, draining well, and set aside. Add the celery strips to the same boiling water and boil for 30 seconds, then scoop them out and set aside. Finally, add the green beans to the boiling water and boil for 2 minutes, then drain well and set aside.

In a frying pan over medium heat, melt the butter with the olive oil. Add the onion and sauté, stirring, until soft and slightly browned, 3–5 minutes. (The recipe can be prepared up to this point and set aside for up to 4 hours at room temperature before continuing.) Add the carrots, celery, and green beans to the onions and continue to sauté until the vegetables are tender but not too soft, about 3 minutes. Add $^1/_2$ teaspoon salt, pepper to taste, and the parsley and mix well.

Transfer to a warmed serving dish and serve immediately.

Serves 6

Fresh Peas and Water Chestnuts

Fresh mint and a little cream bring these two diverse vegetables together in a pleasantly flavorful union. If fresh peas are available, shelling them is worth the effort. This step can be done 4–6 hours in advance, or even the day before dinner.

Shell the peas and refrigerate until needed.

In a saucepan over medium heat, melt 2 tablespoons of the butter. Add the onion and sauté gently until translucent, about 2 minutes. Add the water chestnuts and cook, stirring, about 2 minutes. Set aside.

In another saucepan, combine ¼ cup (2 fl oz/60 ml) water, the remaining 2 tablespoons butter, and salt to taste. Bring to a boil and add the peas. Cover and cook until just tender, 2–3 minutes.

Meanwhile, return the saucepan with the onions and water chestnuts to medium-low heat. Add the mint and cream and stir until heated through.

When the peas are tender, drain well and combine with the onions, water chestnuts, and cream. Toss well until mixed. Season to taste with salt, transfer to a warmed serving dish, and serve.

Serves 8–10

3–4 lb (1.5–2 kg) peas in the shell (about 4 cups/1¼ lb/625 g shelled)

4 tablespoons (2 oz/60 g) unsalted butter

¼ cup (1½ oz/45 g) chopped yellow onion

1–1½ cups (8–10 oz/250–300 g) well-drained canned water chestnuts, thinly sliced

Salt

1 tablespoon finely minced fresh mint

¼ cup (2 fl oz/60 ml) heavy (double) cream

Brussels Sprouts with Orange Butter and Hazelnuts

Grated orange zest lends a lively touch and hazelnuts add a wonderful crunch to this traditional holiday vegetable. Cutting the Brussels sprouts in half allows the densely layered leaves to absorb the flavorful zest-laced butter.

2½ lb (1.25 kg) Brussels sprouts, trimmed and halved lengthwise

6 tablespoons (3 oz/90 g) unsalted butter

4 teaspoons grated orange zest

Salt and freshly ground pepper

½ cup (2½ oz/75 g) hazelnuts (filberts), toasted and skinned (page 328), then coarsely chopped

Bring a large pot three-fourths full of lightly salted water to a boil over high heat. Add the Brussels sprouts and boil until tender when pierced with a fork, about 8 minutes. Drain well.

In a large, heavy saucepan over medium heat, melt the butter. Add the orange zest and Brussels sprouts and stir until the Brussels sprouts are heated through, about 5 minutes. Season to taste with salt and pepper.

Transfer to a large bowl. Sprinkle with the hazelnuts and serve at once.

Serves 8–10

Green Beans with Ham and Shallots

To make advance preparations for this dish, boil the beans the day before, cool completely, and drain well, then wrap in plastic and refrigerate. Sauté the shallots and add the beans and ham just before serving.

3 lb (1.5 kg) green beans, trimmed

6 tablespoons (3 oz/90 g) unsalted butter

6 shallots, sliced

1/4 lb (125 g) cooked ham, cut into slivers

Salt and freshly ground pepper

Bring a large pot three-fourths full of lightly salted water to a boil over high heat. Add the green beans and cook until just tender-crisp, about 5 minutes. Drain and rinse with cold water to cool; drain again.

In a large, heavy frying pan over medium-high heat, melt 4 tablespoons (2 oz/60 g) of the butter. Add the shallots and sauté, stirring frequently, until they begin to brown, about 5 minutes. Add the remaining 2 tablespoons butter, the beans, and the ham and toss until heated through, about 5 minutes.

Season with salt and pepper. Transfer to a warmed serving platter and serve at once.

Serves 8–10

Baked Onions with Tomato Sauce

This dish is best served the moment it comes out of the oven. Use a good-quality extra-virgin olive oil. If fresh plum (Roma) tomatoes are unavailable, use canned diced tomatoes with some of their liquid.

6–8 yellow onions

6–8 plum (Roma) tomatoes

1 teaspoon dried oregano

Salt and freshly ground pepper

3 tablespoons extra-virgin olive oil, plus extra for greasing

Preheat the oven to 350°F (180°C). Select a baking dish large enough to hold the whole onions in a single layer and brush the bottom and sides with olive oil.

Peel each onion and cut a shallow X in the root end. (The X keeps the inner segments from protruding from the top during baking.) Place the onions in the baking dish, root ends down.

Bring a saucepan three-fourths full of water to a boil. Core each tomato and cut a shallow X in the base. Plunge the tomatoes into the boiling water and leave for 1 minute. Using a slotted spoon, remove the tomatoes. When cool enough to handle, peel off the skins. Cut the tomatoes in half crosswise and squeeze out the seeds. Chop coarsely and arrange around the onions in the baking dish.

Sprinkle the onions and tomatoes with the oregano and salt and pepper to taste. Drizzle with the olive oil. Cover the dish loosely with aluminum foil. Bake until the onions are tender, 45–50 minutes.

Transfer the onions to a warmed serving dish and equally top each onion with some of the tomato sauce.

Serves 6–8

Braised Cabbage and Lentils

The lentils can be cooked a day in advance and even the cabbage can be shredded several hours ahead of time. Do not overcook the lentils; they should be tender but remain whole.

Combine the lentils, 4 cups (32 fl oz/1 l) water, and 1 teaspoon salt in a large saucepan over medium heat. Bring just to a simmer, then adjust the heat so the lentils barely simmer, cover partially, and cook until just tender, 25–30 minutes. Drain well and set aside.

Cut the cabbage in half and then slice lengthwise into thin shreds or slice on a mandoline. In a large frying pan over medium heat, melt the butter. Add the cabbage, cover, and let steam over very low heat, stirring several times, 8–10 minutes.

Stir in the lentils, $1/2$ teaspoon salt, and the wine. Cover partially and cook gently, stirring occasionally, until the cabbage is just tender, about 15 minutes.

Stir in the lemon juice and nutmeg. Taste and adjust the seasoning. Transfer to a serving dish and serve immediately.

Serves 6–8

1 cup (7 oz/220 g) lentils, picked over, rinsed, and drained

Salt

1 green cabbage, about 1$1/2$ lb (750 g)

4 tablespoons (2 oz/60 g) unsalted butter

$1/2$ cup (4 fl oz/125 ml) dry white wine

1 tablespoon fresh lemon juice

Pinch of freshly grated nutmeg

Swiss Chard with Ham

Swiss chard is one vegetable that deserves more attention from cooks. It is easy to prepare and goes well with most roasts. Select young, tender leaves if possible. Buy a slice of freshly cut ham about 3/8 inch (9 mm) thick from a good meat market.

4 large bunches red or green Swiss chard, about 4–5 lb (2–2.5 kg) total weight

2 tablespoons unsalted butter

1 yellow onion, diced

3/4–1 lb (375–500 g) cooked ham, trimmed of excess fat and cut into short strips

Salt and freshly ground pepper

2 lemons

Cut off the tough stems from the Swiss chard leaves, including 1–2 inches (2.5–5 cm) into the leaves; discard the stems. Wash the leaves well, drain, and shake off the excess water. Stack the leaves flat and slice into strips 1 inch (2.5 cm) wide. Set aside.

In a large saucepan over medium heat, melt the butter. Add the onion and sauté until translucent, 3–4 minutes. Add the ham and cook for 3–4 minutes, stirring frequently. Add the Swiss chard, reduce the heat, cover, and cook for about 10 minutes. Uncover, stir, and check for doneness by tasting a piece of ham; it should be tender to the bite. If further cooking is needed or too much liquid has collected, raise the heat and cook, uncovered, for 1–2 minutes.

Season to taste with salt and pepper. Using 1 of the lemons, squeeze in juice to taste. Transfer to a warmed serving dish. Cut the remaining lemon into wedges for garnish, if you like.

Serves 8–10

Pies, Fruit Desserts & Cookies

Apple Pie with Lemon and Vanilla

To make the pastry, in a food processor, combine the flour, sugar, and salt. Process to mix. Add the shortening and butter and, using on-off pulses, cut them in until the mixture resembles coarse meal. In a small bowl, whisk together the egg and 3 tablespoons ice water until blended. With the motor running, gradually pour into the flour mixture and process until moist clumps form. Add more water by teaspoons if the dough is too dry. Form into a ball and divide in half. Flatten each half into a disk. Wrap separately in plastic wrap and refrigerate for 1 hour or for up to 1 day.

Position a rack in the lower third of the oven and preheat to 400°F (200°C). To make the filling, in a large bowl, combine the apples, sugar, flour, lemon zest and juice, cinnamon, and nutmeg. Scrape the vanilla bean seeds into the bowl. Mix well.

Roll 1 dough disk between sheets of waxed paper into a round 13 inches (33 cm) in diameter. Transfer the pastry to a deep pie dish 9 inches (23 cm) in diameter and 2 inches (5 cm) deep, discarding the paper, and gently press into the pan. Trim the overhang to 1/2 inch (12 mm). Brush the edges lightly with water. Transfer the filling to the pie shell, mounding it slightly in the center. Similarly roll out the second dough disk 12 inches (30 cm) in diameter. Place atop the filling and trim the overhang to 1 inch (2.5 cm). Fold the top crust edge under the bottom crust edge; press and crimp decoratively. Cut several slits in the top crust. Place the pie on a baking sheet. Bake for 45 minutes.

To make the glaze, in a small bowl, stir together the sugar, cinnamon, and nutmeg. Remove pie from oven. Brush the top crust with the milk, then sprinkle with the sugar mixture. Return to oven and bake until the crust is golden brown, about 20 minutes longer; cover the edges with foil if browning too quickly. Cool on a wire rack, then serve.

Makes one 9-inch (23-cm) double-crust deep-dish pie; serves 8

FOR THE PASTRY:

2 2/3 cups (13 1/2 oz/425 g) all-purpose (plain) flour

2 tablespoons sugar

1/2 teaspoon salt

1/2 cup (4 oz/125 g) vegetable shortening, chilled and diced

1/2 cup (4 oz/125 g) cold unsalted butter, diced

1 egg

3–4 tablespoons ice water

FOR THE FILLING:

7–8 mixed large sweet and tart apples, peeled, quartered, cored, and cut into slices 1/4 inch (6 mm) thick

3/4 cup (6 oz/185 g) sugar

1/4 cup (1 1/2 oz/45 g) all-purpose (plain) flour

1 teaspoon grated lemon zest

1 tablespoon fresh lemon juice

1/2 teaspoon *each* ground cinnamon and ground nutmeg

1 vanilla bean, split

FOR THE GLAZE:

1 tablespoon sugar

1/4 teaspoon *each* ground cinnamon and ground nutmeg

1 tablespoon milk

Maple Spice Pecan Pie

FOR THE PASTRY:

1½ cups (7½ oz/235 g)
all-purpose (plain) flour

1 tablespoon granulated sugar

½ teaspoon salt

¼ teaspoon ground nutmeg

1 tablespoon lemon zest

5 tablespoons (2½ oz/75 g)
cold unsalted butter, cut into
½-inch (12-mm) pieces

3 tablespoons vegetable
shortening, chilled and cut
into ½-inch (12-mm) pieces

3–4 tablespoons ice water

FOR THE FILLING:

3 eggs

¾ cup (6 oz/185 g) firmly
packed dark brown sugar

1 cup (11 oz/345 g) maple syrup

3 tablespoons unsalted butter,
melted

1 tablespoon fresh lemon juice

1 teaspoon vanilla extract
(essence)

¾ teaspoon ground nutmeg

¼ teaspoon salt

1½ cups (6 oz/185 g) coarsely
chopped pecans

To make the pastry, in a food processor, combine the flour, granulated sugar, salt, nutmeg, and lemon zest. Process to mix. Add the butter and shortening and, using on-off pulses, cut them in until pea-sized pieces form. With the motor running, gradually add 3 tablespoons ice water and process just until the dough begins to hold together, adding more water, if needed. Form into a ball and flatten into a disk. Wrap in plastic wrap and refrigerate for at least 1 hour or for up to 1 day.

Place the dough disk between sheets of waxed paper and roll out into a round 12 inches (30 cm) in diameter. Peel off the top sheet of paper and, using the bottom sheet, transfer the round to a pie pan 9 inches (23 cm) in diameter. Peel off the paper and press the pastry gently onto the bottom and sides of the pan. Fold the edges under and crimp decoratively. Pierce the bottom and sides of the pastry in a few places with a fork. Freeze the crust for at least 30 minutes or cover and freeze for up to 3 days.

Preheat the oven to 450°F (230°C). Bake until the crust is pale gold, 15 minutes. Transfer to a wire rack to cool. Reduce the oven temperature to 350°F (180°C).

To make the filling, in a large bowl, whisk together the eggs and brown sugar until the sugar dissolves. Add the maple syrup, butter, lemon juice, vanilla, nutmeg, and salt and whisk to blend. Mix in the pecans. Pour the filling into the baked pie crust. Bake until the filling is puffed and set, about 35 minutes. Transfer to the wire rack and let cool completely before serving.

Makes one 9-inch (23-cm) pie; serves 8–10

Gingered Apple-Cranberry Pie

This pie tastes best when still slightly warm, but it can be baked 3 or 4 hours in advance and served at room temperature. Pippin, Granny Smith, or McIntosh apples work best for baking.

1 recipe (2 disks) Pie or Tart Pastry (page 317)

5 large tart apples, peeled, quartered, cored, and thinly sliced lengthwise

1 cup (4 oz/125 g) fresh cranberries, coarsely chopped

1/3 cup (2 oz/60 g) finely chopped crystallized ginger

Finely grated zest of 1 lemon

3 tablespoons all-purpose (plain) flour

1 cup (8 oz/250 g) granulated sugar

1/4 teaspoon salt

1/4 teaspoon ground allspice

3 tablespoons unsalted butter, cut into small bits

2–3 tablespoons heavy (double) cream

1–2 tablespoons demerara sugar or raw sugar

Lemon Whipped Cream (page 318) for serving

Preheat the oven to 425°F (220°C). On a lightly floured surface, roll out 1 pastry disk into an 11-inch (28-cm) round. Fit carefully into a 9-inch (23-cm) pie pan. Trim the pastry so there is about 1 inch (2.5 cm) overhang. Fold the overhang under and press it down against the pan rim. Roll out the remaining pastry into a 10-inch (25-cm) round for the top crust. Set the prepared pie pan and top crust aside.

In a large bowl, combine the apples, cranberries, ginger, and lemon zest. In a small bowl, toss together the flour, granulated sugar, salt, and allspice. Add to the bowl of fruit and toss well. Arrange the fruit in the pie shell, piling it high in the center. Dot with the butter. Brush the pastry rim with water and lay the top crust over the fruit. Press down around the rim, then trim and flute or leave a plain edge. Make 2 or 3 slits in the top.

Press together the pastry scraps and roll out 1/8 inch (3 mm) thick. Cut out leaf and berry shapes for the the top crust. Brush the top with cream where you wish to place decoration. Press the leaves and berries in place. Lightly brush the top crust, including the decorations, with cream. Sprinkle with the demerara or raw sugar. Bake for 15 minutes. Reduce the heat to 350°F (180°C) and continue baking until the crust is golden and the fruit is tender when pierced through one of the slits, 50–55 minutes longer.

Transfer to a wire rack to cool. Serve slightly warm or at room temperature. Accompany with the lemon whipped cream.

Makes one 9-inch (23-cm) double-crust pie; serves 8–10

Pumpkin-Orange Tart

The pastry dough can be made 3 days ahead and frozen until needed. Prebaking the crust ensures a crisp, flaky pastry. Use a 9-inch (23-cm) pie pan if you like; in this case, the tart must be served from the pan.

On a lightly floured surface, roll out the pastry dough into a 13-inch (33-cm) round. Fit into a 10-inch (25-cm) round fluted tart pan with a removable bottom. There should be about 1 inch (2.5 cm) overhang. Fold the overhang under and press it against the sides to make them thicker and build them higher than the pan rim by about 3/8 inch (1 cm). The shell should be about 1 1/4 inches (3 cm) deep to hold the filling. Prick the bottom a few times with the tines of a fork. Prepare a double thickness of foil large enough to line the tart shell. Poke a couple of holes in it, carefully fit it into the shell and fold the excess over the rim. Refrigerate for 20–30 minutes.

Meanwhile, preheat the oven to 425° (220°C). Place the orange marmalade in a small saucepan over low heat until melted. Set aside.

Remove the pastry shell from the refrigerator and bake for 10 minutes. Remove the foil and continue to bake until lightly golden, 10–12 minutes longer. If the bottom puffs up during baking, prick it with a fork. Transfer to a wire rack. Brush the inside bottom and sides with the melted marmalade. Let cool.

In a bowl, stir together the pumpkin, sugar, orange zest, cloves, ginger, allspice, and salt. Mix in the eggs and then the cream; stir until smooth. Pour into the tart shell and smooth the top. Bake for 15 minutes. Reduce the heat to 325°F (165°C) and bake until a knife inserted in the center comes out clean, about 35 minutes longer.

Cool on a wire rack. Remove the pan sides and place the tart on a serving plate. Serve with the orange sabayon cream.

Makes one 10-inch (25-cm) tart; serves 8–10

1/2 recipe (1 disk) Pie or Tart Pastry (page 317)

1/3 cup (4 oz/125 g) orange marmalade

2 cups (1 lb/500 g) canned pumpkin purée

3/4 cup (6 oz/185 g) sugar

Finely grated zest of 1 orange

1/2 teaspoon ground cloves

1/4 teaspoon ground ginger

1/2 teaspoon ground allspice

1/2 teaspoon salt

3 eggs, lightly beaten

1 cup (8 fl oz/250 ml) heavy (double) cream

Orange Sabayon Cream (page 318) for serving

Poached Winter Fruit

This dish can be prepared a day ahead and assembled just before serving. If you pierce the cranberries with a toothpick, most of them will not burst during cooking. Comice pears are good for poaching because of both their flavor and their texture.

In a large sauté pan over medium heat, combine 2 cups (1 lb/500 g) of the sugar and 4 cups (32 fl oz/1 l) water. Bring to a boil, stirring to dissolve the sugar. Stir in the juice of 1 of the lemons. Set aside and keep warm.

Squeeze the juice of the remaining lemon into a large bowl. Peel, halve, and core the pears. Immediately place each pear half in the bowl, turning it in the juice to coat. When all the halves are coated, transfer them to the hot syrup along with any lemon juice left in the bowl. Bring to a simmer and cook gently, uncovered, turning each pear half a couple of times to poach evenly, until tender, 10–15 minutes. Let the pears cool in their poaching liquid.

In a separate saucepan, combine the remaining 1 cup ($^1/_2$ lb/250 g) sugar and $^1/_2$ cup (4 fl oz/125 ml) water. Bring to a boil, stirring constantly. Reduce the heat to low and add the cranberries. Simmer gently, stirring a couple of times, until the cranberries are just tender and the syrup thickens, 4–5 minutes; do not overcook. Remove from the heat and let cool.

To serve, use a slotted spoon to transfer the pears, core side up, to a deep serving platter or serving dish. Add about one-third of their syrup to the dish. Using the slotted spoon to drain off some of their syrup, arrange cranberries over each pear half. Then, using tongs, place the orange slices over and in between the pears. Garnish with the mint. Serve the lemon whipped cream in a bowl on the side.

Serves 6–8

3 cups (1½ lb/750 g) sugar

2 lemons

4–6 ripe but firm pears

2 cups (8 oz/250 g) fresh cranberries

Poached Orange Slices made from 1 orange (page 319)

Fresh mint sprigs for garnish

Lemon Whipped Cream (page 318) for serving

Sour Cream–Pumpkin Pie

The addition of sour cream gives an added twist as well as a wonderful light and creamy texture to this old Thanksgiving favorite. While fresh pumpkin purée can be used, it is much easier and less time consuming to purchase it canned.

½ recipe (1 disk) Pie or Tart Pastry (page 317)

2 cups (1 lb/500 g) canned pumpkin purée

1 cup (8 oz/250 g) sour cream

⅔ cup (5 oz/155 g) sugar

3 eggs, lightly beaten

1 tablespoon all-purpose (plain) flour

1 teaspoon ground cinnamon

½ teaspoon ground nutmeg

½ teaspoon ground ginger

FOR THE TOPPING:

1 cup (8 fl oz/250 ml) cold heavy (double) cream

2 tablespoons sugar

½ cup (4 oz/125 g) sour cream

On a lightly floured work surface, roll out the pastry dough into a round 13 inches (33 cm) in diameter and ⅛ inch (3 mm) thick. Drape the pastry round over the rolling pin and carefully transfer it to a 9-inch (23-cm) pie pan. Press the pastry gently into the pan. Trim the edge so there is about a 1-inch (2.5-cm) overhang. Fold the overhang under and flute the edges. Freeze the pastry shell until firm, about 20 minutes.

Position a rack in the lower third of the oven and preheat to 400°F (200°C).

Line the pastry shell with parchment (baking) paper or aluminum foil and fill with dried beans or pie weights. Bake until the crust is set, about 15 minutes. Remove the beans or weights and the paper or foil. Continue baking until the crust is golden brown, about 20 minutes longer. Transfer to a wire rack and let cool completely. Reduce the oven temperature to 325°F (165°C).

In a large bowl, combine the pumpkin, sour cream, sugar, eggs, flour, cinnamon, nutmeg, and ginger. Whisk until smooth. Pour the pumpkin mixture into the baked pie crust. Bake until the filling is just set, about 45 minutes. Check periodically and cover the edges with aluminum foil if the crust browns too quickly. Transfer to the wire rack and let cool completely.

To make the topping, in a chilled bowl, using an electric mixer set on high speed, beat together the cream and sugar until stiff peaks form. Using a rubber spatula, fold the sour cream into the whipped cream.

Cut the pie into wedges and serve with the topping.

Makes one 9-inch (23-cm) pie; serves 8

Sweetheart Raspberry Tart

½ recipe (1 disk) Pie or Tart Pastry (page 317)

2 oz (60 g) semisweet (plain) chocolate, chopped

½ teaspoon unflavored gelatin

1 tablespoon framboise eau de vie

1 cup (8 fl oz/250 ml) Vanilla Pastry Cream, hot (page 319)

⅓ cup (3 fl oz/80 ml) cold heavy (double) cream

3 cups (12 oz/375 g) raspberries

On a lightly floured work surface, roll out the pastry dough into a round about 12 inches (30 cm) in diameter and ⅛ inch (3 mm) thick. Drape the pastry round over the rolling pin and ease it into a 9-inch (23-cm) tart pan with a removable bottom. Trim the edges even with the rim. Freeze the pastry shell until firm, about 20 minutes.

Preheat the oven to 400°F (200°C). Line the pastry shell with parchment (baking) paper or aluminum foil and fill with dried beans or pie weights. Bake until the pastry shell is set, about 15 minutes. Remove the beans or weights and the paper or foil. Continue baking until the crust is golden brown, about 20 minutes longer. Transfer to a wire rack and let cool completely.

Place the chocolate in a heatproof bowl or the top pan of a double boiler. Set over (but not touching) gently simmering water. Stir with a wooden spoon until the chocolate is melted and smooth. Using the back of a spoon, generously coat the inside bottom and sides of the pastry shell with the chocolate. Refrigerate until set, about 20 minutes.

Meanwhile, in a small bowl, dissolve the gelatin in the framboise and let stand for 10 minutes. Stir the gelatin mixture into the hot pastry cream. Let stand at room temperature, stirring occasionally, until cool but not set.

In a chilled bowl, using an electric mixer set on medium-high speed, whip the cream to form stiff peaks. Using a rubber spatula, fold the whipped cream into the pastry cream. Spread in the chocolate-lined shell. Refrigerate until set, about 1 hour.

Arrange the raspberries over the pastry cream filling. Serve within 4 hours.

Makes one 9-inch (23-cm) tart; serves 6

Apple-Cranberry Crisp

This deep-dish dessert of seasonal fruit baked with a crumbly oat, almond, sugar, and spice topping is as simple to make as it is delicious. Use green, tart apples such as pippin or Granny Smith, which are best for baking.

Preheat the oven to 375°F (190°C). Grease a 13-by-9-by-2-inch (33-by-23-by-5-cm) baking dish or a 3-qt (3-l) baking dish with sides 2 inches (5 mm) deep.

In a bowl, combine the oats, brown sugar, the 3/4 cup (4 oz/125 g) flour, 1/2 teaspoon of the cinnamon, 1/2 teaspoon of the cardamom, and the salt. Add the butter and, using your fingers, rub the ingredients together until the mixture is the consistency of coarse crumbs. Mix in the almonds.

In a large bowl, combine the apples, cranberries, granulated sugar, the remaining 1 tablespoon flour, the remaining 3/4 teaspoon cinnamon, and the remaining 3/4 teaspoon cardamom. Stir to mix well. Transfer to the prepared baking dish. Spread the oat mixture evenly over the fruit.

Bake until the topping is golden brown and the apples are tender, about 55 minutes. Serve warm or at room temperature with scoops of vanilla ice cream.

Serves 8–10

1¼ cups (4 oz/125 g) old-fashioned rolled oats

1 cup (7 oz/220 g) plus 2 tablespoons firmly packed dark brown sugar

3/4 cup (4 oz/125 g) all-purpose (plain) flour, plus 1 tablespoon

1¼ teaspoons ground cinnamon

1¼ teaspoons ground cardamom

1/4 teaspoon salt

3/4 cup (6 oz/185 g) unsalted butter, at room temperature, plus extra for greasing

3/4 cup (3 oz/90 g) sliced (flaked) almonds

8–10 tart apples, about 4 lb (2 kg) total weight peeled, quartered, cored, and sliced

3 cups (12 oz/375 g) fresh cranberries

2/3 cup (5 oz/155 g) granulated sugar

Vanilla ice cream for serving

Miniature Truffle Tartlets

Make these small, delicate sweets for putting out on your annual New Year's or Christmas Eve buffet table. Sugared violets, orange peel, or rose petals would also make beautiful garnishes.

FOR THE PASTRY:

1 cup (5 oz/155 g) all-purpose (plain) flour

¼ cup (2 oz/60 g) sugar

3 tablespoons unsweetened cocoa powder

¼ teaspoon salt

6 tablespoons (3 oz/90 g) cold unsalted butter, cut into pieces

1 egg yolk

1 cup (8 fl oz/250 ml) Bittersweet Chocolate Ganache, warmed (page 317)

About 22 fresh raspberries or toasted and skinned hazelnuts (filberts) (page 328), or a combination

To make the pastry, in a bowl, combine the flour, sugar, cocoa, and salt. Add the butter and, using your fingertips or a pastry blender, blend the ingredients together until the mixture resembles coarse meal. Using a fork, stir in the egg yolk until fully combined. The dough should be soft but not wet.

Spray about twenty-two 2-to-3-inch (5-to-7.5-cm) tartlet pans or muffin-pan cups with cooking spray. Pinch off tablespoon-sized portions of the dough and, using your fingertips, press the dough evenly onto the bottom and up the sides of each pan or cup. Freeze until firm, about 15 minutes.

Preheat the oven to 400°F (200°C).

Place the pans on baking sheets and bake until the crusts just begin to brown on the edges, about 20 minutes. Transfer the baking sheets holding the pans to wire racks and let cool completely.

With the tip of a sharp knife, carefully loosen the crusts, then lift the crusts out of the pans and place on the baking sheets. Pour the ganache into the crusts, dividing it evenly. Refrigerate until the ganache is almost set, about 4 minutes.

Top each tartlet with a raspberry, hazelnut, or other decoration. Cover tightly and refrigerate until firm, about 1 hour. Serve immediately, or wrap in plastic wrap and store in the refrigerator for up to 1 day.

Makes twenty-two 2–3-inch (5–7.5-cm) tartlets

Orange-Spice Nut Tartlets

The flavors in this sophisticated dessert are reminiscent of the Italian dried-fruit-and-nut Christmas confection called *panforte*. Serve with whipped cream, if desired.

On a lightly floured work surface, roll out the pastry dough into a round about 14 inches (35 cm) in diameter and 1/8 inch (3 mm) thick. Cut the round into quarters. Ease each quarter into a tartlet pan with a removable bottom 4 1/2 inches (11.5 cm) in diameter and 3/4 inch (2 cm) deep. Trim the edges even with the rim and patch any holes with the scraps. Place on a baking sheet and freeze until firm, about 20 minutes.

Position a rack in the middle of the oven and preheat to 400°F (200°C). Line the pastry shells with parchment (baking) paper or aluminum foil and fill with dried beans or pie weights. Bake until the crusts are set, about 15 minutes. Remove the beans or weights and the paper or foil. Transfer the baking sheet holding the shells to a wire rack and let cool. Leave the oven set at 400°F (200°C).

In a saucepan, combine the cream, granulated sugar, brown sugar, honey, and cocoa. Bring to a boil over high heat, stirring to dissolve the sugars. Boil, stirring often, until very thick, about 4 minutes. Remove from the heat and let cool slightly. Stir in all the nuts, the figs, orange zest, cinnamon, nutmeg, coriander, and cloves.

Divide the filling evenly among the pastry shells. Bake until the filling is bubbling and darker around the edges, about 25 minutes. Transfer the baking sheet to the wire rack and let cool slightly.

Run a small, sharp knife around the edges of the pans to loosen the crusts, then remove the pan sides. Let cool completely.

Makes four 4 1/2-inch (11.5-cm) tartlets; serves 4

1/2 recipe (1 disk) Pie or Tart Pastry (page 317)

3/4 cup (6 fl oz/180 ml) heavy (double) cream

1/3 cup (3 oz/90 g) granulated sugar

3 tablespoons firmly packed light brown sugar

3 tablespoons honey

1 tablespoon unsweetened cocoa powder

1/3 cup *each* (1/2 oz/45 g) chopped walnuts and almonds, toasted (page 328)

1/3 cup (2 oz/60 g) hazelnuts (filberts), toasted and skinned (page 328), then chopped

1/3 cup (2 oz/60 g) diced dried Calimyrna figs

2 teaspoons grated orange zest

1/2 teaspoon *each* ground cinnamon, nutmeg, and coriander

Pinch of ground cloves

Pear and Mince Pie

This dessert is a light version of the traditional wintertime mince pie. Use pears that are ripe but firm and not bruised. Bosc, Comice, or Anjou are good choices. You can also top the pie with a solid crust rather than the lattice crust specified here.

Position a rack in the lower third of the oven and preheat to 400°F (200°C). On a lightly floured work surface, roll out 1 pastry disk into a round 11 inches (28 cm) in diameter and 1/8 inch (3 mm) thick. Drape the pastry round over the rolling pin and carefully transfer it to a 9-inch (23-cm) pie pan. Press the pastry firmly but gently into the pan and trim the edges flush with the pan rim.

In a large bowl, combine the pears, mincemeat, brown sugar, flour, cinnamon, orange zest, allspice, and cloves. Stir to mix well and set aside.

On the lightly floured work surface, roll out the remaining pastry disk into a second round about 1/8 inch (3 mm) thick. Using a pastry cutter or a knife, cut into strips about 1/2 inch (12 mm) wide. Following the instructions on page 317, use the pastry strips to make a lattice top on a lightly floured sheet of waxed paper. Spoon the filling into the pie shell. Secure the lattice on top as directed on page 317.

In a small bowl, whisk together the egg and milk until blended. Brush the egg mixture evenly over the crust. Bake until the crust is golden brown and the juices are bubbling, about 1 hour. Check periodically and cover the edges with aluminum foil if they brown too quickly.

Transfer to a wire rack and let cool briefly. Serve warm or at room temperature.

Makes one 9-inch (23-cm) lattice-top pie; serves 8

1 recipe (2 disks) Pie or Tart Pastry (page 317)

5 large pears, peeled, halved, cored, and chopped

1¼ cups (10 oz/315 g) prepared mincemeat

¼ cup (2 oz/60 g) firmly packed dark brown sugar

1 tablespoon all-purpose (plain) flour

1 teaspoon ground cinnamon

1 teaspoon grated orange zest

½ teaspoon ground allspice

⅛ teaspoon ground cloves

1 egg

1 tablespoon milk

Summer Berry Pie

A celebration of the berries of summer, this colorful pie is perfect for a picnic or barbecue. Cover the edges of the pie with aluminum foil if they start to brown too quickly while in the oven before the filling is finished baking.

1½ cups (6 oz/185 g) sugar

¼ cup (1 oz/30 g) cornstarch (cornflour)

3 tablespoons fresh lemon juice

4½ cups (18 oz/560 g) raspberries

4½ cups (18 oz/560 g) blackberries or boysenberries

1 recipe (2 disks) Pie or Tart Pastry (page 317)

In a large, heavy saucepan, stir together the sugar, cornstarch, and lemon juice. Add the berries and toss gently with the sugar mixture. Place over medium heat and bring to a boil, stirring very gently. Boil, stirring, until the mixture becomes thick and clear, about 6 minutes. Transfer to a bowl and let cool.

Position a rack in the lower third of the oven and preheat to 400°F (200°C).

On a lightly floured work surface, roll out 1 pastry disk into a round about 14 inches (35 cm) in diameter and ¹/8 inch (3 mm) thick. Drape the pastry round over the rolling pin and carefully transfer it to a 9-inch (23-cm) deep pie dish with 2-inch (5-cm) sides. Press the pastry firmly but gently into the dish.

Roll out the remaining pastry disk into a round 13 inches (33 cm) in diameter and ¹/8 inch (3 mm) thick. Using a knife, cut vents decoratively into the pastry round.

Pour the cooled filling into the pastry shell. Drape the top pastry round over the rolling pin and carefully transfer it to the pie, positioning it over the filling. Trim the edges of the pastry rounds so that there is about a 1-inch (2.5-cm) overhang. Press firmly around the rim of the pan to seal the crusts together, then fold the overhang under and flute the edges.

Bake until the crust is golden and the juices are bubbling, about 45 minutes. Check periodically (see note). Transfer to a wire rack and let cool completely before serving.

Makes one 9-inch (23-cm) double-crust deep-dish pie; serves 8

Dried Fruit Compote

Dried fruits have an intensity of flavor that makes this compote a wonderful finish to a holiday meal. For an alcohol-free version, omit the Marsala and increase the orange juice to 3⅓ cups (27 fl oz/840 ml).

4 cups (1½ lb/750 g) mixed dried fruits such as pitted prunes, apples, peaches, apricots, pears, figs, and cherries

½ cup (3 oz/90 g) golden raisins (sultanas)

1⅓ cups (11 fl oz/340 ml) sweet Marsala wine

2 cups (16 fl oz/500 ml) fresh orange juice

1 cinnamon stick, about 3 inches (7.5 cm) long

In a large, heavy pot over medium heat, combine the mixed dried fruits, raisins, Marsala, orange juice, cinnamon stick, and 1 cup (8 fl oz/250 ml) water. Cover and, when the liquid starts to simmer, reduce the heat to low and cook, stirring gently once or twice, until the fruit is quite soft but not disintegrated, about 30 minutes.

Remove from the heat and let cool to room temperature. Remove the cinnamon stick and discard. Transfer to a glass serving bowl and serve warm. The compote may be covered and refrigerated; let it come to room temperature before serving.

Serves 8

Eggnog Tart

On a lightly floured work surface, roll out the pastry dough into a round 12 inches (30 cm) in diameter and 1/8 inch (3 mm) thick. Drape the pastry round over the rolling pin and ease it into a 9-inch (23-cm) tart pan with a removable bottom. Trim the edges even with the rim. Freeze the shell until firm, about 20 minutes.

Preheat the oven to 400°F (200°C). Line the pastry shell with parchment (baking) paper or aluminum foil and fill with dried beans or pie weights. Bake until the crust is set, about 15 minutes. Remove the beans or weights and the paper or foil. Continue baking until golden brown, about 20 minutes longer. Transfer to a wire rack and let cool completely. Reduce the oven temperature to 325°F (165°C).

In a heavy saucepan over medium heat, combine the cream, milk, and vanilla bean and bring to a simmer. Remove from the heat. Cover and let stand for 10 minutes. In a large bowl, whisk together the egg yolks and sugar until blended. Return the cream mixture to medium-high heat and bring to a boil. Remove from the heat. Gradually add the cream mixture to the egg yolk mixture, whisking constantly. Place over low heat and cook, stirring constantly, until the mixture thickens and coats the back of a spoon, about 4 minutes; do not allow it to boil. Remove from the heat and whisk in the brandy. Remove the vanilla bean and discard. Let cool slightly.

Pour the custard into the cooled crust and sprinkle nutmeg lightly over the top. Bake until just set, about 20 minutes. Let cool on the wire rack before serving.

Makes one 9-inch (23-cm) tart; serves 8

1/2 recipe (1 disk) Pie or Tart Pastry (page 317)

1 cup (8 fl oz/250 ml) heavy (double) cream

1/4 cup (2 fl oz/60 ml) milk

1 piece vanilla bean, about 3 inches (7.5 cm) long, split in half lengthwise

5 egg yolks

1/4 cup (2 oz/60 g) sugar

1 tablespoon brandy

Pinches of ground nutmeg

Twelfth Night Jam Tart

For centuries, star-shaped tarts like this one have been served at the celebration of Twelfth Night, which marks the twelfth day after Christmas. This tart is good served warm with vanilla ice cream.

1 recipe (2 disks) Pie or Tart
Pastry (page 317)

1 egg

2 tablespoons heavy (double)
cream

About ¼ cup (2½ oz/75 g)
each of 5 assorted jams,
such as apricot, raspberry,
blueberry, plum, cherry,
blackberry, or marmalade,
in any combination

Position a rack in the middle of an oven and preheat to 400°F (200°C). On a lightly floured work surface, roll out 1 pastry disk into a round 11 inches (28 cm) in diameter and ⅛ inch (3 mm) thick. Drape the pastry round over the rolling pin and transfer it to a heavy baking sheet. Using a small, sharp knife and starting about 1½ inches (4 cm) in from the edge, mark the points of a clock face on the pastry round. Using the knife, draw a line (without cutting all the way through) from 12 o'clock to 4 o'clock, from 4 to 8 o'clock, and from 8 to 12 o'clock. Then draw a line from 6 to 2 o'clock, from 2 to 10 o'clock and from 10 to 6 o'clock, to form a 6-point star.

On the floured surface, roll out the remaining dough disk into a round 11 inches (28 cm) in diameter and about ⅛ inch (3 mm) thick. Using the knife, cut the round into strips ½ inch (12 mm) wide. Lay a dough strip on each of the lines you just cut onto the pastry round, to form the 6-point star. Cut off the edges of the strips evenly with the outline of the clock face. Fold the uncovered edge of the bottom crust inward so that the edge is even with the points of the star and forms a rim.

In a small bowl, whisk together the egg and cream until well blended. Brush the egg mixture over the surface of the pastry. Bake until golden brown, about 20 minutes. Remove from the oven and fill the indentations with the assorted jams. Return to the oven and bake until the jams are set, about 5 minutes.

Transfer to a wire rack and let cool slightly. Serve warm or at room temperature.

Makes one 9-inch (23-cm) tart; serves 8

Apple-Cinnamon Pie

Here is an old-fashioned American pie that will shine on your Fourth of July or Thanksgiving table. Serve with ice cream or whipped cream. Use tart green apples such as pippin or Granny Smith.

Position a rack in the bottom third of the oven and preheat to 400°F (200°C). On a lightly floured work surface, roll out 1 pastry disk into a round 13 inches (33 cm) in diameter and 1/8 inch (3 mm) thick. Drape the pastry round over the rolling pin and transfer it to a 9-inch (23-cm) pie pan. Press firmly but gently into the pan.

In a large bowl, combine the apples, the 2/3 cup (5 oz/155 g) sugar, the tapioca, cinnamon, and nutmeg. Toss gently until all ingredients are evenly distributed. Spoon the filling into the crust.

On the lightly floured surface, roll out the remaining pastry disk into a round about 12 inches (30 cm) in diameter. Carefully drape the pastry round over the rolling pin and position it over the filling. Trim the edges of the pastry rounds so there is about a 1-inch (2.5-cm) overhang. Press firmly around the rim of the pan to seal the crusts together, then fold the overhang under and flute the edges. Using a small, sharp knife, cut 4 equidistant vents around the center of the top crust for the steam to escape. Gather up and reroll the scraps, then cut into decorative shapes. Moisten the bottoms lightly with water and place the cutouts on the pie top.

Sprinkle the top crust with the 1 tablespoon sugar and a little cinnamon. Bake until the crust is golden brown and the juices are bubbling, about 1 hour. Check often and cover the edges with aluminum foil if they brown too quickly.

Transfer to a wire rack and let cool slightly. Serve warm or at room temperature.

Makes one 9-inch (23-cm) double-crust pie; serves 8

1 recipe (2 disks) Pie or Tart Pastry (page 317)

7–8 large tart green apples, quartered, cored, and thinly sliced

2/3 cup (5 oz/155 g) sugar, plus 1 tablespoon for sprinkling

2 tablespoons quick-cooking granulated tapioca

1 tablespoon ground cinnamon, plus extra for sprinkling

1/2 teaspoon ground nutmeg

Baked Pears with Custard Sauce

This light and delicious recipe comes from Chuck Williams. The liqueur in the custard sauce can be replaced with vanilla extract (essence). Be sure to use ripe but firm pears. Comice, Bartlett (Williams'), or Bosc are all good choices.

FOR THE CUSTARD SAUCE:

2 cups (16 fl oz/500 ml) milk

6 egg yolks

1/2 cup (4 oz/125 g) sugar

1 tablespoon crème de cacao, Cointreau, Grand Marnier, or other liqueur

2 cups (1 lb/500 g) sugar

1 piece fresh ginger, about 3 inches (7.5 cm) long, peeled and cut into 4 pieces

Juice of 1 lemon

8–10 small or medium ripe but firm pears such as Comice, Bartlett (Williams'), or Bosc

Small fresh mint sprigs for garnish

To make the custard sauce, in a heavy saucepan over medium heat, warm the milk just until bubbles appear along the edges of the pan. Remove from the heat. In a bowl, combine the egg yolks and sugar and whisk until very light. Continuing to beat, gradually add the hot milk. Pour into the saucepan and place over medium-low heat. Cook, stirring, just until the mixture thickens enough to coat the back of a spoon. Remove from the heat and pour into a clean bowl; stir for a few seconds. Stir in the liqueur and cover with plastic wrap placed directly on the surface of the custard to prevent a skin from forming. Set aside to cool.

Preheat the oven to 350°F (180°C).

In a saucepan over medium heat, combine the sugar and 2 cups (16 fl oz/500 ml) water. Bring to a boil, stirring until the sugar dissolves. Add the ginger, reduce the heat to low, and cook at a bare simmer, uncovered, until the ginger is translucent, 20–25 minutes. Remove from the heat.

Meanwhile, place the lemon juice in a large bowl. Peel the pears, cut in half length-wise, and remove the core and the stem and blossom ends. Place in the bowl and turn in the lemon juice to coat well. Arrange the pear halves in a large, shallow baking dish, core side up. Spoon the ginger syrup over the pears. Bake, basting every 5–6 minutes with the pan syrup, until tender, 20–25 minutes. Remove from the oven and let cool to room temperature.

To serve, divide the pear halves among dessert plates. Top with the custard sauce and garnish with the mint sprigs.

Serves 8–10

Pecan-Cranberry Pie

Fresh cranberries add a wonderful tartness to this sweet, rich Southern pie. It's a delicious addition to a Thanksgiving or Christmas menu or to follow the traditional black-eyed peas on New Year's Day.

On a lightly floured work surface, roll out the pastry dough into a round 13 inches (33 cm) in diameter and 1/8 inch (3 mm) thick. Drape the pastry round over the rolling pin and carefully transfer it to a 9-inch (23-cm) pie pan. Press the pastry gently but firmly into the pan. Trim the edge so there is about a 1-inch (2.5-cm) overhang. Fold the overhang under. Flute the edges or gather up and reroll the scraps, cut into decorative shapes, moisten the bottoms lightly with water, and place the cutouts along the pie rim. Freeze until firm, about 20 minutes.

Position a rack in the lower third of the oven and preheat to 400°F (200°C).

In a large bowl, combine the eggs, brown sugar, corn syrup, melted butter, molasses, and vanilla. Whisk until smooth. Stir in the pecans and cranberries.

Pour the pecan-cranberry filling into the pastry shell. Bake until the center of the filling is set, about 45 minutes. Check periodically and cover the edges with aluminum foil if the crust browns too quickly.

Transfer to a wire rack and let cool completely before serving.

Makes one 9-inch (23-cm) pie; serves 8–12

½ recipe (1 disk) Pie or Tart Pastry (page 317)

3 eggs

3/4 cup (6 oz/185 g) firmly packed light brown sugar

½ cup (4 fl oz/125 ml) light corn syrup

4 tablespoons (2 oz/60 g) unsalted butter, melted and cooled

2 tablespoons light molasses

1 teaspoon vanilla extract (essence)

1½ cups (6 oz/185 g) pecans, toasted (page 328), and coarsely chopped

1½ cups (6 oz/185 g) fresh cranberries

Holiday Cutout Cookies

These classic Christmas cookies can be sprinkled with colored sugar crystals and dragées before baking, or decorated with White Icing (page 319) after baking using a pastry bag fitted with a plain tip or a small plastic bag with a corner snipped off.

1 cup (8 oz/250 g) unsalted butter, at room temperature, plus extra for greasing

3/4 cup (6 oz/185 g) sugar

3 egg yolks

1 piece vanilla bean, about 2 inches (5 cm) long

2 1/2 cups (12 1/2 oz/390 g) all-purpose (plain) flour

1 teaspoon baking powder

1/2 teaspoon salt

In a large bowl, using an electric mixer set on medium speed, beat together the butter and sugar until light and fluffy, about 4 minutes. Beat in the egg yolks, one at a time, beating well after each addition. Cut the vanilla bean in half lengthwise and, using a small, sharp knife, scrape the seeds into the butter mixture. Mix well. In a sifter, combine the flour, baking powder, and salt. Sift the flour mixture directly onto the butter mixture. Reduce the mixer speed to low and beat until well mixed.

Divide the dough into 4 equal pieces. Shape each piece into a ball and then flatten the balls into disks. Wrap the disks in plastic wrap and refrigerate overnight. (The dough can be prepared up to 3 days ahead.) Let it soften slightly at room temperature before continuing.

Position a rack in the upper third of the oven and preheat to 350°F (180°C). Grease 2 large baking sheets. On a lightly floured work surface, roll out a dough disk 1/4 inch (6 mm) thick. Using cookie cutters, cut out desired shapes. Transfer the cutouts to the prepared baking sheets. Gather up and reroll the scraps and cut out more cookies. Repeat with the remaining dough disks.

Bake until the cookies are golden on the edges, about 8 minutes. Transfer the cookies to wire racks and let cool completely. Store in an airtight container at room temperature for up to 1 week.

Makes 4–5 dozen cookies

Pfeffernüsse

This German version of the traditional northern European "pepper nut" cookies is a family favorite at Christmastime. These tiny treats are characterized by many spices, such as anise, cinnamon, nutmeg—and the black pepper for which they are named.

In a bowl, sift together the flour, salt, pepper, aniseed, cinnamon, baking soda, allspice, nutmeg, and cloves. In a large bowl, using an electric mixer set on medium speed, beat together the butter, brown sugar, and molasses until light and fluffy, about 4 minutes. Beat in the egg. Reduce the mixer speed to low and beat in the flour mixture. Cover and refrigerate for several hours.

Preheat the oven to 350°F (180°C). Grease 2 baking sheets.

Roll pieces of the dough between your palms into balls about 1 1/2 inches (4 cm) in diameter. Place the balls on the baking sheets, spacing them 2 inches (5 cm) apart.

Bake until the cookies are golden brown on the bottom and firm to the touch, about 14 minutes. Transfer the baking sheets to wire racks and let the cookies cool slightly on the sheets. Place the confectioners' sugar in a sturdy paper bag. Drop a few cookies into the bag, close the top securely, and shake gently to coat the warm cookies with the sugar. Transfer to the wire racks and let cool completely. Repeat with the remaining cookies.

Store in an airtight container at cool room temperature for up to 1 week.

Makes about 2 1/2 dozen cookies

2 1/4 cups (11 1/2 oz/360 g) all-purpose (plain) flour

1/2 teaspoon salt

1/2 teaspoon freshly ground pepper

1/2 teaspoon crushed aniseed

1/2 teaspoon ground cinnamon

1/4 teaspoon baking soda (bicarbonate of soda)

1/4 teaspoon ground allspice

1/4 teaspoon ground nutmeg

1/8 teaspoon ground cloves

1/2 cup (4 oz/125 g) unsalted butter, at room temperature, plus extra for greasing

3/4 cup (6 oz/185 g) firmly packed light brown sugar

1/4 cup (3 oz/90 g) light molasses

1 egg

About 2 cups (8 oz/250 g) confectioners' (icing) sugar for dusting

Honey-Anise Springerle

These cookies were made by Germanic tribes as part of the pagan celebration of Julfest. Wooden springerle rolling pins embossed with decorative shapes are available at specialty food stores and online.

Unsalted butter for greasing

2 eggs

2/3 cup (5 oz/155 g) sugar

1/3 cup (4 oz/125 g) honey

1 teaspoon vanilla extract (essence)

1 teaspoon aniseed

1/2 teaspoon grated orange zest

1/2 teaspoon grated lemon zest

2 3/4 cups (14 oz/440 g) all-purpose (plain) flour

1 teaspoon baking powder

Generous 1/4 teaspoon salt

Grease 3 large baking sheets.

In a bowl, using an electric mixer set on high speed, beat the eggs until very pale and airy, about 3 minutes. Gradually add the sugar and continue beating until the mixture drops from the beaters in a ribbon, about 5 minutes. Gradually beat in the honey, vanilla, aniseed, and orange and lemon zests. In a sifter, combine the flour, baking powder, and salt. Sift the mixture directly onto the egg mixture and, using a rubber spatula, stir gently to incorporate the flour.

Transfer the dough to a lightly floured work surface and knead briefly. Roll out the dough into a rectangle about 1/4 inch (6 mm) thick. Lightly flour a springerle rolling pin, then firmly but gently roll it over the dough. Carefully cut into cookies and transfer to the prepared baking sheets. Gather up and reroll the scraps and cut out more cookies. Cover the baking sheets with plastic wrap and let stand overnight at cool room temperature.

Preheat the oven to 300°F (150°C). Bake until lightly golden and very crisp, about 20 minutes. Transfer to wire racks and let cool completely.

Store in an airtight container at room temperature for up to 2 weeks.

Makes about 6 dozen cookies

Coconut-Almond Macaroons

As moist and chewy as candy bars, these cookies make a nice treat for Passover and will keep in an airtight container at cool room temperature for up to 4 days.

Preheat the oven to 350°F (180°C). Grease 2 large baking sheets.

In a baking pan, combine 1 1/2 cups (6 oz/185 g) of the coconut and the almonds. Bake, stirring occasionally, until golden, about 12 minutes. Remove from the oven; let cool. Leave the oven set at 350°F (180°C).

In a bowl, combine the cooled coconut mixture, the remaining 2 cups (8 oz/250 g) coconut, condensed milk, and almond extract. In another bowl, using an electric mixer set on high speed, beat together the egg whites, sugar, and salt until soft peaks form. Using a rubber spatula, gently fold the egg whites into the coconut mixture.

Using a large spoon, form mounds 2 inches (5 cm) in diameter on the prepared baking sheets, spacing them 2 inches (5 cm) apart. Bake until the cookies are golden brown, about 10 minutes. Transfer to wire racks and let cool completely.

Line 2 baking sheets with waxed paper. Dip the bottoms of the cookies into the melted chocolate and place them, chocolate side down, on the prepared baking sheets. Refrigerate until the chocolate is set. Store in an airtight container at cool room temperature for up to 4 days.

Makes about 18 cookies

Vegetable shortening for greasing

3 1/2 cups (14 oz/435 g) sweetened flaked coconut

1 cup (4 oz/125 g) sliced (flaked) almonds

1/2 cup (4 fl oz/125 ml) sweetened condensed milk

1/2 teaspoon almond extract (essence)

2 egg whites

1 tablespoon sugar

Pinch of salt

Bittersweet chocolate, chopped and melted (page 325)

Raspberry Linzer Heart Cookies

2 cups (8 oz/250 g) walnuts, toasted (page 328) and cooled

2 1/2 cups (12 1/2 oz/390 g) all-purpose (plain) flour

1 cup (8 oz/250 g) unsalted butter, at room temperature, plus extra for greasing

1 cup (4 oz/125 g) confectioners' (icing) sugar, plus extra for dusting

2 egg yolks

1/2 cup (2 oz/60 g) cornstarch (cornflour)

Raspberry jam

In a food processor, process the walnuts and 1 cup (5 oz/155 g) of the flour until the nuts are finely ground; do not overprocess. Set aside.

In a medium bowl, using an electric mixer set on medium speed, beat together the butter and the confectioners' sugar until fluffy, about 4 minutes. Beat in the egg yolks, one at a time, beating well after each addition. Reduce the mixer speed to low and beat in the walnut mixture, the remaining 1 1/2 cups (7 1/2 oz/235 g) flour, and the cornstarch until blended.

Divide the dough into 4 pieces. Shape each piece into a ball and then flatten into disks. Wrap the disks in plastic wrap and refrigerate overnight.

Position a rack in the upper third of the oven and preheat to 325°F (165°C). Grease 2 large baking sheets. On a lightly floured work surface, roll out a dough disk 1/4 inch (6 mm) thick. Using a heart-shaped cookie cutter 2 1/2 inches (6 cm) in diameter, cut out hearts. Transfer half of the hearts to a prepared baking sheet. Using a heart-shaped cookie cutter 1 1/2 inches (4 cm) in diameter, cut out a heart from the center of each of the remaining heart cutouts, creating heart frames to use as cookie tops. Transfer to the other prepared sheet. Gather up and reroll the smaller hearts and scraps, then cut out more tops and bottoms. Repeat with the remaining disks.

Bake until just golden, about 15 minutes for bottoms and 12 minutes for tops. Let cool completely on wire racks.

Using a fine-mesh sieve, dust the heart frames with confectioners' sugar. Using a small butter knife, spread raspberry jam over the tops of the large hearts. Place the sugar-dusted frames atop the larger hearts. Store in an airtight container at cool room temperature for up to 3 days.

Makes about 4 dozen cookies

Gingerbread Cookies

Decorate these cookies using a pastry bag fitted with a plain tip or a small plastic bag with a corner snipped off, or spread each cookie with a thin layer of the icing, let dry, and then, using a tiny brush and food coloring, paint on decorations.

3/4 cup (6 oz/185 g) unsalted butter, at room temperature, plus extra for greasing

3/4 cup (6 oz/185 g) firmly packed light brown sugar

1/4 cup (3 oz/90 g) light molasses

2 egg yolks

2 1/3 cups (12 oz/375 g) unbleached all-purpose (plain) flour

2 teaspoons ground cinnamon

2 teaspoons ground ginger

1 teaspoon ground allspice

1/2 teaspoon baking soda (bicarbonate of soda)

1/4 teaspoon ground cloves

1/4 teaspoon salt

1/2 cup (4 fl oz/125 ml) White Icing (page 319)

In a bowl, using an electric mixer set on medium speed, beat together the butter, brown sugar, and molasses until fluffy, about 3 minutes. Beat in the egg yolks. In a sifter, combine the flour, cinnamon, ginger, allspice, baking soda, cloves, and salt. Sift the flour mixture directly onto the butter mixture. Reduce the mixer speed to low and beat until well combined. Gather the dough into a ball; it will be soft. Form into 3 disks, wrap the disks in plastic wrap, and refrigerate overnight.

Position racks in the upper third of the oven and preheat to 375°F (190°C). Grease 2 large, heavy baking sheets.

Remove one dough disk from the refrigerator. On a lightly floured work surface, roll it out 1/4 inch (6 mm) thick. Using a figure-shaped cookie cutter 5 inches (13 cm) long, cut out gingerbread people. Transfer the cookies to a prepared baking sheet, placing them about 1 inch (2.5 cm) apart. Gather up the scraps into a ball, wrap in plastic wrap, and refrigerate. Repeat rolling and cutting out the cookies with the remaining dough, in 2 batches. Then reroll the scraps and cut out more cookies.

Bake until the cookies begin to turn golden brown on the edges, about 10 minutes. Transfer to wire racks and let cool.

Decorate the cooled cookies with the white icing as desired (see note). Store in an airtight container at room temperature for up to 1 week.

Makes about 20 cookies

Lemon-Cardamom Tuiles

These elegant, wafer-thin French cookies have a citrus and spice fragrance. Tuiles ("tiles") are thin cookies that are pressed around a rolling pin while still hot to produce a shape resembling a curved roof tile.

Preheat the oven to 350°F (180°C). Grease 2 baking sheets.

In a food processor, combine the two sugars and lemon zest. Process until the lemon zest is very finely minced. Transfer to a large bowl and add the butter. Using an electric mixer set on medium speed, beat together the sugar mixture and butter until light and fluffy, about 3 minutes. Beat in the egg whites, cardamom, vanilla, and salt until well mixed. Reduce the mixer speed to low and beat in the flour.

Drop 1 teaspoon of the batter onto a prepared baking sheet. Using the back of a spoon, spread the batter into a round about 3 inches (7.5 cm) in diameter. Repeat 5 more times, spacing the cookies evenly.

Bake until the cookies are golden brown on the edges, about 5 minutes. While the cookies are baking, form the next batch on the second baking sheet.

Remove from the oven and immediately run the tip of a small knife under the edge of a cookie. Carefully pick up the cookie and drape it over a long rolling pin. Quickly repeat with the remaining cookies; let cool completely on the rolling pin.

Continue to bake and form the remaining batter in the same way, generously buttering the baking sheets before each new batch. Store in an airtight container at cool room temperature for up to 2 days.

Makes about 5 dozen cookies

½ cup (4 oz/125 g) granulated sugar

¼ cup (1 oz/30 g) confectioners' (icing) sugar

1 tablespoon minced lemon zest

6 tablespoons (3 oz/90 g) unsalted butter, at room temperature, plus extra for greasing

3 egg whites

2 teaspoons ground cardamom

½ teaspoon vanilla extract (essence)

¼ teaspoon salt

½ cup (2½ oz/75 g) all-purpose (plain) flour

Hazelnut Biscotti

The simplicity of these Italian cookies is appealing, but, if you like, you can add 1 tablespoon grated orange zest and 1 cup (4 oz/125 g) dried pitted sour cherries with the first addition of flour.

1 cup (8 oz/250 g) unsalted butter, at room temperature, plus extra for greasing

3 cups (1½ lb/750 g) sugar

4 eggs

6 cups (30 oz/940 g) all-purpose (plain) flour

2 teaspoons baking soda (bicarbonate of soda)

1 teaspoon salt

2 cups (10 oz/315 g) hazelnuts (filberts), toasted and skinned (page 328)

Bittersweet chocolate, chopped and melted (page 325), for dipping

Preheat the oven to 325°F (165°C). Grease 2 large baking sheets.

In a large bowl, using an electric mixer set on medium speed, beat together the butter and sugar just until combined. Beat in the eggs. In another large bowl, stir together the flour, baking soda, and salt. On low speed, beat half of the flour mixture into the butter mixture until combined. Beat in the hazelnuts and then the remaining flour mixture.

Transfer the dough to a lightly floured work surface and knead briefly until the dough holds together. Divide the dough into 4 equal mounds. Shape each mound into a loaf 9 inches (23 cm) long and 3 inches (7.5 cm) wide. Place the loaves on the prepared baking sheets. Bake until the loaves are golden and firm when the tops are lightly pressed, about 1 hour. Remove from the oven and let cool slightly on the baking sheets. Leave the oven set at 325°F (165°C).

Using a spatula, carefully transfer the loaves to a work surface. Using a long, serrated knife, cut crosswise on a slight diagonal into slices ½ inch (12 mm) thick. Arrange the slices, cut side down, on the baking sheets. Return to the oven and bake until golden and crisp, about 45 minutes. Transfer to wire racks and let cool completely.

Dip one side of each cooled cookie into the melted chocolate and set the cookies, chocolate side up, on baking sheets. Refrigerate until the chocolate is set. Store in an airtight container at room temperature for up to 1 week.

Makes about 5 dozen cookies

Pine Nut Bars

These moist and sophisticated bar cookies are a good addition to a Christmas cookie platter. Store in an airtight container at cool room temperature for up to 3 days.

Preheat the oven to 350°F (180°C). Generously grease a 7-by-11-inch (18-by-28-cm) square baking pan.

In a heavy saucepan over medium heat, melt the butter. Add the pine nuts, vanilla bean, and orange zest. Cook, stirring, until the pine nuts are golden brown, about 3 minutes. Remove from the heat.

Remove the vanilla bean from the saucepan and, using the tip of a sharp knife, scrape the seeds into the pan. Discard the pod. Stir in the brown sugar. Let cool slightly, then whisk in the eggs and stir in the baking soda, salt, and then the flour.

Pour the batter into the prepared pan. Bake until a toothpick inserted into the center comes out clean, about 20 minutes. Transfer to a wire rack and let cool completely. Press down gently on the edges to flatten if necessary.

To make the topping, in a small, heavy saucepan, combine the cream and butter and bring to a boil. Remove from the heat and whisk in the white chocolate. Return the pan to low heat and stir until the chocolate melts and the mixture is smooth, 30 seconds. Pour the topping over the cooled uncut bars in the pan. Tilt the pan to spread the topping evenly. Refrigerate until the topping is almost set, 8 minutes.

With a knife, score the topping into 24 equal bars. Garnish each rectangle with a pine nut and an orange zest curl, if desired. When the topping is set, cut along the marks into bars.

Makes 2 dozen bars

½ cup (4 oz/125 g) unsalted butter, plus extra for greasing

⅔ cup (4 oz/125 g) pine nuts, plus extra for optional garnish

1 piece vanilla bean, about 2 inches (5 cm) long, split in half lengthwise

½ teaspoon orange zest

1 cup (7 oz/220 g) firmly packed light brown sugar

2 eggs

½ teaspoon baking soda (bicarbonate of soda)

¼ teaspoon salt

1 cup (5 oz/155 g) all-purpose (plain) flour

FOR THE TOPPING:

6 tablespoons (3 fl oz/90 ml) heavy (double) cream

1 tablespoon unsalted butter

4½ oz (140 g) white chocolate, chopped

24 small orange zest curls (optional)

Cardamom Molasses Spice Cookies

1 cup (4 oz/125 g) walnuts

4 cups (1¼ lb/625 g) all-purpose (plain) flour

1½ cups (10½ oz/330 g) firmly packed dark brown sugar

1 tablespoon ground cardamom

1 tablespoon ground ginger

2 teaspoons ground cinnamon

1 teaspoon salt

1 teaspoon baking soda (bicarbonate of soda)

½ cup (4 oz/125 g) unsalted butter, at room temperature, plus extra for greasing

½ cup (4 oz/125 g) vegetable shortening

½ cup (5½ oz/170 g) dark molasses

2 eggs

1 tablespoon plus 1 teaspoon vanilla extract (essence)

2 tablespoons orange zest

FOR THE ICING:

6 cups (1½ lb/750 g) confectioners' (icing) sugar

¼ cup (2 fl oz/60 ml) milk

3 tablespoons fresh lemon juice

Place the walnuts in a food processor and process to grind finely (do not process to a paste). Add ½ cup (2½ oz/75 g) of the flour and ½ cup (3½ oz/105 g) of the brown sugar and process to a powder. Set aside.

In a large bowl, sift together the remaining 3½ cups (17½ oz/550 g) flour, the cardamom, ginger, cinnamon, salt, and baking soda. Set aside. In another large bowl, combine the butter, shortening, and the remaining 1 cup (7 oz/ 225 g) brown sugar. Using an electric mixer set on high speed, beat the butter mixture until light and fluffy, about 3 minutes. Add the molasses, eggs, vanilla, and orange zest and again beat until light and fluffy. Add the flour and nut mixtures and beat on low speed just until incorporated. Gather the dough into a ball, form into 4 disks, wrap the disks in plastic wrap, and refrigerate for at least 1 hour or up to 2 days.

Position a rack in the upper third of the oven and another rack in the middle; preheat to 350°F (180°C). Grease 2 baking sheets. Dust 1 disk with flour and place between 2 sheets of waxed paper. Roll out ¼ inch (6 mm) thick. Using decoratively shaped cutters about 2 inches (5 cm) in diameter, cut out cookies. Transfer to the prepared baking sheets, spacing them ½ inch (12 mm) apart. Refrigerate any scraps.

Bake until firm on the edges and browned on the bottom, about 10 minutes. Let cool on wire racks. Repeat with the remaining dough and scraps.

Meanwhile, to make the icing, stir together all the ingredients until smooth. If the mixture is too thick to pipe or spread, thin with a little more milk.

Spread the icing onto the cooled cookies. To make the plaid pattern shown here, mix separate, smaller batches of icing and tint with different food colorings. Then use a pastry bag fitted with a small tip to apply the colored icing to the hardened white base. A plastic bag with a hole snipped in the corner also works well.

Let stand until the icing sets, about 2 hours.

Makes about 6 dozen cookies

Spicy Ginger Bars

These soft and chewy bars are addictive. For a variation, fold in a rounded 6 cups (5 oz/155 g) semisweet chocolate chips with the crystallized ginger. The bars can be made 2 days in advance, covered with foil, and stored at room temperature.

3/4 cup (6 oz/185 g) unsalted butter, at room temperature, plus extra for greasing

3/4 cup (5 1/2 oz/170 g) firmly packed dark brown sugar

1/2 cup (4 oz/125 g) granulated sugar

2 eggs

1 tablespoon dark molasses

2 1/4 cups (11 1/2 oz/360 g) all-purpose (plain) flour

1/4 teaspoon salt

1 teaspoon baking soda (bicarbonate of soda)

1 1/2 teaspoons ground ginger

1/2 teaspoon ground cloves

1/2 cup (2 1/2 oz/75 g) crystallized ginger, cut into 1/4-inch (6-mm) dice

Preheat the oven to 375°F (190°C). Grease a 9-by-13-inch (23-by- 33-cm) baking pan. Dust with flour, tapping out the excess.

In a bowl, using an electric mixer set on medium speed, beat together the butter, brown sugar, and granulated sugar until light, creamy, and smooth, 3–4 minutes. Add the eggs, one at a time, beating thoroughly after each addition until creamy. Beat in the molasses.

In a separate bowl, sift together the flour, salt, baking soda, ground ginger, and cloves. Add the flour mixture to the butter mixture and beat well on low speed until thoroughly combined. Add the crystallized ginger and stir to mix well. Pour the batter into the prepared pan.

Bake until the top is golden in color, about 30 minutes. Remove from the oven and let cool completely in the pan on a wire rack. Cut into bars, each about 1 1/2 inches (4 cm) square.

Makes 4 dozen bars

Dora Apter's Mandlebread

Position 2 racks in the middle of the oven and preheat to 350°F (180°C). Line 2 baking sheets with aluminum foil.

In a large bowl, using an electric mixer on high speed, beat together the eggs and 1 cup (8 oz/250 g) of the sugar until light and fluffy, 3 minutes. Reduce the speed to low and beat in the oil until incorporated. In another bowl, sift together the flour, baking soda, and salt. With the mixer set on low, add the flour mixture to the egg mixture, beating just until incorporated. Mix in the almond extract and the nuts.

Turn out the dough onto a floured work surface. Knead 5 or 6 turns until a ball forms, adding a little flour if the dough is very sticky. Divide into 5 equal pieces. Stir together the remaining 2/3 cup sugar and the cinnamon in a small bowl. Knead 1 tablespoon of the cinnamon sugar into each dough piece, then form into flat logs 12 inches (30 cm) long and 2 inches (5 cm) wide. Carefully transfer the logs to the prepared baking sheets, spacing them 3 inches (7.5 cm) apart. Brush the tops with the egg-water mixture, then sprinkle with the remaining cinnamon sugar.

Bake until the tops are dry and slightly cracked, about 30 minutes. At the halfway point, switch the baking sheets between the shelves, turning them 180 degrees as well. Transfer the logs to a work surface. Using a serrated knife, cut crosswise into slices 1 1/2 inches (4 cm) wide. Place the slices on the baking sheets, cut sides down. Return them to the oven until lightly golden brown, 4–5 minutes. Turn the cookies over and bake until lightly browned on the second side. Let cool completely on wire racks. Store in an airtight container for up to 2 weeks at room temperature.

Makes about 4 dozen cookies

4 extra-large eggs

1 2/3 cups (13 oz/410 g) sugar

1 cup (8 fl oz/250 ml) vegetable oil

4 cups (1 lb/500 g) sifted all-purpose (plain) flour, plus extra for kneading

4 teaspoons baking soda (bicarbonate of soda)

1 teaspoon salt

2 teaspoons almond extract (essence)

1 generous cup (5 oz/155 g) hazelnuts (filberts), toasted and skinned (page 328), or almonds, toasted (page 328), or a mixture

3 tablespoons ground cinnamon

1 egg, lightly beaten with 1 tablespoon water

Cakes, Puddings & Tea Breads

Mocha Bûche de Noël

6 eggs

3/4 cup (6 oz/185 g) granulated sugar

1 teaspoon instant espresso powder

3/4 cup (4 oz/125 g) all-purpose (plain) flour, plus extra for dusting

2 tablespoons unsweetened cocoa powder

1/4 teaspoon salt

2 tablespoons unsalted butter, melted and cooled, plus extra for greasing

Confectioners' (icing) sugar for dusting

1 1/2 cups (12 fl oz/375 ml) Coffee Buttercream Frosting (page 318)

1 cup (8 fl oz/250 ml) Bittersweet Chocolate Ganache (page 317)

Preheat the oven to 350°F (180°C). Grease a 10-by-15-by-1 inch (25-by-38-by-2.5-cm) jelly-roll pan. Line the bottom with parchment (baking) paper. Grease and flour the paper and pan sides.

In the top pan of a double boiler or large, heatproof bowl, combine the eggs, granulated sugar, and espresso powder. Place over (but not touching) gently boiling water and whisk until just warm to the touch. Remove from the heat. Using an electric mixer set on high speed, beat until tripled in volume and soft peaks form, about 3 minutes. In a sifter, combine the flour, cocoa, and salt. Sift directly onto the egg mixture. Using a rubber spatula, gently fold the mixtures together. Drizzle on the melted butter and fold it in.

Pour the batter into the prepared pan. Bake until a toothpick inserted into the center of the cake comes out clean, about 15 minutes. Transfer to a wire rack and let cool completely in the pan.

Place a large sheet of waxed paper on a work surface. Using a sifter or sieve, generously dust the paper with confectioners' sugar. Invert the jelly-roll pan onto the paper and lift off the pan. Peel off the parchment paper. Spread the buttercream frosting evenly over the cake. Beginning at a long side, roll up the cake jelly-roll style. Using a sharp knife, cut off the ends on the diagonal so that each piece is 1 inch (2.5 cm) long on one side and 3 inches (7.5 cm) long on the other. Place one piece, cut side down, on top of the cake toward one end. Place the other piece, cut side down, on the side of the cake toward the other end. The cake should resemble a log with cut limbs.

Stir the ganache until spreadable, then frost the cake, including all the ends. Using a fork, run the tines in circles on the ends and cut limbs of the log. Then run the tines the length of the log to simulate bark. Just before serving, sift confectioners' sugar over the log, to simulate snow. Slice crosswise to serve.

Serves 12

Warm Lemon Rice Custards

These custards can be served warm, or you can bake them several hours in advance and serve at room temperature. Let the custards cool completely, cover, and store in the refrigerator, then remove from the refrigerator about 20 minutes before serving.

Preheat the oven to 400°F (200°C). Using 1 tablespoon of the butter, grease twelve 5–fl oz (160-ml) ramekins. Bring a 2-qt (2-l) saucepan three-fourths full of water to a boil. Add the rice, bring just to a boil, reduce the heat to medium, and simmer for 5 minutes. Drain and transfer to a bowl.

Pour the milk into the same pan and bring to a boil over medium heat. Return the rice to the pan and add the lemon zest. Cook, stirring occasionally, until the rice is tender and the milk is absorbed, about 20 minutes. Remove from the heat. Add the granulated sugar and the remaining 2 tablespoons butter. Stir until the sugar is completely dissolved.

In a large bowl, whisk together the whole eggs, egg yolks, and lemon juice until blended. Add one-fourth of the hot rice to the eggs and stir together. Continue to add the rice slowly, stirring constantly, until all of the rice has been added; do not add the hot rice to the eggs too quickly or the eggs will scramble. Spoon the mixture into the prepared ramekins, dividing it evenly. (The custards can be prepared up to this point 1 day in advance, covered, and refrigerated. About 20 minutes before you are ready to bake them, remove from the refrigerator.)

Set the ramekins in a baking pan and pour boiling water into the pan to reach halfway up the sides of the dishes. Cover the pan with aluminum foil and bake until a skewer inserted into the center of a custard comes out clean, 30–35 minutes. Remove from the oven and let cool for 10–20 minutes. Using a sieve, dust the tops with confectioners' sugar and serve.

Serves 12

3 tablespoons unsalted butter

1 cup (7 oz/220 g) short-grain white rice

3 cups (24 fl oz/750 ml) milk

1 tablespoon grated lemon zest

3/4 cup (6 oz/185 g) granulated sugar

3 whole eggs, plus 3 egg yolks

1 tablespoon fresh lemon juice

Boiling water, as needed

Confectioners' (icing) sugar for dusting

Pumpkin Cheesecake

Make this cheesecake the day before serving. The cream cheese, pumpkin purée, and eggs must be at room temperature before mixing. Use confectioners' (icing) sugar to stencil leaf or other designs on top.

1½ cups (5 oz/155 g) graham cracker crumbs

3 tablespoons (8 oz/250 g) sugar, plus 1 cup

1 teaspoon ground ginger

6 tablespoons (3 oz/90 g) unsalted butter, melted, plus extra for greasing

1½ lb (750 g) cream cheese, at room temperature

2 cups (1 lb/500 g) canned pumpkin purée

1 teaspoon finely grated orange zest

1 tablespoon ground cinnamon

½ teaspoon ground cloves

½ teaspoon ground nutmeg

6 eggs, lightly beaten

Preheat the oven to 325°F (165°C). Cover the outside bottom and sides of a 9-inch (23-cm) springform pan with heavy-duty aluminum foil, shiny side out. Grease the inside of the pan and set aside.

In a bowl, stir together the graham cracker crumbs, the 3 tablespoons sugar, and the ginger. Stir and toss while gradually adding the melted butter. Continue to stir and toss until well mixed. Press the crumb mixture evenly over the inside of the pan to reach about 2 inches (5 cm) up the sides. Refrigerate for 30 minutes.

Place the cream cheese in a large bowl. Using an electric mixer set on medium speed, beat until light and fluffy, 2–3 minutes. Slowly add the 1 cup (8 oz/250 g) sugar while continuously beating; occasionally scrape down the bowl sides. Add the pumpkin, orange zest, cinnamon, cloves, and nutmeg and beat until smooth. Add the eggs, a little at a time, beating well after each addition and scraping down the bowl sides. Using a rubber spatula, stir slowly to dispel some of the bubbles.

Pour the batter into the chilled crust and smooth the surface. Bake until the top is lightly puffed all over, 60–70 minutes. The center may be slightly underset; it will firm up during cooling. Cool on a wire rack, then remove the foil and the pan sides and refrigerate overnight. Before serving, carefully slip the chilled cake onto a large, flat serving plate.

Makes one 9-inch (23-cm) cheesecake; serves 6–8

Cranberry-Orange Steamed Pudding

If you do not have a steamed pudding mold, use a small, ovenproof mixing bowl. Cover the filled bowl with a piece of buttered aluminum foil, buttered side in, and fasten securely with kitchen string.

Grease the inside of a 1½–2-qt (48–64–fl oz/1.5–2-l) pudding mold and its cover. Select a lidded pot large enough to hold the mold. Place a low trivet or jar lid in the pot bottom.

In a small saucepan, combine the cold water with ⅓ cup (3 oz/90 g) of the sugar. Bring to a boil, stirring to dissolve the sugar. Add the cranberries, cover, and simmer for 2–3 minutes. Set aside. In a bowl, stir together the flour, baking soda, cloves, allspice, and ground ginger. Set aside.

In a large bowl, combine the butter and the remaining 1 cup (8 oz/250 g) sugar. Using an electric mixer set at medium speed, beat until light and fluffy, about 3 minutes, scraping down the bowl sides as needed. Add the eggs, a little at a time, beating well after each addition. Beat until increased in volume slightly, 5–6 minutes, again scraping down the bowl sides. Using a rubber spatula, fold the flour mixture, one-third at a time, into the egg mixture, alternating with the orange juice and the cranberries and their liquid. Quickly beat in the crystallized ginger and orange zest. Spoon into the prepared mold, avoiding air bubbles. Cover the mold and place on the trivet in the pot. Add boiling water to reach two-thirds up the mold sides. Cover the pot and simmer gently for 1½ hours. Add boiling water as needed to maintain the original level.

Remove the mold and let stand for 5 minutes. Invert onto a serving plate and lift off the mold. Cut into wedges and serve warm with the brandy butter sauce.

Serves 8–10

½ cup (4 fl oz/125 ml) cold water

1⅓ cups (11 oz/340 g) sugar

1 cup (4 oz/125 g) dried cranberries

2½ cups (12½ oz/390 g) all-purpose (plain) flour

1½ teaspoons baking soda (bicarbonate of soda)

¼ teaspoon ground cloves

⅛ teaspoon *each* ground allspice and ground ginger

½ cup (4 oz/125 g) unsalted butter, at room temperature, plus extra for greasing

3 eggs, lightly beaten

½ cup (4 fl oz/125 ml) fresh orange juice

⅓ cup (2 oz/60 g) crystallized ginger, chopped

1 tablespoon finely grated orange zest

Boiling water, as needed

Brandy Butter Sauce (page 319) for serving

Pear Upside-Down Spice Cake

Preheat the oven to 350°F (180°C). Line the inside of a springform pan 10 inches (25 cm) in diameter with aluminum foil. Use one piece of foil for the bottom and another for the sides, cutting the foil to fit and pressing it tightly into the pan. Grease the foil.

In a small, heavy saucepan over low heat, melt the 6 tablespoons (3 oz/90 g) butter. Add ³/₄ cup (6 oz/185 g) of the brown sugar and stir until well blended. Pour into the foil-lined pan. Arrange the pear slices atop the syrup in the pan.

Sift together the flour, baking powder, baking soda, cinnamon, ground ginger, cloves, and salt into a bowl. Combine the milk and vanilla in a small bowl. In a large bowl, using an electric mixer set on high speed, beat together the ¹/₂ cup (4 oz/125 g) butter and the remaining ¹/₂ cup (3 oz/90 g) brown sugar until light and fluffy, about 3 minutes. Add the egg and beat until well blended. Add the molasses and orange zest and beat until fully combined. Mix in the dry ingredients in 2 batches alternating with the milk mixture, beginning and ending with the dry ingredients. Using a rubber spatula, fold in the crystallized ginger. Pour the batter evenly over the pears in the pan, being careful not to disturb the pears.

Bake the cake until a toothpick inserted into the center comes out clean, about 55 minutes. Transfer to a wire rack to cool for 5 minutes. Run a small knife between the cake and the foil to loosen the cake. Turn out the cake onto the rack. Let cool for at least 30 minutes.

Serve the cake warm or at room temperature with whipped cream or ice cream.

Makes one 10-inch (25-cm) cake; serves 8–10

6 tablespoons (3 oz/90 g) plus ¹/₂ cup (4 oz/125 g) unsalted butter, plus extra for greasing

1¹/₄ cups (9 oz/275 g) firmly packed golden brown sugar

2 ripe but firm pears such as Anjou or Bartlett (Williams'), peeled, quartered, cored, and thinly sliced

1¹/₂ cups (6 oz/185 g) cake (soft-wheat) flour

1¹/₈ teaspoons baking powder

¹/₄ teaspoon baking soda (bicarbonate of soda)

4 teaspoons ground cinnamon

1 teaspoon ground ginger

¹/₂ teaspoon ground cloves

¹/₂ teaspoon salt

¹/₂ cup (4 fl oz/125 ml) milk

1 teaspoon vanilla extract (essence)

1 egg

¹/₂ cup (5¹/₂ oz/170 g) light molasses

1 tablespoon grated orange zest

¹/₄ cup (1¹/₄ oz/37 g) chopped crystallized ginger

Whipped cream or vanilla ice cream for serving

Chocolate-Almond Cheesecake

1 cup (3 oz/90 g) chocolate cookie crumbs

1 cup (4 oz/125 g) sliced (flaked) almonds

4 tablespoons (2 oz/60 g) unsalted butter, melted and cooled

4 tablespoons (2 oz/60 g) plus 1¹/₂ cups (12 oz/375 g) sugar

10 oz (315 g) bittersweet chocolate, chopped, plus 2 oz (60 g) chopped, for optional garnish

2 lb (1 kg) cream cheese, at room temperature

¹/₂ cup (1¹/₂ oz/45 g) unsweetened cocoa powder

4 eggs

¹/₂ cup (4 fl oz/125 ml) heavy (double) cream

1 tablespoon vanilla extract (essence)

1¹/₂ teaspoons almond extract (essence)

2 cups (16 oz/500 g) sour cream

Marzipan fruits (optional) for garnish

Preheat the oven to 350°F (180°C).

In a bowl, mix together the cookie crumbs, almonds, melted butter, and 1 tablespoon of the sugar. Press evenly over the bottom of a 10-inch (25-cm) springform pan. Bake until just golden, about 12 minutes. Let cool on a wire rack. Leave the oven set at 350°F (180°C).

In the top pan of a double boiler or a heatproof bowl placed over (but not touching) simmering water, place the 10 oz (315 g) chopped chocolate. Heat, stirring, until melted and smooth. Let cool. In a large bowl, using an electric mixer set on medium speed, beat together the cream cheese, the 1¹/₂ cups (12 oz/375 g) sugar, and the cocoa until blended, about 3 minutes. Beat in the cooled chocolate. Add the eggs, one at a time, beating well after each addition. Beat in the cream, vanilla, and 1 teaspoon of the almond extract.

Pour the chocolate mixture over the cooled crust. Bake until puffy and gently set in the center, about 1 hour. Let cool on the wire rack until the cake deflates slightly, about 20 minutes. Leave the oven temperature set at 350°F (180°C).

In a bowl, stir together the sour cream and the remaining 3 tablespoons sugar and ¹/₂ teaspoon almond extract. Spread over the settled cheesecake. Return to the oven and bake until just set, about 8 minutes. Let cool completely on the wire rack.

If desired, melt the 2 oz (60 g) chocolate as above. Dip fork tines into the melted chocolate and wave the fork back and forth over the cheesecake to create a zigzag pattern. Cover and refrigerate overnight.

Before serving, arrange marzipan fruits around the top or alongside the cheesecake.

Makes one 10-inch (25-cm) cheesecake; serves 12–16

Galette des Rois

The bean or porcelain figure hidden in the center of this cake is believed to bring good fortune to the person who finds it. Warn all who sample the cake about the surprise inside before they take a bite.

²/₃ cup (3¹/₂ oz/105 g) blanched almonds, toasted (page 328) and cooled

¹/₃ cup (¹/₂ oz/45 g) confectioners' (icing) sugar

1 tablespoon cornstarch (cornflour)

2 eggs

1 tablespoon dark rum

¹/₄ teaspoon almond extract (essence)

1 cup (8 fl oz/250 ml) Vanilla Pastry Cream, cooled to room temperature (page 319)

6 tablespoons (3 oz/90 g) unsalted butter, at room temperature

1 package (17¹/₄ oz/537 g) frozen puff pastry sheets (2 sheets), thawed at room temperature

1 dried bean or a tiny porcelain figure

1 tablespoon milk

Preheat the oven to 400°F (200°C).

In a food processor, process the almonds, confectioners' sugar, and cornstarch until the nuts are finely ground. Add 1 of the eggs, the rum, and the almond extract and process, using on-off pulses, until blended. Add the pastry cream and process just until blended. With the motor running, add the butter, 1 tablespoon at a time, and process until smooth.

On a lightly floured work surface, roll out each puff pastry sheet into a 12-inch (30-cm) square. Using a piece of waxed paper cut to size as a guide, cut out a round 11 inches (28 cm) in diameter from each square. Discard the pastry scraps.

Transfer 1 pastry round to a baking sheet. Spread the filling over the round, leaving a 1-inch (2.5-cm) border uncovered around the edges. Place the dried bean or porcelain figure atop the filling. In a small bowl, whisk together the remaining egg and the milk. Brush some of the mixture on the uncovered border. Place the other pastry round on top and press the edges together. Brush the top with the remaining mixture. Using a knife, score the top in a diamond pattern, being careful not to cut through to the filling.

Bake until the crust is golden brown, about 35 minutes. Transfer to a wire rack and let cool completely. To serve, cut into wedges.

Makes one 11-inch (28-cm) cake; serves 12

Sweet Potato–Ginger Pudding

Here is an ideal vegetable accompaniment to baked ham or turkey. If tan sweet potatoes are not available, use the orange-fleshed ones (also called yams). Brush off any excess sugar from the crystallized ginger.

Place the sweet potatoes in a large saucepan with water to cover. Bring to a boil, reduce the heat to medium-low, cover, and cook until tender, 30–40 minutes. Drain and let cool.

Preheat the oven to 350°F (180°C). Grease a 2-qt (2-l) soufflé dish or baking dish.

Peel the cooled sweet potatoes and place in a food processor. Process to a smooth purée. You should have about 2 1/2 cups (1 1/4 lb/625 g). Transfer the purée to a large bowl and stir in the lemon zest, salt, and ginger, then stir in the cream and nutmeg.

In a separate bowl, using an electric mixer set on medium speed, beat the egg whites until soft folds form. Add about one-fourth of the beaten whites to the potato mixture and stir in the remaining whites, being careful not to deflate the mixture. Spoon into the prepared baking dish.

Bake until risen and slightly golden on top, 40–50 minutes. Serve immediately.

Serves 8–10

2 lb (1 kg) tan-skinned sweet potatoes, unpeeled

Unsalted butter for greasing

Finely grated zest of 1 lemon

1/2 teaspoon salt

1/3 cup (2 oz/60 g) crystallized ginger, finely chopped

1 1/2 cups (12 fl oz/375 ml) heavy (double) cream

Pinch of ground nutmeg

4 egg whites

Bittersweet Chocolate Valentine Cake

If your loved one is a chocolate addict, bake this for Valentine's Day. The cake can be sprinkled with chocolate curls or piped with melted white chocolate. Buy top-quality chocolate for best results. Garnish with strawberries, if desired.

8 oz (250 g) bittersweet chocolate, chopped

1 cup (8 oz/250 g) unsalted butter, plus extra for greasing

5 eggs

1⅓ cups (11 oz/345 g) sugar

2 tablespoons all-purpose (plain) flour, plus extra for dusting

1 tablespoon vanilla extract (essence)

¼ teaspoon salt

1 cup (8 fl oz/250 ml) Bittersweet Chocolate Ganache, warm (page 317)

2 oz (60 g) white chocolate, melted (page 325) (optional)

Preheat the oven to 325°F (165°C). Grease a heart-shaped cake pan 9 inches (23 cm) in diameter and 3 inches (7.5 cm) deep. Line the bottom of the pan with parchment (baking) paper cut to fit precisely. Butter the paper, then dust the paper and pan sides with flour.

In a heavy saucepan over medium-low heat, combine the chopped bittersweet chocolate and butter. Stir until melted and smooth, about 2 minutes. Remove from the heat and let cool slightly. In a large bowl, whisk together the eggs and sugar until well blended. Whisk in the chocolate mixture, then stir in the flour, vanilla, and salt until combined.

Pour the batter into the prepared pan. Bake until the cake is set and slightly puffed in the center, about 1 hour and 10 minutes. Transfer to a wire rack and let cool until warm. Invert onto a serving plate. Carefully lift off the pan and peel off the paper. Let cool completely.

Tuck strips of waxed paper under the edges of the cake. Pour the warm ganache over the top and, using an icing spatula, coax it down the sides. When the glaze stops dripping, remove the paper strips. Let cool and then refrigerate until set, about 1 hour.

If using the white chocolate, spoon it into a small pastry bag fitted with a plain tip (or a small plastic bag with a corner snipped off) and pipe decoratively on top. Refrigerate overnight before serving.

Makes one 9-inch (23-cm) cake; serves 8

Lemon-Blueberry Bundt Cake

If possible, use Meyer lemons for this summertime cake to give it a sweet-tart flavor.
This cake is perfect for a summer holiday picnic. If you like, place fresh blueberries
in the center and lemon leaves and paper-thin lemon slices around the sides.

Preheat the oven to 350°F (180°C). Grease and lightly flour a 10-inch (25-cm) Bundt pan completely.

In a large bowl, sift together the flour, baking soda, and salt. Set aside. In another bowl, using an electric mixer set on medium speed, beat together the butter, sugar, and lemon zest until light and fluffy, about 4 minutes. Add the eggs, one at a time, beating well after each addition. Beat in the lemon juice. Reduce the speed to low and beat in the flour mixture in two batches alternating with the buttermilk, beginning and ending with the flour mixture. Stir in the dried blueberries.

Spoon the batter into the prepared pan. Bake until a toothpick inserted near the center of the cake comes out clean, about 55 minutes. Transfer the pan to a wire rack and let cool slightly.

To make the glaze, in a small saucepan over high heat, combine the sugar, lemon juice, and butter. Bring to a boil, stirring to dissolve the sugar, then boil the mixture until syrupy, about 5 minutes.

Brush some of the glaze over the surface of the warm cake. Invert the cake onto a serving plate and carefully lift off the pan. Drizzle the top of the cake with the remaining glaze. Let cool completely before serving.

Makes one 10-inch (25-cm) cake; serves 12

3 cups (12 oz/375 g) cake
(soft-wheat) flour

1/2 teaspoon baking soda
(bicarbonate of soda)

1/2 teaspoon salt

3/4 cup (6 oz/185 g) unsalted
butter, at room temperature,
plus extra for greasing

1 3/4 cups (14 oz/440 g) sugar

2 tablespoons minced
lemon zest

3 eggs

1/4 cup (2 fl oz/60 ml) fresh
lemon juice

3/4 cup (6 fl oz/180 ml) plus
2 tablespoons buttermilk

3/4 cup (3 oz/90 g) dried
blueberries

FOR THE GLAZE:

1/4 cup (2 oz/60 g) sugar

1/4 cup (2 fl oz/60 ml) fresh
lemon juice

2 tablespoons unsalted butter

Chocolate Brownie Pudding Cakes

Although rich and chocolatey, this dessert is not overly heavy. It is particularly well suited to a New Year's Eve menu because it can be assembled completely in advance and then popped into the oven to bake just before serving.

5½ oz (170 g) bittersweet chocolate, chopped

½ cup (4 oz/125 g) plus 1 tablespoon unsalted butter, plus extra for greasing

3 whole eggs, plus 3 egg yolks

⅓ cup (3 oz/90 g) granulated sugar

5 tablespoons (½ oz/45 g) all-purpose (plain) flour

Confectioners' (icing) sugar for dusting

Whipped cream for serving (optional)

Preheat the oven to 375°F (190°C). Lightly grease six 1-cup (8–fl oz/250-ml) ramekins and set aside.

Place the chocolate and butter in the top pan of a double boiler or a heatproof bowl set over (but not touching) gently simmering water. Stir with a wooden spoon until the chocolate is melted and smooth. Remove from the pan of water and let cool.

In a large bowl, combine the whole eggs, egg yolks, and granulated sugar. Using an electric mixer set on medium speed, beat until the mixture is a light lemon color, about 5 minutes. Add the flour and continue to beat on medium speed until fully blended. Add the cooled chocolate-butter mixture and beat again until blended. Divide the batter among the prepared ramekins, filling each halfway. (The recipe can be prepared up to this point, lightly covered with aluminum foil or plastic wrap, and set aside at room temperature for up to 3 hours before baking.)

Set the ramekins on a baking sheet and place in the oven. Bake until the cakes are set but the centers still move slightly when the ramekins are shaken, about 10 minutes. Be careful to not overbake or the cakes will be dry instead of creamy in the center. Remove from the oven and, using a sieve, lightly dust the tops with confectioners' sugar.

Place the ramekins on dessert plates and top each with a dollop of whipped cream, if desired. Serve immediately.

Serves 6

Date-Walnut Pudding

Select a baking dish that measures about 11½-by-8-by-2-inches (29-by-20-by-5.5-cm). If the dish is too large, the pudding will not be thick enough and will bake too quickly.

½ cup (2½ oz/75 g) all-purpose (plain) flour

2 teaspoons baking powder

¼ teaspoon salt

1¼ cups (9 oz/280 g) firmly packed light brown sugar

3 eggs, at room temperature

½ cup (4 oz/125 g) unsalted butter, at room temperature, plus extra for greasing

2 teaspoons finely grated orange zest

2 tablespoons dark rum

1½ cups (12 fl oz/375 ml) milk, at room temperature

1½ cups (12 oz/375 g) firmly packed, coarsely chopped pitted dates

1½ cups (6 oz/185 g) coarsely broken walnuts

Whole dates and walnut halves for garnish

Ginger Sabayon Cream (page 318) for serving

Preheat the oven to 350°F (180°C). Generously grease a 2–2½-qt (2–2.5-l) earthenware, porcelain, or heatproof glass baking dish.

In a bowl, stir together the flour, baking powder, and salt. Set aside.

In a large bowl, combine the brown sugar and eggs. Using an electric mixer set on medium speed, beat until fluffy and thickened, about 3 minutes, scraping down the sides of the bowl at regular intervals. Add the butter and beat until well blended, 3 minutes longer. Beat in the orange zest and the rum. Using a rubber spatula, stir in the flour mixture and then beat in the milk. Stir in the dates and walnuts, being sure the date pieces are well distributed and not clinging together. The mixture will separate, but do not worry; it will come together during baking.

Pour the mixture into the prepared baking dish. Bake until golden brown and a knife inserted in the center comes out dry, 40–50 minutes. Remove from the oven and place on a wire rack. Garnish with the whole dates and walnut halves. Let cool slightly. Serve warm with the ginger sabayon cream.

Serves 6–8, with leftovers

Dried Fruit and Nut Fruitcake

This cake does not call for the traditional candied fruits that make most fruitcakes taste old-fashioned. Wrapped in plastic wrap, it can be stored in a cool place for several days.

In a bowl, combine the pears, apricots, prunes, dark and golden raisins, cherries, dates, orange peel, and crystallized ginger. Pour the $^{1}/_{2}$ cup (4 fl oz/ 125 ml) brandy over the top. Let stand for at least 4 hours or as long as overnight at room temperature, stirring occasionally.

Preheat the oven to 325°F (165°C). Grease a tube pan 10 inches (25 cm) in diameter and $4^{1}/_{4}$ inches (10.5 cm) deep. Line the bottom with parchment (baking) paper or waxed paper cut to fit precisely. Butter the paper, then flour the paper and pan sides. In a large bowl, using an electric mixer set on medium speed, beat the butter until light and fluffy, about 7 minutes. Add the sugar and continue beating until once again fluffy, about 4 minutes. Beat in the eggs, one at a time, beating well after each addition. Beat in the vanilla and salt. Reduce the mixer speed to low and beat in the flour. After the nuts have cooled, chop them up. Using a wooden spoon, fold in the nuts and the brandy-fruit mixture until fully incorporated.

Spoon the batter into the pan. Using the back of a wooden spoon, spread the batter evenly and smooth the top. Bake until a toothpick inserted near the center of the cake comes out clean, about 1 hour and 50 minutes. Transfer to a wire rack. Brush 1 tablespoon of the remaining brandy over the cake. Let cool for 5 minutes.

Invert the cake onto the rack. Carefully lift off the pan and then peel off the paper. Brush the remaining 2 tablespoons brandy over the top and sides. Let cool completely before serving.

Makes one 10-inch (25-cm) cake; serves 12–20

1 cup *each* (6 oz/185 g) chopped dried pears, apricots, and pitted prunes

$^{1}/_{2}$ cup *each* (3 oz/90 g) dark raisins and golden raisins (sultanas)

$^{1}/_{2}$ cup *each* (2 oz/60 g) dried pitted sour cherries and chopped pitted dates

3 tablespoons finely chopped candied orange peel

2 tablespoons finely chopped crystallized ginger

$^{1}/_{2}$ cup (4 fl oz/125 ml) plus 3 tablespoons brandy

$1^{1}/_{2}$ cups (12 oz/375 g) unsalted butter, at room temperature, plus extra for greasing

$2^{1}/_{2}$ cups ($1^{1}/_{4}$ lb/625 g) sugar

8 eggs, at room temperature

1 tablespoon vanilla extract (essence)

$^{1}/_{2}$ teaspoon salt

3 cups (9 oz/280 g) sifted cake (soft-wheat) flour

2 cups (8–10 oz/250–315 g) nuts, toasted (page 328)

Devil's Food Cupcakes

Perfect for kids and adults alike, this recipe is a delightful treat for a large group. Beets give these cupcakes a nice, moist texture and a slightly reddish hue. For a festive touch, lightly sprinkle colored sugar crystals over the frosting.

2 beets

2 cups (10 oz/315 g) all-purpose (plain) flour

2/3 cup (2 oz/60 g) unsweetened cocoa powder

1 teaspoon baking soda (bicarbonate of soda)

1/2 teaspoon salt

3/4 cup (6 oz/185 g) unsalted butter, at room temperature

1 1/2 cups (12 oz/375 g) sugar

2 eggs

1 teaspoon vanilla extract (essence)

1 cup (8 fl oz/250 ml) hot water

1 recipe Buttercream Frosting, at room temperature (page 318) or Bittersweet Chocolate Ganache, warm (page 317)

Trim the stems from the beets, leaving 1/2 inch (12 mm) intact. Place the beets in a saucepan with water to cover, bring to a boil, reduce the heat to medium-low, and simmer until tender when pierced with a knife, about 30 minutes. Drain and let cool. Peel the beets and finely grate. You should have about 3/4 cup (5 oz/155 g). Set aside. Reserve any left over for another use.

Preheat the oven to 350°F (180°C). Line 24 standard-sized muffin cups with fluted paper liners. In a large bowl, sift together the flour, cocoa, baking soda, and salt. In another bowl, using an electric mixer set on medium speed, beat together the butter and sugar until light and fluffy, about 4 minutes. Add the eggs, one at a time, beating well after each addition. Beat in the beets and vanilla. Reduce the mixer speed to low and beat in the flour mixture in two batches alternating with the hot water, beginning and ending with the flour mixture.

Spoon the batter into the prepared cups, filling each about two-thirds full. Bake until a toothpick inserted into the center of a cupcake comes out clean, about 20 minutes. Remove from the oven and immediately invert onto a wire rack. Turn the cupcakes right side up and let cool completely.

Using an icing spatula, frost the cooled cupcakes with buttercream frosting or drizzle with warm ganache. Serve immediately, or store, loosely draped with plastic wrap, at room temperature for up to 1 day.

Makes 24 cupcakes

Passover Vanilla-Orange Sponge Cake

Passover cake meal is a fine matzoh meal specifically formulated for cake baking. Look for it in kosher markets or well-stocked food stores. Serve the cake with a strawberry-orange compote and whipped cream, if you like.

Preheat the oven to 325°F (165°C). In a food processor, combine the sugar and vanilla bean and process until fine; set aside.

In a bowl, using an electric mixer set on high speed, beat the egg yolks until very thick and pale, about 4 minutes. Place the vanilla sugar in a sifter and gradually sift directly onto the yolks, discarding any large pieces of vanilla bean. Continue to beat until the mixture is thick and pale and tripled in volume, about 5 minutes. Gradually beat in the orange juice and zest.

In a clean bowl, using clean, dry beaters, beat the egg whites and salt until stiff but not dry. Set aside. Combine the cake meal and potato starch in the sifter and sift the mixture directly onto the egg yolk mixture. Using a rubber spatula, fold in gently but thoroughly. Then fold in the egg whites, again working gently but thoroughly.

Spoon into a tube pan 10 inches (25 cm) in diameter and 4 inches (10 cm) deep. Bake until golden and the top springs back when gently touched, about 50 minutes. Invert the cake in its pan onto the neck of a bottle. Let cool completely.

To remove the cake from the pan, run a sharp knife around the edges of the pan to loosen the cake, then invert onto a serving plate. Carefully lift off the pan. Serve immediately, or cover with a cake dome and store at cool room temperature for up to 8 hours.

Makes one 10-inch (25-cm) cake; serves 8

1½ cups (12 oz/375 g) sugar

1 piece vanilla bean, about 2 inches (5 cm) long

10 eggs, separated, at room temperature

½ cup (4 fl oz/125 ml) fresh orange juice

1 tablespoon grated orange zest

¼ teaspoon salt

¾ cup (4 oz/125 g) Passover cake meal (see note)

½ cup (2 oz/60 g) potato starch

Steamed Plum Pudding

This steamed pudding is lighter and easier to make than the traditional Christmastime recipe. To reheat the pudding, return it to the mold and steam just until heated through. Serve with lightly whipped cream.

1 cup (6 oz/185 g) pitted prunes

3 eggs

1/2 cup (4 oz/125 g) unsalted butter, at room temperature, plus extra for greasing

1 3/4 cups (14 oz/440 g) sugar, plus extra for dusting

2 tablespoons brandy

2 teaspoons vanilla extract (essence)

2 cups (10 oz/315 g) all-purpose (plain) flour

2 teaspoons ground cinnamon

1 1/2 teaspoons baking soda (bicarbonate of soda)

1 teaspoon ground allspice

3/4 teaspoon salt

1/4 teaspoon ground cloves

1/2 cup (3 oz/90 g) *each* golden raisins (sultanas) and dark raisins

1/2 cup (2 oz/60 g) chopped walnuts

Grease the bottom and sides of a 2-qt (2-l) steamed pudding mold, then dust with sugar. Butter and sugar the inside lid as well. In a small, heavy saucepan over high heat, combine the prunes and 1 cup (8 fl oz/250 ml) water. Bring to a simmer, reduce the heat to medium-low, cover, and simmer until the prunes are very soft, about 15 minutes. Transfer the prunes and liquid to a blender and let cool briefly. Add the eggs and purée until smooth. Set aside.

In a large bowl, using an electric mixer set on medium speed, beat together the butter and sugar until light and fluffy, about 4 minutes. Beat in the prune mixture, brandy, and vanilla.

In a sifter, combine the flour, cinnamon, baking soda, allspice, salt, and cloves. Sift directly onto the prune mixture. Reduce the mixer speed to low and beat until blended. Beat in the golden and dark raisins and walnuts. Spoon the batter into the prepared mold and attach the lid. Fill the bottom chamber of a 2-chambered steamer or a deep soup pot with water and bring to a boil over medium-high heat. Place the pudding mold in the top chamber or on a steamer rack set over (but not touching) the water. Cover and steam until a toothpick inserted near the center comes out clean, about 2 hours. Check the water level periodically, adding more boiling water as necessary to maintain its original level.

Detach the mold lid and invert the pudding onto a serving plate. Lift off the mold. Serve warm or at room temperature.

Serves 8

Cranberry-Orange Cheesecake

This Thanksgiving cheesecake needs to be prepared a day ahead of time and then refrigerated overnight. If you like, garnish with orange slices just before serving.

Place the dried cranberries in a small, heavy saucepan and add water to cover. Place over low heat, cover, and bring to a simmer. Cook the cranberries until soft and plump, about 4 minutes. Remove from the heat and let cool. Drain off any liquid.

Preheat the oven to 350°F (180°C). In a bowl, combine the graham cracker crumbs, melted butter, and 1/4 cup (2 oz/60 g) of the sugar. Using a fork, stir to mix well. Press the crumb mixture over the bottom and 2 inches (5 cm) up the sides of a springform pan 10 inches (25 cm) in diameter and 3 inches (7.5 cm) deep. Bake until the crust is just golden, about 12 minutes. Transfer to a wire rack and let cool. Leave the oven set at 350°F (180°C).

In a bowl, using an electric mixer set on medium speed, beat together the cream cheese and 1 cup (8 oz/250 g) of the sugar until smooth. Beat in the orange juice concentrate, orange zest, and liqueur until well mixed. Add the eggs, one at a time, beating well after each addition. Using a rubber spatula, fold in the drained cranberries. Spoon the cream cheese mixture into the cooled crust. Bake until the cheesecake is just set when the pan is gently shaken, about 1 hour. Transfer to the wire rack and let cool slightly. Leave the oven set at 350°F (180°C).

In a small bowl, stir together the sour cream and 2 tablespoons sugar. Pour over the cheesecake, spreading evenly. Bake until the sour cream is set, about 8 minutes.

Transfer to the wire rack and let cool. Cover and refrigerate overnight. To serve, remove the pan sides, carefully slip the cheesecake onto a serving plate, and cut.

Makes one 10-inch (25-cm) cheesecake; serves 12

1 cup (4 oz/125 g) dried cranberries

2 cups (6 oz/185 g) graham cracker crumbs

1/2 cup (4 oz/125 g) unsalted butter, melted and cooled

1 1/4 cups (10 oz/310 g) plus 2 tablespoons sugar

2 lb (1 kg) cream cheese, at room temperature

1/2 cup (4 fl oz/125 ml) thawed, undiluted frozen orange juice concentrate

1 tablespoon grated orange zest

2 tablespoons orange-flavored liqueur, such as Grand Marnier

5 eggs

2 cups (16 fl oz/500 ml) sour cream

Orange, Walnut, and Pear Pumpkin Bread

The recipe makes 2 loaves of bread; enjoy the second one for breakfast the next day or give it as a gift. The loaves can also be tightly wrapped in aluminum foil and refrigerated for up to 3 days.

2 cups (14 oz/440 g) firmly packed light brown sugar

1½ cups (12 oz/375 g) canned pumpkin purée

½ cup (4 fl oz/125 ml) vegetable oil, plus extra for greasing

2 eggs, lightly beaten

2 teaspoons baking soda (bicarbonate of soda)

1¼ teaspoons ground ginger

¾ teaspoon ground cardamom

4 teaspoons grated orange zest

½ teaspoon salt

1 cup (4 oz/125 g) walnuts, chopped

½ lb (250 g) dried pears, chopped (about 1½ cups)

2½ cups (12½ oz/390 g) all-purpose (plain) flour, plus extra for dusting

Orange zest strips (optional)

Preheat the oven to 350°F (180°C). Grease and flour two 4½-by-8½-by-2½-inch (11.5-by-21.5-by-6-cm) loaf pans.

In a large bowl, using a wooden spoon, stir together the brown sugar, pumpkin, oil, eggs, baking soda, ginger, cardamom, grated orange zest, and salt until well mixed. Add the walnuts and pears and stir to distribute evenly. Add the flour and stir just until blended; do not overmix. Divide the batter evenly between the prepared pans.

Bake until a toothpick inserted into the center comes out clean, about 55 minutes. Transfer to wire racks to cool for 10 minutes. Turn out the loaves onto the racks and let cool completely. Cut into slices, arrange on a serving platter, and garnish with orange zest strips, if desired.

Makes 2 loaves

Chocolate Bread

Here is a rich, decadent loaf that is a welcome addition to any holiday breakfast, especially when chocolate lovers are seated around the table. It is best eaten on the day it is made. The white icing can be made a day ahead and refrigerated.

Pour the warm water into a large bowl. Sprinkle the yeast over the top and let stand until the yeast dissolves, about 1 minute. Using a wire whisk, stir in the sugar and salt. Whisk in the eggs and melted butter until well mixed. Using a wooden spoon, beat in the cocoa and then the flour to make a soft dough.

Gather the dough into a ball, place in a large greased bowl, turn to coat with butter, and cover the bowl with a clean kitchen towel. Place in a warm, draft-free area and let rise until doubled in bulk, about 1 1/2 hours.

Using a wooden spoon, stir the chocolate into the dough, removing any air pockets at the same time. Transfer the dough to a lightly floured work surface and knead briefly until the chocolate is incorporated and the dough is smooth. Divide the dough in half and form each half into a rectangular loaf, tucking under the ends. Generously grease two 4-by-8-inch (10-by-20-cm) loaf pans. Place the loaves in the prepared pans. Cover with the kitchen towel and let rise in a warm, draft-free area until doubled in bulk, about 1 hour.

Meanwhile, preheat the oven to 375°F (190°C). Bake until the breads sound hollow when thumped on the bottom, about 40 minutes. Immediately turn out the loaves onto a wire rack.

While the loaves are still warm, using a small icing spatula, spread the white icing on top and partly down the sides of the loaves. Let cool completely before serving.

Makes 2 loaves

1/2 cup (4 fl oz/125 ml) warm water (105°–115°F/40°–46°C)

1 tablespoon active dry yeast

1/3 cup (3 oz/90 g) sugar

1 1/2 teaspoons salt

4 eggs

3/4 cup (6 oz/185 g) unsalted butter, melted and cooled, plus extra for greasing

3 tablespoons unsweetened cocoa powder

3 3/4 cups (19 oz/590 g) all-purpose (plain) flour

8 oz (250 g) bittersweet chocolate, coarsely chopped

1/2 cup (4 fl oz/125 ml) White Icing (page 319)

Pear Kuchen

Kuchen, the traditional German coffee cake, is perfect for any autumn or winter holiday. During the summertime, substitute 8 large, red plums, halved, pitted, and sliced, for the pears, and cinnamon for the nutmeg.

½ cup (4 oz/125 g) unsalted butter, at room temperature, plus extra for greasing

½ cup (4 oz/125 g) plus 2 tablespoons sugar

7 oz (220 g) almond paste

4 eggs, at room temperature

1 cup (5 oz/155 g) all-purpose (plain) flour

¼ teaspoon salt

4 large, ripe but firm pears, peeled, halved, cored, and cut into eighths

Ground nutmeg

Preheat the oven to 350°F (180°C). Lightly grease a 9-by-12-inch (23-by-30-cm) rectangular baking dish.

In a bowl, using an electric mixer set on medium speed, beat together the butter and the ½ cup (4 oz/125 g) sugar until light and fluffy, about 4 minutes. Gradually beat in the almond paste. Add the eggs, one at a time, beating well after each addition. Continue beating until the mixture is light, about 3 minutes. Reduce the mixer speed to low and beat in the flour and salt until well blended.

Spoon the batter into the prepared baking dish, spreading it evenly. Arrange the pear wedges in attractive rows over the surface, pressing them gently into the batter. Sprinkle the pears with the 2 tablespoons sugar and a light dusting of nutmeg. Bake until the pears are tender when pierced with a knife and the cake is golden brown, about 55 minutes.

Transfer to a wire rack and let cool slightly. Cut into squares to serve.

Makes one 9-by-12-inch (23-by-30-cm) cake; serves 12

Blueberry Crumb Coffee Cake

Any mother would love to be served this simple, delicate coffee cake on Mother's Day — or any other special day. It can also be baked in an 8-inch (20-cm) square pan. Use fresh or frozen, unthawed blueberries.

Preheat the oven to 350°F (180°C). Grease a springform pan 8 inches (20 cm) in diameter and 3 inches (7.5 cm) deep.

In a small saucepan, melt the butter. To make the topping, in a small bowl, combine the brown sugar, 2 tablespoons flour, and cinnamon. Add 3 tablespoons of the melted butter and, using your fingertips or a pastry blender, blend the ingredients together until the mixture resembles coarse meal. Using a fork, stir in the pecans. Set aside.

To make the cake, in a bowl, sift together the remaining 1 1/2 cups (7 1/2 oz/235 g) flour, baking powder, baking soda, salt, and nutmeg. In a large bowl, whisk together the granulated sugar, eggs, lemon zest, and 2 tablespoons melted butter until light and pale, about 1 minute. Using a wooden spoon, stir in the flour mixture in two batches alternating with the sour cream, beginning and ending with the sour cream. Fold in the blueberries. Spoon the batter into the prepared pan. Sprinkle the topping evenly over the surface.

Bake until a toothpick inserted into the center comes out clean, 35–40 minutes. Transfer to a wire rack and let cool until warm, about 15 minutes, then transfer to a serving plate and remove the pan sides. Cut into wedges and serve warm.

Makes one 8-inch (20-cm) coffee cake; serves 8

1/4 cup (2 oz/60 g) firmly packed light brown sugar

1 1/2 cups (7 1/2 oz/235 g) plus 2 tablespoons all-purpose (plain) flour

1/2 teaspoon ground cinnamon

5 tablespoons unsalted butter, plus extra for greasing

1/4 cup (1 oz/30 g) finely chopped pecans

2 teaspoons baking powder

1/2 teaspoon baking soda (bicarbonate of soda)

1/4 teaspoon *each* salt and ground nutmeg

3/4 cup (6 oz/185 g) granulated sugar

2 eggs

1 1/2 teaspoons grated lemon zest

1 cup (8 oz/250 g) sour cream

1/3 cup (3 oz/90 g) blueberries

Cherries and Cream Sweetheart Scones

Laced with dried cherries, these rich, heart-shaped scones are great for a Valentine's Day breakfast or an afternoon tea. They are best enjoyed on the day they are made.

Preheat the oven to 400°F (200°C).

In a large bowl, combine the 2 cups (10 oz/315 g) flour, the ⅓ cup (3 oz/90 g) sugar, baking powder, and salt. Add the butter and, using your fingertips or a pastry blender, blend the ingredients together until the mixture resembles coarse meal. Using a fork, stir in the cherries and then the cream to form a soft dough. Let stand for 2 minutes.

Transfer the dough to a lightly floured surface. Sprinkle the top of the dough with the 2 tablespoons flour. Using your fingertips, gently press out the dough into a round ½ inch (12 mm) thick. Using a lightly floured heart-shaped cookie cutter 3 inches (7.5 cm) in diameter, cut out the scones. Transfer the scones to ungreased baking sheets, spacing them about 2 inches (5 cm) apart. Gather up the remaining dough scraps, press out into a round ½ inch (12 mm) thick and cut out as many more scones as possible. Transfer to the baking sheets. Sprinkle the scones evenly with the 2 tablespoons sugar.

Bake until golden brown, about 15 minutes. Remove from the oven and serve warm, or transfer to a wire rack, let cool, and serve at room temperature.

Makes about 12 scones

2 cups (10 oz/315 g) plus 2 tablespoons all-purpose (plain) flour

⅓ cup (3 oz/90 g) sugar, plus 2 tablespoons

1 tablespoon baking powder

½ teaspoon salt

6 tablespoons (3 oz/90 g) cold unsalted butter, cut into 12 pieces

⅔ cup (3 oz/90 g) dried pitted sour cherries

1 cup (8 fl oz/250 ml) heavy (double) cream

Orange-Cranberry Bread

This holiday bread can be made a day in advance, cooled, wrapped in plastic wrap or foil, and stored at room temperature. This bread would be good served with roast lamb, turkey, or chicken.

1¹/₂ cups (6 oz/185 g) fresh cranberries

Grated zest of 1 orange

1 cup (8 oz/250 g) sugar

1¹/₂ cups (7¹/₂ oz/235 g) all-purpose (plain) flour

¹/₂ cup (2¹/₂ oz/75 g) yellow cornmeal, preferably stone-ground

¹/₂ teaspoon salt

1¹/₂ teaspoons baking powder

¹/₂ teaspoon baking soda (bicarbonate of soda)

3 tablespoons unsalted butter, at room temperature, plus extra for greasing

1 egg

¹/₂ cup (4 fl oz/ 125 ml) fresh orange juice

Preheat the oven to 325°F (165°C). Lightly grease an 8¹/₂-by-4¹/₂-by-2¹/₂-inch (21.5-by-11-by-6-cm) loaf pan.

Sort the cranberries and discard any soft ones. Coarsely chop the cranberries and place in a small saucepan over low heat. Add the orange zest and ¹/₂ cup (4 oz/125 g) of the sugar and heat slowly just to a simmer, stirring to dissolve the sugar. Set aside to cool.

In a large bowl, stir together the flour, cornmeal, salt, baking powder, and baking soda. Set aside.

In a separate bowl, combine the butter and the remaining ¹/₂ cup (4 oz/125 g) sugar. Beat until light and fluffy, about 3 minutes. Beat in the egg. Stir in half of the flour mixture and then the orange juice and ¹/₂ cup (4 fl oz/125 ml) water. Stir in the remaining flour mixture and then the cooled cranberry mixture. Do not overmix. Spoon the batter into the prepared loaf pan. Place in the oven and bake until a toothpick inserted in the center of the loaf comes out clean, 55–60 minutes.

Remove from the oven and let stand for 5 minutes. Turn out onto a wire rack and let cool. Slice and serve.

Makes 1 loaf

Golden Panettone

This sweet yeast bread is a popular Italian favorite at Christmastime. It can be given as a gift or enjoyed with dinner. If you don't have a charlotte mold, use two 1-lb (500-g) coffee cans with the tops removed.

In a small, heavy saucepan, combine the raisins and Marsala. Bring to a boil. Remove from the heat, cover, and let stand at room temperature to plump.

Meanwhile, in a heavy-duty mixer fitted with the dough hook, combine 1 1/2 cups (7 1/2 oz/235 g) of the flour, the sugar, yeast, and salt. In a small saucepan over low heat, combine the 1 cup (8 fl oz/250 ml) milk and butter and stir until the butter melts and the mixture is 125°F (52°C). Add the milk mixture to the flour mixture and beat on medium speed until well mixed. Beat in 3 of the eggs, then stir in the reserved raisins and Marsala, pine nuts, and orange zest. Beat in the remaining 3 cups (15 oz/470 g) flour to make a soft dough.

Place the dough in a large, greased bowl. Cover with a kitchen towel and place in a warm, draft-free area and let rise until doubled in bulk, about 2 hours.

Stir down the dough to remove the air pockets. Generously grease two 7-inch (18-cm) charlotte molds. Line the bottoms with parchment (baking) paper. Grease the paper. Divide the dough evenly between the molds. Cover with the towel and let rise in a warm, draft-free area until doubled in bulk, about 1 hour.

Preheat the oven to 375°F (190°C). In a small bowl, beat the remaining egg with the 1 tablespoon milk. Brush evenly over the tops of the loaves. Bake until golden brown and a toothpick inserted near the center comes out clean, about 45 minutes. Transfer the pans to a wire rack and let cool slightly. Then invert onto the wire rack, lift off the pans, and peel off the paper. Turn right side up and let cool completely.

Makes 2 loaves

1 cup (6 oz/185 g) golden raisins (sultanas)

1/2 cup (4 fl oz/125 ml) dry Marsala wine

4 1/2 cups (22 1/2 oz/705 g) all-purpose (plain) flour

1/2 cup (4 oz/125 g) sugar

1 tablespoon active dry yeast

1 teaspoon salt

1 cup (8 fl oz/250 ml) plus 1 tablespoon milk

1/2 cup (4 oz/125 g) unsalted butter, plus extra for greasing

4 eggs

3/4 cup (4 oz/125 g) pine nuts, lightly toasted (page 328)

2 teaspoons grated orange zest

Pumpkin-Spice Layer Cake

Preheat the oven to 350°F (180°C). Grease and flour 3 cake pans each 9 inches (23 cm) in diameter. In a large bowl, using an electric mixer set on medium speed, beat together the pumpkin purée and buttermilk until blended. Beat in the eggs, sugar, oil, and vanilla.

In a sifter, combine the flour, baking soda, cinnamon, ginger, and salt and sift the mixture directly onto the batter. Reduce the mixer speed to low and beat in the flour mixture, stopping occasionally to scrape down the sides, just until combined. Fold in the currants.

Divide the batter among the prepared pans. Bake until a toothpick inserted into the center of each cake comes out clean, about 25 minutes. Transfer to wire racks to cool for 10 minutes. Invert the cakes onto the racks, lift off the pans, and let cool.

In a large bowl, using the electric mixer set on medium-high speed, beat the cream cheese until very light and fluffy, about 4 minutes. Gradually beat in the butter-cream frosting until well blended.

Place a cake layer on a cake stand or serving plate. Using an icing spatula, spread the top with about 3/4 cup (6 fl oz/185 ml) of the frosting. Top with a second cake layer and spread it with about 3/4 cup (6 fl oz/185 ml) of the remaining frosting. Place the final cake layer on top. Spread the top and sides of the cake decoratively with the remaining frosting.

Slice into wedges and serve immediately, or cover with a cake dome and store overnight at cool room temperature.

Makes one 9-inch (23-cm) cake; serves 8

Unsalted butter for greasing

2 cups (16 oz/500 g) canned pumpkin purée

3/4 cup (6 fl oz/180 ml) buttermilk

4 eggs

2 cups (1 lb/500 g) sugar

3/4 cup (6 fl oz/180 ml) vegetable oil

1 teaspoon vanilla extract (essence)

3 cups (15 oz/470 g) all-purpose (plain) flour, plus extra for dusting

2 teaspoons baking soda (bicarbonate of soda)

2 teaspoons ground cinnamon

1 teaspoon ground ginger

1 teaspoon salt

1/2 cup (3 oz/90 g) dried currants

3/4 lb (375 g) cream cheese, at room temperature

2 recipes Orange Buttercream Frosting (page 318) (3 cups/ 24 fl oz/750 ml)

Apricot-Almond Chocolate Chunk Coffee Ring

In a heavy-duty mixer fitted with the dough hook, combine 2 cups (10 oz/315 g) of the flour, the sugar, yeast, and salt. In a saucepan over low heat, stir together the milk and butter. Clip a candy thermometer onto the pan and heat until the butter melts and the thermometer registers 130°F (54°C). Add the milk mixture to the flour mixture and beat on medium-high speed until well mixed. Beat in the eggs and the almond extract. Beat in about 2 1/2 cups (12 1/2 oz/390 g) more flour to make a dough that is semisoft but no longer sticky.

Transfer the dough to a lightly floured work surface and knead, adding flour as necessary to prevent sticking, until smooth and elastic, 5 minutes. Cover with a clean kitchen towel and let rest for 10 minutes.

Grease a baking sheet. Knead the dough briefly, then roll it out into a 16-by-20-inch (40-by-50-cm) rectangle. Spread evenly with the preserves, leaving a 1/2-inch (12-mm) border uncovered. Sprinkle evenly with the apricots, chocolate, and half of the almonds. Starting at a long side, roll up jelly-roll style and pinch the seam to seal. Bring the ends together, forming a ring, and place seam side down on the prepared baking sheet. Press the ends together to seal. Using a sharp knife, cut gashes on the bias around the top of the ring about 1 inch (2.5 cm) apart, 2 inches (5 cm) deep, and to within 1 inch (2.5 cm) of the inner rim of the ring. Gently pull open the gashes. Cover with the kitchen towel and let rise in a warm, draft-free area until doubled in bulk, about 40 minutes.

Preheat the oven to 375°F (190°C). Bake until golden brown, about 50 minutes. Transfer to a serving plate and let cool slightly. Drizzle with the icing and sprinkle evenly with the remaining almonds. Serve warm.

Makes one 12-inch (30-cm) coffee cake; serves 10

About 4 2/3 cups (23 1/2 oz/735 g) all-purpose (plain) flour

1/3 cup (3 oz/90 g) sugar

1 tablespoon quick-rise active dry yeast

1/2 teaspoon salt

3/4 cup (6 fl oz/180 ml) milk

1/2 cup (4 oz/125 g) unsalted butter, plus extra for greasing

2 eggs

1/2 teaspoon almond extract (essence)

3/4 cup (7 1/2 oz/235 g) apricot preserves

1/2 cup (3 oz/90 g) minced dried apricots

3 oz (90 g) bittersweet chocolate, chopped

1 cup (4 oz/125 g) sliced (flaked) almonds, toasted (page 328)

1/2 cup (4 fl oz/125 ml) White Icing (page 319)

Old-Fashioned Gingerbread
with Rum Whipped Cream

3 cups (15 oz/470 g)
all-purpose (plain) flour

1¹/₂ teaspoons baking powder

4 teaspoons ground ginger

2 teaspoons ground cinnamon

¹/₂ teaspoon *each* ground
allspice and cloves

³/₄ teaspoon *each* baking soda
(bicarbonate of soda) and salt

³/₄ cup (6 oz/185 g) unsalted
butter, at room temperature,
plus extra for greasing

³/₄ cup (6 oz/185 g) firmly
packed light brown sugar

2 eggs

1 cup (11 oz/345 g) plus
2 tablespoons dark molasses

4 teaspoons grated orange zest

1 cup (8 fl oz/250 ml) plus
2 tablespoons buttermilk

¹/₂ cup (2¹/₂ oz/75 g)
crystallized ginger, chopped

1 cup (8 fl oz/250 ml) cold
heavy (double) cream

3 tablespoons firmly packed
light brown sugar

1 tablespoon dark rum

1 tablespoon vanilla extract
(essence)

Preheat the oven to 350°F (180°C). Grease and flour a 13-by-9-by-2-inch (33-by-23-by-5-cm) baking dish.

Sift together the flour, baking powder, ground ginger, cinnamon, allspice, cloves, baking soda, and salt into a bowl. In a large bowl, using an electric mixer set on high speed, beat the butter until light and fluffy, about 2 minutes. Add the brown sugar and beat until fluffy, about 2 minutes longer. Beat in the eggs one at a time, then beat in the molasses and orange zest until well combined. Mix in the dry ingredients in 3 batches alternately with the buttermilk, beginning and ending with the dry ingredients. Using a rubber spatula, fold in the crystallized ginger.

Pour the batter into the prepared baking dish, spreading it evenly and smoothing the surface. Bake until springy to the touch, about 50 minutes. Transfer to a wire rack to cool.

In a large bowl, combine the cream and brown sugar. Using an electric mixer set on high speed, beat until stiff peaks form. Add the rum and vanilla and beat again until stiff peaks form.

Cut the gingerbread into squares and serve warm or at room temperature with the whipped cream.

Serves 12

Gifts from the Kitchen

Vanilla Bean Caramels

For this recipe, you will need 3 dozen pieces of cellophane, waxed paper, or colored waxed paper (sold at kitchenware shops) — each measuring 4½ by 6 inches (12 by 15 cm) — for wrapping the caramels.

Vegetable oil for greasing

½ cup (3½ oz/105 g) firmly packed light brown sugar

½ cup (4 oz/125 g) granulated sugar

½ cup (5 fl oz/160 ml) light corn syrup

¼ cup (2 fl oz/60 ml) plus 2 tablespoons whole milk

¼ cup (2 fl oz/60 ml) plus 2 tablespoons condensed milk

¼ cup (2 fl oz/60 ml) heavy (double) cream

¼ cup (2 oz/60 g) unsalted butter

1 vanilla bean, split lengthwise

Pinch of salt

Line an 8-inch (20-cm) square baking pan with aluminum foil, covering the bottom and sides. Grease generously with vegetable oil.

In a heavy 3-qt (3-l) saucepan over medium heat, combine the brown sugar, granulated sugar, corn syrup, whole milk, condensed milk, cream, butter, vanilla bean, and salt. Stir constantly until the sugars dissolve and the mixture comes to a boil. Using a pastry brush dipped in water, brush down the sides of the pan to prevent sugar crystals from forming. Raise the heat to medium-high and clip a candy thermometer onto the side of the pan. Cook, stirring slowly but constantly, until the thermometer registers 240°F (115°C), about 10 minutes.

Remove the pan from the heat. Remove the vanilla bean and discard. Immediately pour the caramel into the prepared baking pan all at once; do not scrape the residue from the pan bottom. Let the caramel cool completely, about 2 hours.

Grease a cutting board with vegetable oil. Turn out the cooled caramel onto the board and peel off the foil. Oil a large knife and cut the caramel into strips about 1½ inches (4 cm) wide. Cut the strips crosswise into pieces 1 inch (2.5 cm) long, reoiling the knife occasionally to prevent sticking. Wrap each candy in a piece of clear cellophane, waxed paper, or colored waxed paper (see note), twisting the ends. Store in an airtight container at room temperature for up to 2 weeks.

Makes about 3 dozen

Maple-Nut Pralines

These are New Orleans—style candies enriched with the New England accent of pure maple syrup. Stacked on a plate or piled in a decorated canister, they make a wonderful hostess gift or snack for a buffet table.

Vegetable oil for greasing

2 cups (22 fl oz/690 ml) pure maple syrup

1 cup (8 fl oz/250 ml) heavy (double) cream, plus 2 tablespoons if needed

1 tablespoon unsalted butter

1 cup (4 oz/125 g) walnuts, chopped

1 cup (4 oz/125 g) pecans, chopped

1/2 teaspoon ground nutmeg

Grease 2 baking sheets. In a saucepan over medium heat, stir together the maple syrup and the 1 cup (8 fl oz/250 ml) cream. Clip a candy thermometer onto the side of the pan. Boil until the thermometer registers 238°F (114°C), about 15 minutes.

Remove from the heat and let cool to 220°F (104°C), about 5 minutes.

Add the butter and stir just until melted and the mixture is creamy, about 1 minute. Stir in the walnuts, pecans, and nutmeg. Immediately, using a tablespoon, scoop up spoonfuls of the mixture and drop onto the prepared baking sheets, spacing evenly. (If the mixture becomes too dry to drop, add 2 tablespoons cream and stir over low heat until melted.)

Let the candies cool completely. Store in an airtight container at room temperature for up to 3 weeks.

Makes about 2 1/2 dozen

Chocolate-Almond Caramels

These rich candies have a luxurious flavor and are sure to disappear quickly. Try presenting them on plates wrapped in festive cellophane. For a sweet gift, wrap them loosely in cellophane or package in a festive holiday tin.

Line a 9-inch (23-cm) square baking pan with aluminum foil, covering the bottom and sides. Generously grease the foil.

In a heavy 3-qt (3-l) saucepan over medium-high heat, combine 1 cup (8 fl oz/250 ml) of the cream and the coffee. Bring to a boil, then remove from the heat. Cover and let steep for 30 minutes.

Return the pan to medium-high heat and bring the cream-coffee mixture to a boil again. Strain through a very fine-mesh sieve into a glass measuring cup. Discard the coffee grounds. Add enough cream to measure 1 cup (8 fl oz/250 ml). Return to the saucepan and add the chocolate, sugar, corn syrup, and butter. Stir over medium heat until the chocolate and butter melt and the sugar dissolves. Clip a candy thermometer onto the side of the pan and boil, gently stirring occasionally, until the thermometer registers 242°F (117°C), about 10 minutes.

Remove the pan from the heat and stir in the vanilla, salt, and almonds. Pour the mixture into the prepared baking pan. Let cool until firm enough to cut, 2 hours.

Coat a cutting board with vegetable oil. Turn out the cooled caramel onto the board and peel off the foil. Oil a large knife and cut the caramel into pieces about 1 inch (2.5 cm) square, reoiling the knife occasionally to prevent sticking. Wrap each square in a piece of clear cellophane or waxed paper, twisting the ends. Store in an airtight container at room temperature for up to 1 month.

Makes about 6 dozen

Unsalted butter for greasing

About 1 1/4 cups (10 fl oz/ 310 ml) heavy (double) cream

3 tablespoons freshly ground (medium-grind) coffee

3 oz (90 g) unsweetened chocolate, chopped

1 1/2 cups (12 oz/375 g) sugar

3/4 cup (7 1/2 fl oz/230 ml) light corn syrup

4 tablespoons (2 oz/60 g) unsalted butter

2 teaspoons vanilla extract (essence)

1/4 teaspoon salt

1 3/4 cups (9 1/2 oz/295 g) whole almonds, toasted (page 328) and coarsely chopped

Vegetable oil for greasing

Pine Nut Brittle

The secret to making good brittle is low humidity, since the candy becomes sticky in humid weather. So wait for a dry day, then whip up a batch. Pack in airtight glass jars tied with ribbon to give as a gift.

Grease a baking sheet. In a bowl, combine the pine nuts, orange zest, butter, and salt. Set aside.

In a heavy 2-qt (2-l) saucepan over low heat, combine the sugar and $^1/_3$ cup (3 fl oz/ 80 ml) water. Stir constantly until the sugar dissolves. Using a pastry brush dipped in water, brush down the sides of the pan to prevent sugar crystals from forming. Raise the heat to high and bring the mixture to a rolling boil. Continue to boil without stirring, swirling the pan occasionally, until the mixture turns a deep golden color, about 10 minutes.

Add the nut mixture and stir until coated with the syrup. Immediately pour onto the prepared baking sheet. Spread out slightly with a wooden spoon, forming a thin sheet of brittle. Let cool completely, about 30 minutes.

Break into pieces. Serve immediately, or store in an airtight container at room temperature for up to 1 week.

Makes about 10 oz (315 g)

1 cup (5 oz/155 g) pine nuts

1 tablespoon finely grated orange zest

1½ teaspoons unsalted butter, plus extra for greasing

¼ teaspoon salt

1 cup (8 oz/250 g) sugar

Double-Chocolate and Orange Truffles

For an extra-special touch, dust these confections with cocoa powder or drizzle with melted milk chocolate. Serve in paper candy cups, which can be bought in specialty-food or baking supply stores. Store in an airtight container for up to 3 weeks.

In a heavy saucepan over medium-low heat, combine the milk chocolate and orange juice concentrate. Stir constantly until smooth. Add the butter and stir until incorporated. Pour into a bowl; this mixture is the truffle filling. Cover and freeze until firm enough to mound in a spoon, about 40 minutes.

Line a baking sheet with aluminum foil. Using a tablespoon, scoop out rounded spoonfuls of the filling and drop onto the sheet, spacing evenly. Cover and freeze until almost firm but still pliable, about 30 minutes. Roll each chocolate mound between your palms into a smooth ball, then roll in cocoa. Return to the baking sheet. Freeze while preparing the coating.

Line another baking sheet with foil. Place the bittersweet or semisweet chocolate in the top pan of a double boiler or in a heatproof bowl. Set over (but not touching) barely simmering water. Heat, stirring frequently, until melted and smooth. Remove from the heat.

Drop 1 truffle ball into the chocolate, tilting the pan if necessary to coat the ball completely. Slip a fork under the truffle, lift it from the chocolate, and tap the fork gently against the side of the pan to allow any excess chocolate to drip off. Using a knife, gently slide the truffle off the fork and onto the prepared baking sheet. Repeat with the remaining truffles.

Refrigerate uncovered until firm, about 1 hour. Store in an airtight container.

Makes about 1 1/2 dozen

12 oz (375 g) milk chocolate, chopped

1/2 cup (4 fl oz/125 ml) frozen orange juice concentrate, thawed

2 tablespoons unsalted butter, at room temperature

Unsweetened cocoa powder for dusting

12 oz (375 g) bittersweet or semisweet (plain) chocolate, finely chopped

Caramel-Nut Popcorn

This is likely the most luxurious popcorn you could ever want. For a variation, spread the clumps (after baking and cooling) on a baking sheet and drizzle with Bittersweet Chocolate Ganache (page 317); store the chocolate-coated popcorn in the refrigerator.

3 cups (3 l) freshly popped corn (about 1/2 cup/3 oz/90 g unpopped)

1 cup (5 oz/155 g) unsalted roasted cashews

1 cup (5 oz/155 g) salted roasted macadamia nuts

1 cup (5 1/2 oz/170 g) whole almonds or 1 cup (4 oz/125 g) pecan halves

1 cup (7 oz/220 g) firmly packed dark brown sugar

1/2 cup (5 fl oz/160 ml) light corn syrup

1/2 cup (4 oz/125 g) unsalted butter, plus extra for greasing

1 tablespoon finely grated orange zest

1/2 teaspoon salt

1 teaspoon vanilla extract (essence)

1/2 teaspoon baking soda (bicarbonate of soda)

Preheat the oven to 250°F (120°C). Grease a large roasting pan. Combine the popped corn and nuts in the prepared pan, mixing well. Place in the oven as it heats while you prepare the glaze.

In a large heavy saucepan over medium heat, combine the brown sugar, corn syrup, butter, orange zest, and salt. Bring to a boil, stirring constantly until the sugar dissolves. Boil for 4 minutes without stirring. Remove from the heat and mix in the vanilla and baking soda. Gradually pour the glaze over the popped corn mixture, stirring to coat well.

Bake until dry, stirring occasionally, about 1 hour. Remove from the oven. Using a metal spatula, free the popcorn from the bottom of the pan. Let cool completely in the pan.

Break into clumps. Serve immediately or store in an airtight container at room temperature for up to 1 week.

Makes about 4 qt (4 l)

Espresso, White Chocolate, and Macadamia Nut Bark

If you prefer, chopped toasted almonds can be substituted for the macadamia nuts. Either way, the result is an elegant, beautifully marbled after-dinner candy. Purchase a high-quality white chocolate, such as Lindt or Callebaut, for the best texture.

Lightly butter a 10-by-15-by-1-inch (25-by-38-by-2.5-cm) jelly-roll pan. Line the pan with waxed paper.

Place the white chocolate in the top pan of a double boiler or in a heatproof bowl set over (but not touching) barely simmering water. Place the bittersweet or semisweet chocolate in the top pan of another double boiler or in a heatproof bowl set over (but not touching) barely simmering water. Stir both frequently with separate spoons until melted and smooth.

Stir 3/4 cup (4 oz/120 g) of the nuts into the white chocolate. Pour the mixture onto the prepared jelly-roll pan to form 3 stripes the full length of the pan, one down each side and one down the center. Mix 1/2 cup (2 1/2 oz/80 g) of the nuts and the coffee into the bittersweet or semisweet chocolate. Pour the nut-chocolate mixture onto the prepared pan, forming 2 stripes the length of the pan, between the white chocolate stripes. Draw the tip of a small knife back and forth across both chocolates to form a marble pattern. Tilt the pan to swirl the chocolates together. Sprinkle with the remaining 1/2 cup nuts. Refrigerate uncovered until firm, at least 1 hour.

Gently peel the candy from the waxed paper. Holding the candy with the waxed paper (to prevent fingerprints on the chocolate), break into large irregular pieces. Store in an airtight container in the refrigerator for up to 2 weeks.

Makes about 1 1/3 lb (660 g)

Unsalted butter for greasing

10 oz (315 g) white chocolate, finely chopped

8 oz (250 g) bittersweet or semisweet (plain) chocolate, finely chopped

1 3/4 cups (9 oz/280 g) unsalted macadamia nuts, toasted (page 328) and halved

2 teaspoons freshly ground espresso (fine-grind) coffee

Macadamia and Coconut Clusters

Here is an easy-to-make treat with a delightful taste of the tropics. You can vary the ratio of milk chocolate and bittersweet chocolate, or use only one or the other. Place the individual pieces in paper candy cups for gift giving.

Line a baking sheet with parchment (baking) paper or waxed paper.

Place the milk chocolate and the bittersweet or semisweet chocolate in the top pan of a double boiler or in a heatproof bowl set over (but not touching) hot (not simmering) water. Heat, stirring constantly, until melted and smooth.

Pour out the hot water from the bottom pan and replace it with lukewarm water. Replace the top pan or heatproof bowl. Let the chocolate stand uncovered, stirring frequently, until it cools slightly and begins to thicken, about 10 minutes.

Stir the macadamia nuts and coconut into the chocolate, mixing thoroughly. Using a small spoon, scoop out slightly rounded teaspoonfuls of the mixture and drop onto the prepared baking sheet, spacing evenly. Refrigerate uncovered until set, about 2 hours.

Store in an airtight container in the refrigerator for up to 1 month or in the freezer for up to 2 months.

Makes about 4 dozen

10 oz (315 g) milk chocolate, chopped

3 oz (90 g) bittersweet or semisweet (plain) chocolate, chopped

2 cups (10 oz/315 g) coarsely chopped, lightly salted roasted macadamia nuts

1 1/2 cups (6 oz/185 g) sweetened shredded coconut, lightly toasted

Milk Chocolate and Toasted-Almond Fudge

Pecans, walnuts, hazelnuts, or just about any other nut would also be great
in these candies. Purchase a high-quality milk chocolate for the best results.
Store in an airtight container in the refrigerator for up to 2 weeks.

1 oz (30 g) unsweetened
chocolate, chopped

6 oz (185 g) milk chocolate,
chopped

1 teaspoon vanilla extract
(essence)

1½ cups (12 oz/375 g) sugar

2/3 cup (5 fl oz/160 ml)
sweetened condensed milk

½ cup (4 fl oz/125 ml)
heavy (double) cream

¼ cup (2 oz/60 g) unsalted
butter, cut into pieces

3/4 cup (4 oz/125 g) whole
almonds, toasted (page 328)
and very coarsely chopped,
plus 28 whole almonds,
toasted (page 328)

Line a 5-by-9-by-3-inch (13-by-23-by-7.5-cm) loaf pan with aluminum foil, allowing
the foil to overhang the sides slightly.

In a metal bowl, combine the unsweetened and milk chocolates and the vanilla.
Set aside. In a heavy 3-qt (3-l) saucepan over medium-low heat, combine the sugar,
condensed milk, cream, butter, and 2/3 cup (5 fl oz/160 ml) water. Stir until the sugar
dissolves. Using a pastry brush dipped in water, brush down the sides of the pan to
prevent sugar crystals from forming. Raise the heat to high and bring to a rolling
boil. Reduce the heat to medium-high and clip a candy thermometer onto the side
of the pan. Using a wooden spoon, stir constantly but slowly until the thermometer
registers 230°F (110°C), about 16 minutes.

Pour the boiling mixture over the chocolate; do not scrape the syrupy residue from
the pan bottom. Stir vigorously with a wooden spoon until the chocolate melts
and the fudge thickens slightly, about 1 minute. Mix in the 3/4 cup (4 oz/125 g)
chopped almonds. Pour immediately into the prepared loaf pan and smooth with
a rubber spatula. Immediately press the whole almonds into the surface, spacing
evenly. Refrigerate uncovered until firm enough to cut, about 1 hour.

Using the foil overhang as an aid, carefully lift the fudge from the pan. Peel the foil
from the sides. Trim the edges of the fudge evenly and cut into 28 pieces. Serve at
room temperature.

Makes 28 pieces

Walnut-Date Clusters

Place these sweet treats in candy cups and pack into gift tins. If fresh dates are unavailable, purchase chopped, dried dates. Store in the refrigerator for up to 1 month or in the freezer for up to 2 months.

Line a baking sheet with parchment (baking) paper or waxed paper.

In a bowl, mix together the dates and walnuts. Set aside. Place the chocolate in the top pan of a double boiler or in a heatproof bowl set over (but not touching) hot (not simmering) water. Heat, stirring constantly, until melted and smooth.

Pour out the hot water from the bottom pan and replace it with lukewarm water. Replace the top pan or heatproof bowl. Let the chocolate stand, stirring frequently, until it cools slightly and begins to thicken, about 10 minutes.

Stir the date-walnut mixture into the chocolate, mixing thoroughly. Using a small spoon, scoop out slightly rounded teaspoonfuls of the mixture and drop onto the prepared baking sheet, spacing evenly. Refrigerate uncovered until set, about 2 hours. Store in an airtight container.

Makes about 4 dozen

1¹/₂ cups (6 oz/185 g) coarsely chopped pitted dates

1¹/₂ cups (6 oz/185 g) coarsely chopped walnuts

1¹/₂ oz (375 g) milk chocolate, finely chopped

Olive Oil with Lemon and Bay Leaf

Flavored oils have many uses. Include a gift tag suggesting brushing this on toasted Italian bread, mixing it with pasta and grated pecorino romano cheese, or tossing it with a salad. Use the highly aromatic California bay leaves in this recipe if you can.

Scrub the lemon with an abrasive sponge to remove all surface impurities. Rinse thoroughly and dry well.

Pour the olive oil into a small heavy saucepan. Using a zester and working directly over the pan, remove the zest from the lemon, letting it fall into the oil. Add the bay leaf and peppercorns. Clip a candy thermometer onto the side of the pan. Heat the oil over medium-low heat until the thermometer registers 200°F (93°C). Cook at 200°–225°F (93°–107°C) for 10 minutes. Remove from the heat and let cool slightly.

Sterilize a 1-cup (8–fl oz/250-ml) bottle (page 323). Carefully transfer the oil to the hot, sterilized bottle. Cover tightly. Store at room temperature for up to 2 months.

Makes about 1 cup (8 fl oz/250 ml)

1 large fresh lemon

1 cup (8 fl oz/250 ml) extra-virgin olive oil

1 bay leaf

1/4 teaspoon whole peppercorns

Hot Spiced Cider Sachets

Present these sachets with a gift card that reads: "To make great spiced cider, simmer 2 quarts (2 l) cider with 1 sachet in a covered pan for 30 minutes. Ladle into mugs and enjoy. Sweeten to taste."

6 cinnamon sticks, each about 3 inches (7.5 cm) long

30 whole cardamom pods

30 whole cloves

18 crystallized ginger slices, each about 1 inch (2.5 cm) in diameter

12 small bay leaves

Cut out six 5-inch (13-cm) squares of cheesecloth (muslin). Break the cinnamon sticks into pieces and divide them evenly among the squares. Place 5 cardamom pods, 5 cloves, 3 ginger slices, and 2 bay leaves atop each square. Bring the corners of each square together and tie with kitchen string, white thread, or twine. Use immediately or place in an airtight container and store at room temperature for up to 2 months.

Makes 6 sachets

Olives with Orange and Fennel

This easy-to-make appetizer adds an unusual touch to any hors d'oeuvre tray. Make gifts of these by filling glass jars or ceramic crocks. Quality brine-cured olives can be found at well-stocked food stores.

Pat the olives dry with paper towels. Place on a firm work surface and, using the side of a large knife, crush each olive just until the skin cracks. Place in a container with a tight-fitting cover.

Lightly crush the fennel seeds in a mortar with a pestle. Add the seeds to the olives, along with the orange zest strips and bay leaves. Pour in enough olive oil to cover the olives. Let stand for 4 hours at room temperature.

Cover tightly and refrigerate for at least 2 days to allow the flavors to marry. Store refrigerated for up to 2 months. Serve at room temperature.

Makes about 2 cups (10 oz/315 g)

1¹/₂ cups (8 oz/250 g) brine-cured black olives such as Kalamata or Niçoise

1 teaspoon fennel seeds

3 orange zest strips, each 2 inches (5 cm) long by 1 inch (2.5 cm) wide

2 large bay leaves, preferably California

³/₄ cup (6 fl oz/180 ml) olive oil, or as needed

Orange and Rosemary Vinegar

Select an interesting bottle for this flavored vinegar, pair it with a bottle of your favorite olive oil, and you have a wonderful gift. Mix them together to make an outstanding vinaigrette for fresh greens and vegetables, or for dipping bread.

2 fresh rosemary sprigs

About 1½ cups (12 fl oz/ 375 ml) red wine vinegar

3 orange zest strips, each 2 inches (5 cm) long and 1 inch (2.5 cm) wide

Wash a 1½-cup (12–fl oz/375-ml) bottle in hot soapy water. Rinse well. Fill the bottle with hot water and set aside.

Rinse the rosemary sprigs and pat dry. In a small saucepan over medium heat, warm the vinegar until it is hot.

Drain the bottle well. While the bottle is still hot, place the rosemary and orange zest strips in it. Carefully pour in the hot vinegar. Cover tightly and let stand at room temperature for at least 2 weeks to let the flavors to marry. Store indefinitely at room temperature.

Makes about 1½ cups (12 fl oz/375 ml)

Kitchen Potpourri

The same spices that lend so much character to cooked foods can also be kept around to fill the kitchen with a pleasant scent. Place the mixture in a decorative bowl, or a cachepot for setting out on a kitchen counter.

1/4 cup (1 1/4 oz/37 g) whole cloves

1 cup (1 1/4 oz/37 g) whole allspice

10 cinnamon sticks, each 3 inches (7.5 cm) long, broken into pieces

8 small bay leaves

4 whole nutmegs

3 tablespoons star anise

2 tablespoons whole cardamom pods

Combine all the ingredients in a bowl, mixing well. Store indefinitely at room temperature, stirring occasionally.

Makes about 2 cups (6 oz/185 g)

Spiced Nuts

Spiced nuts are best served hot, so enclose a gift card instructing recipients to spread the nuts on a baking sheet and reheat in a 300°F (150°C) oven for about 5 minutes.

Preheat the oven to 300°F (150°C). Place the nuts in a bowl.

Pour the oil into a small, heavy saucepan and place over medium-low heat until warm. Add the cumin and cayenne and stir until the mixture is aromatic, about 15 seconds. Pour the flavored oil over the nuts. Add the sugar and salt and stir to coat evenly. Transfer the nuts to a baking pan.

Bake, stirring occasionally, until the nuts are toasted, about 20 minutes. Store in an airtight container for up to 2 weeks.

Makes about 2 1/2 cups (10 oz/315 g)

2 1/2 cups (10–12 oz/315–375 g) nuts of your choice

2 tablespoons vegetable oil

1 1/2 teaspoons ground cumin

1/4 teaspoon cayenne pepper

2 tablespoons sugar

1 teaspoon salt

Blueberry-Orange Marmalade

1¹/₂ cups (12 oz/375 g) sugar

¹/₂ cup (4 fl oz/125 ml) fresh orange juice

2 cups (8 oz/250 g) fresh or frozen blueberries

3¹/₄ cups (2 lb/1 kg) orange marmalade

1 teaspoon ground allspice

In a heavy nonaluminum saucepan over low heat, combine the sugar and orange juice. Stir until the sugar dissolves. Raise the heat to medium-high and bring to a boil. Add the blueberries and boil, stirring frequently, until the mixture reaches the jelling stage, about 10 minutes. To test for doneness, remove the pan from the heat. Fill a chilled spoon with the mixture, then slowly pour it back into the pan; the last 2 drops should merge and fall in a sheet. Alternatively, spoon 1 tablespoon of the mixture onto a chilled plate and place in the freezer for 2 minutes; it should wrinkle when gently pushed with a fingertip.

Add the marmalade and allspice to the blueberries. Clip a candy thermometer onto the pan and boil, stirring often, until it registers 220°F (104°C), about 15 minutes.

Meanwhile, wash canning jars and lids in hot soapy water and rinse well. Fill the jars with hot water. Place the lids in a small saucepan. Add water to cover and bring to a simmer. Remove from the heat.

Drain 1 jar well. Spoon the hot marmalade into the jar to within ¹/₄ inch (6 mm) of the top. Using a hot, damp kitchen towel, wipe the rim of the jar clean. Drain 1 lid and place atop the jar; seal tightly with the screw band. Repeat with the remaining marmalade and jars.

Process the jars in a hot-water bath (page 323), check the seals, label, and store. (If the preserves will be used within 3 weeks, omit the water bath and simply store in the refrigerator.)

Makes about 2¹/₂ pints (40 fl oz/1.25 l)

Pine Nut and Honey Spread

Use this spread on toasted country bread or English muffins for a breakfast or teatime treat. In a mouthwatering innovation, sweet and resinous pine nuts are enlisted for a role more commonly given to peanuts, almonds, or cashews.

Sterilize jars and lids (page 323).

In a 4-cup (32–fl oz/1-l) glass measuring cup, combine the pine nuts, honey, orange zest, and cloves and stir to mix well.

Using tongs, remove 1 jar from the water, draining well. Pour the honey spread into the jar. Remove 1 lid from the water and place atop the jar; seal tightly. Repeat with the remaining honey spread and jars.

Mix well before using.

Makes about 2 cups (24 oz/750 g)

1¼ cups (6½ oz/200 g) pine nuts

1¼ cups (15 oz/470 g) honey

2½ teaspoons finely grated orange zest

½ teaspoon ground cloves

Cappuccino Fudge Sauce

This sauce makes a superb topping for slices of cake or vanilla, chocolate, or coffee ice cream. Spoon it into canning jars or ceramic containers for a winning holiday-time gift.

1 cup (8 fl oz/250 ml) half-and-half (half cream), or as needed

2 tablespoons freshly ground (medium-grind) coffee

8 whole cloves

2 orange zest strips, each 2 inches (5 cm) long and 1 inch (2.5 cm) wide

1 cinnamon stick, about 3 inches (7.5 cm) long

1/8 teaspoon ground nutmeg

1/4 cup (2 oz/60 g) plus 2 tablespoons firmly packed light brown sugar

6 oz (185 g) bittersweet or semisweet (plain) chocolate, finely chopped

2 tablespoons brandy or Grand Marnier (optional)

Thoroughly wash jars and lids in hot soapy water and rinse well. Fill the jars with hot water. Set aside.

In a heavy saucepan over high heat, combine the 1 cup (8 fl oz/250 ml) half-and-half, the coffee, cloves, orange zest strips, cinnamon, and nutmeg. Bring to a boil. Remove from the heat, cover, and let stand for 30 minutes.

Return the mixture to high heat and again bring to a boil. Strain through a fine-mesh sieve into a glass measuring cup, pressing against the spices with the back of a wooden spoon to extract all the liquid. If necessary, add more half-and-half to measure 3/4 cup (6 fl oz/180 ml).

Pour the strained liquid into a clean, heavy saucepan. Add the brown sugar and simmer, stirring constantly, until dissolved. Remove from the heat. Add the chocolate and stir until melted and smooth. Stir in the brandy or Grand Marnier, if desired.

Drain 1 jar well. While the jar is still hot, spoon in the hot sauce. Using a hot, damp kitchen towel, wipe the rim of the jar clean. Place 1 lid atop the jar and seal tightly. Repeat process with the remaining sauce and jars. Let cool to room temperature.

Store in the refrigerator for up to 2 weeks.

Makes about 1 1/2 cups (12 fl oz/375 ml)

Pear and Cranberry Chutney

Here's something for those who like a little sweet pizzazz with their savory treats: a spicy variation on cranberry sauce that makes an excellent accompaniment to turkey, pork, or grilled chicken.

In a heavy nonaluminum saucepan over medium heat, combine the brown sugar, dried cranberries, orange juice, shallots, ginger, vinegar, orange zest, cinnamon, red pepper flakes, and salt. Stir until the sugar dissolves. Add the pears and simmer, stirring occasionally, until the pears are tender, about 10 minutes. Increase the heat to medium-high. Add the cranberries and boil, stirring frequently, until they begin to burst, about 5 minutes.

Meanwhile, wash canning jars and lids in hot soapy water and rinse well. Fill the jars with hot water. Place the lids in a small saucepan. Add water to cover and bring to a simmer. Remove from the heat.

Drain 1 jar. Spoon the hot chutney into the jar to within $1/4$ inch (6 mm) of the top. Run a nonmetallic spatula between the chutney and the jar sides to remove air bubbles. Using a kitchen towel dipped into hot water, immediately wipe the rim clean. Drain 1 lid and place atop the jar. Seal tightly with the screw band. Repeat with the remaining chutney and jars.

Following the directions on page 323, process the jars in a hot-water bath, check the seals, label, and store. (If the chutney will be used within 3 weeks, omit the water bath and simply store in the refrigerator.)

Makes about 2 1/2 pints (40 fl oz/1.25 l)

2 cups (14 oz/440 g) firmly packed light brown sugar

$3/4$ cup (3 oz/90 g) dried cranberries

$1/2$ cup (4 fl oz/125 ml) fresh orange juice

3 shallots, minced

3 tablespoons minced, peeled fresh ginger

2 tablespoons balsamic vinegar

1 tablespoon finely grated orange zest

$1/2$ teaspoon ground cinnamon

$1/4$ teaspoon red pepper flakes

$1/4$ teaspoon salt

1 lb (500 g) pears, peeled, halved, cored, and cut into $1/2$-inch (12-mm) dice

4 cups (1 lb/500 g) fresh or frozen cranberries

Raspberry–Red Wine Sauce

This elegant, ruby-colored sauce is perfect spooned over vanilla ice cream or a slice of pound cake and garnished with fresh raspberries. If the sauce will be used within 3 weeks, omit the water bath and simply store in the refrigerator.

3 cups (24 fl oz/750 ml) dry red wine

3 cups (12 oz/375 g) frozen unsweetened raspberries

1½ cups (12 oz/375 g) sugar

1 vanilla bean, broken in half and then split lengthwise

In a heavy nonaluminum saucepan over medium heat, combine the wine, raspberries, sugar, and vanilla bean. Stir until the sugar dissolves, then simmer for 10 minutes. Raise the heat to medium-high and boil until the mixture is reduced to 2½ cups (20 fl oz/625 ml), about 30 minutes longer.

Meanwhile, wash canning jars and lids in hot soapy water and rinse well. Fill the jars with hot water. Place the lids in a small saucepan. Add water to cover and bring to a simmer. Remove from the heat.

Pour the berry mixture through a sieve into a bowl, pressing on the berries with the back of a wooden spoon to extract as much juice as possible. Retrieve the vanilla bean pieces and rinse them. Return the sauce to the pan along with the vanilla bean pieces. Bring to a boil.

Drain 1 jar well. Spoon the hot sauce into the jar to within ¼ inch (6 mm) of the top. Using a hot, damp kitchen towel, wipe the rim of the jar clean. Drain 1 lid and place atop the jar. Seal tightly with the screw band. Repeat with the remaining sauce and canning jars.

Following the directions on page 323, process the jars in a hot-water bath, check the seals, label, and store.

Makes about 2 cups (16 fl oz/500 ml)

Dried-Fruit Chutney

The use of dried fruits means you can make this delicious spicy condiment any time of the year. If you decide to put the chutney into jars that are not standard canning jars, omit the water bath and store in the refrigerator.

In a bowl, combine the dried peaches, apricots, and figs. Pour in enough hot water to cover and let stand for 30 minutes. Drain, reserving 1 1/4 cups (10 fl oz/310 ml) of the soaking water.

In a large, heavy nonaluminum saucepan over high heat, combine the soaked fruits, the reserved soaking water, vinegar, dates, prunes, onion, sugar, curry powder, ginger, red pepper flakes, and salt. Bring to a boil, stirring until the sugar dissolves. Reduce the heat and simmer, stirring frequently, until the chutney is thick and the fruits are tender, about 10 minutes.

Meanwhile, wash canning jars and lids in hot soapy water and rinse well. Fill the jars with hot water. Place the lids in a small saucepan. Add water to cover and bring to a simmer. Remove from the heat.

Drain 1 jar. Spoon the hot chutney into the jar to within 1/4 inch (6 mm) of the top. Run a nonmetallic spatula between the chutney and the jar sides to remove air bubbles. Using a kitchen towel dipped into hot water, immediately wipe the rim clean. Drain 1 lid and place atop the jar. Seal tightly with the screw band. Repeat with the remaining chutney and jars.

Following the directions on page 323, process the jars in a hot-water bath, check the seals, label, and store. (If the chutney will be used within 3 weeks, omit the water bath and simply store in the refrigerator.)

Makes about 3 1/2 pints (56 fl oz/1.75 l)

1/2 lb (250 g) dried peaches, chopped

1/2 lb (250 g) dried apricots, chopped

1/2 lb (250 g) dried Calimyrna figs, stems removed and chopped

2 cups (16 fl oz/500 ml) cider vinegar

1/2 lb (250 g) pitted dates, chopped

1/2 lb (250 g) pitted prunes, chopped

1 large yellow onion, chopped

1 cup (8 oz/250 g) sugar

1 1/2 teaspoons Madras curry powder

1 teaspoon ground ginger

1/4 teaspoon red pepper flakes

1/4 teaspoon salt

Plum-Vanilla Preserves

Make these preserves in mid-summer, when plums are at their best. If the preserves will be used within 3 weeks, omit the water bath and store in the refrigerator.

10–12 plums, about 4 lb (2 kg) total weight, preferably purple-fleshed Santa Rosa

1 cup (8 fl oz/250 ml) fresh orange juice

1/2 cup (4 fl oz/125 ml) fresh lemon juice

4 whole allspice

2 cinnamon sticks, each about 3 inches (7.5 cm) long

7 cups (3 1/2 lb/1.75 kg) sugar

1 vanilla bean, broken in half and then split lengthwise

Halve and pit the plums, then cut into slices 1/2 inch (12 mm) thick. Place in a heavy nonaluminum saucepan and add the orange and lemon juices, allspice, and cinnamon. Bring to a boil over high heat. Reduce the heat, cover, and simmer, stirring occasionally, until very tender, about 20 minutes.

Add the sugar and vanilla bean and stir until the sugar dissolves. Simmer, uncovered, stirring and crushing the fruit with the back of a wooden spoon occasionally at first and then more frequently near the end of cooking, about 45 minutes longer, until the jelling stage is reached. To test, remove from the heat. Fill a chilled spoon with the preserves, then slowly pour the preserves back into the pan; the last 2 drops should merge and fall from the spoon in a sheet.

Meanwhile, wash four 1-pint (16–fl oz/500-ml) canning jars and lids in hot soapy water; rinse well. Fill the jars with hot water. Place the lids in a small saucepan. Add water to cover and bring to a simmer. Remove from the heat.

Drain 1 jar. Spoon the hot preserves and 1 vanilla bean piece into the jar to within 1/4 inch (6 mm) of the top. Using a kitchen towel dipped into hot water, immediately wipe the rim clean. Drain 1 lid and place atop the jar. Seal tightly with the screw band. Repeat with the remaining preserves and jars.

Following the directions on page 323, process the jars in a hot-water bath, check the seals, label, and store.

Makes about 4 pints (64 fl oz/2 l)

Orange-Lemon Curd

Here's something you might not have thought of lately: an old-fashioned citrus custard that is superb on scones, English muffins, in tarts, with fruit, or drizzled over cakes.

Thoroughly wash jars and lids in hot soapy water and rinse well. Fill the jars with hot water. Set aside.

Combine the sugar, orange and lemon juices, butter, orange zest and cardamom in the top pan of a double boiler or in a heatproof bowl. Set over (but not touching) simmering water and stir until the sugar dissolves and the butter melts.

Strain the beaten eggs through a fine-mesh sieve. Whisk into the juice-butter mixture. Cook, stirring constantly, until the custard thickens and leaves a path on the back of a spoon when a finger is drawn across, about 15 minutes; do not boil.

Drain 1 jar well. While the jar is still hot, spoon in the hot curd. Place a lid atop the jar and seal tightly. Repeat with the remaining curd and jars. Let cool to room temperature. Store in the refrigerator for up to 3 weeks.

Makes about 1 pint (16 fl oz/500 ml)

1 cup (8 oz/250 g) sugar

6 tablespoons (3 fl oz/90 ml) strained fresh orange juice

2 tablespoons (1 fl oz/30 ml) strained fresh lemon juice

6 tablespoons (3 oz/90 g) unsalted butter, cut into pieces

3 tablespoons finely grated orange zest

1/4 teaspoon ground cardamom

3 eggs, lightly beaten

Peaches-and-Spice Jam

Have ready a large bowl three-fourths full of cold water. Bring a large saucepan three-fourths full of water to a boil. Add half the peaches and blanch for 30 seconds. Using a slotted spoon, transfer the peaches to the bowl of water. Repeat with the remaining peaches. Drain the peaches, then peel, halve, and pit them. Working over a large, heavy nonaluminum saucepan, cut the peaches lengthwise, allowing their juices and the slices to fall into the pan. Stir in the sugar, lemon juice, cinnamon, cardamom, and cloves. Let stand for 1 hour.

Place the pan over medium heat and cook, stirring, until the sugar dissolves. Raise the heat and bring to a slow boil. Cook, uncovered, to the jelling stage, stirring occasionally at first and then more frequently near the end of cooking, about 30 minutes. To test for doneness, remove from the heat. Fill a chilled spoon with the jam, then slowly pour it back into the pan; the last 2 drops should merge and fall in a sheet. Alternatively, spoon 1 tablespoon jam onto a chilled plate and freeze for 2 minutes; it should wrinkle when gently pushed with a fingertip.

Meanwhile, wash canning jars and lids in hot soapy water and rinse well. Fill the jars with hot water. Put the lids in a pan with water to cover and bring to a simmer. Remove from the heat.

Drain 1 jar. Spoon in the hot jam and a few spices to within 1/4 inch (6 mm) of the top. Using a hot, damp kitchen towel, wipe the rim clean. Drain 1 lid and place on the jar. Seal tightly with the screw band. Repeat with the remaining jam and jars. Process the jars in a hot-water bath (page 323), check the seals, label, and store. (If the jam will be used within 3 weeks, omit the water bath and store in the refrigerator until ready for use.)

Makes about 2 1/2 pints (40 fl oz/1.25 l)

8 peaches, about 4 lb (2 kg) total weight

4 cups (2 lb/1 kg) sugar

1/4 cup (2 fl oz/60 ml) fresh lemon juice

2 cinnamon sticks, each 3 inches (7.5 cm) long

10 whole cardamom pods

4 whole cloves

Chocolate, Caramel, and Pecan Sauce

This luscious sauce is a perfect topping for ice cream. For gift giving, enclose a card that reads: "Before serving, warm in a heavy saucepan over low heat, stirring constantly and thinning with a small amount of water if necessary."

2½ cups (1¼ lb/625 g) sugar

1½ cups (12 fl oz/375 ml) heavy (double) cream

6 tablespoons (3 oz/90 g) unsalted butter

3 oz (90 g) semisweet (plain) chocolate, chopped

2 cups (8 oz/250 g) pecan halves and pieces

Wash jars and lids in hot soapy water and rinse well. Fill the jars with hot water. Set aside.

In a deep, heavy saucepan over low heat, combine the sugar and ⅔ cup (5 fl oz/ 160 ml) water. Stir until the sugar dissolves. Using a pastry brush dipped in water, brush down the sides of the pan to prevent sugar crystals from forming. Raise the heat to medium-high and bring to a boil. Continue to boil without stirring, swirling the pan occasionally, until the mixture turns a deep amber, about 15 minutes.

Remove from the heat. Add the cream (the mixture will bubble up; be careful to avoid splashes) and whisk until smooth. Return the pan to high heat and bring to a boil, whisking constantly. Remove from the heat, add the butter and chocolate, and stir until melted and smooth. Stir in the pecans.

Drain 1 jar well. While the jar is still hot, spoon in the hot sauce. Place 1 lid atop the jar and seal tightly. Repeat with the remaining sauce and jars. Let cool to room temperature. Store in the refrigerator for up to 2 weeks.

Makes about 4 cups (32 fl oz/1 l)

Basic Recipes & Techniques

The following basic recipes are found throughout *Holiday Favorites*. All are quite simple to prepare and you will find the results quite rewarding. Use the freshest ingredients that you can find.

Roasted Vegetable Stock

7 large carrots, unpeeled, cut into chunks

3 yellow onions, unpeeled, quartered

8 celery stalks, cut into chunks

1/2 lb (250 g) fresh mushrooms with stems intact, brushed clean and quartered

1 large russet potato, unpeeled, cut into chunks

4–6 fresh thyme or parsley sprigs, or a mixture

1/4 teaspoon whole peppercorns, crushed

1 bay leaf

Preheat the oven to 350°F (180°C). Coat a large roasting pan with nonstick cooking spray.

Spread the carrots, onions, celery, mushrooms, and potato in the pan. Roast for 45 minutes to 1 hour, or for up to 1 1/2 hours if you want a stronger flavored stock, stirring once or twice.

Remove from the oven and transfer the vegetables to a large stockpot. Pour 2 cups (16 fl oz/500 ml) hot water into the roasting pan, bring to a simmer, and deglaze the pan by stirring to dislodge

any browned bits. Add to the stockpot along with 4 1/2 qt (4.5 l) water, the thyme and/or parsley, peppercorns, and bay leaf. Bring to a boil over high heat, skimming off scum from the surface. Reduce the heat to low, cover partially and simmer for about 2 hours.

Carefully pour the hot stock through a strainer. Discard all of the solids. Line the strainer with cheesecloth (muslin) and strain the stock again. Let cool, then store in an airtight container.

Makes about 4 qt (4 l)

Chicken or Turkey Stock

2 lb (1 kg) chicken wings or turkey wings or other parts

2 celery stalks, cut into pieces

1 yellow onion, quartered

1 bay leaf

2 or 3 fresh thyme sprigs or 1/2 teaspoon dried thyme

3 fresh flat-leaf (Italian) parsley sprigs

2 strips, lemon zest each 2 inches (5 cm) long and 1/2 inch (12 mm) wide

2 teaspoons salt, or to taste

Rinse the poultry parts and place in a large saucepan with 8 cups (64 fl oz/2 l) water. Bring to a boil over high heat, regularly skimming off the foam from the surface. Reduce the heat to a simmer and add the celery, onion, bay leaf, thyme, parsley, lemon zest, and salt. Cover partially and simmer until the meat is falling from the bones, about 1 1/2 hours.

Remove from the heat and strain. Let the stock cool to room temperature, then refrigerate it in a tightly covered container. Just before using, remove the fat that solidifies on the top and discard.

Makes 6–7 cups (48–56 fl oz/1.5–1.75 l)

Beef Stock

6 lb (3 kg) meaty beef shanks (shins), plus beef scraps or other trimmings, if available

2 yellow onions, coarsely chopped

1 leek, trimmed, carefully washed, and coarsely chopped

2 carrots, peeled and coarsely chopped

Mushroom stems (optional)

6 cloves garlic

4 fresh flat-leaf (Italian) parsley sprigs

10 whole peppercorns

3 fresh thyme sprigs

2 small bay leaves

Preheat the oven to 450°F (230°C). Place the beef shanks in a large roasting pan and roast, turning often, until browned, about 1 1/2 hours.

Transfer the shanks to a large stockpot, reserving the juices in the pan, and add cold water to cover. Add any beef scraps you have on hand. Bring to a boil and skim off any scum and foam on the surface. Reduce the heat and simmer, uncovered, for 2 hours. Add water as needed to keep the bones immersed and skim the scum from the surface.

Place the roasting pan on the stove top. Add the onions, leek, carrots, and celery to the fat remaining in the pan. Brown over high heat, stirring often, until the vegetables caramelize, 15–20 minutes. When the shanks have simmered for 2 hours, add the vegetables to the stockpot. Pour 1 cup (8 fl oz/250 ml) hot water into the roasting pan, bring to a simmer, and deglaze the pan by stirring to dislodge any browned bits. Add these juices to the pot.

Place the mushroom stems, if using, garlic, parsley, peppercorns, thyme, and bay leaves on a square of cheesecloth (muslin) and tie into a small bag with kitchen string. Add to the stockpot. Simmer, uncovered, over low heat, for 6 hours longer (for a total of 8 hours), or preferably the whole day.

Remove from the heat and remove the solids with a slotted spoon or skimmer. Pour the stock through a strainer. Line the strainer with cheesecloth (muslin) and strain again. Refrigerate, uncovered, until cool, then cover tightly.

Before using stock, remove the fat that solidifies on the top and discard.

Makes 4–5 qt (4–5 l)

Chicken or Turkey Gravy

For added flavor, stir in 1 or 2 tablespoons sherry at the last minute.

¼ cup (2 fl oz/60 ml) dry white wine

5 tablespoons all-purpose (plain) flour

4 cups chicken or turkey stock, heated (page 314)

salt and freshly ground pepper

After removing the chicken or turkey from the roasting pan, skim or pour off the fat from the pan juices, reserving about 3–4 tablespoons of the fat. To the remaining pan juices, add the wine and ¼ cup (2 fl oz/60 ml) water and place over medium heat. Bring to a simmer and deglaze the pan by stirring to dislodge any browned bits. Strain into a bowl and set aside.

In a saucepan over medium heat, warm the reserved fat until it is bubbly. Add the flour and stir rapidly for a few seconds. Add the strained pan juices and 3½ cups (28 fl oz/875 ml) of the stock. Cook, while rapidly stirring, until smooth and thickened, 1–2 minutes. Add the remaining stock as needed to achieve the desired gravy consistency.

Season to taste with salt and pepper. Pour into a warmed sauceboat and serve at once.

Makes about 4 cups (32 fl oz/1 l)

Herbed Bread Crumbs

The best bread to use for crumbs is a coarse-textured white bread that can be purchased sliced in 1- or 1½-pound (500- or 750-g) loaves.

4 slices white bread (see note)

Pinch of salt

Pinch of freshly ground pepper

¼ teaspoon chopped fresh thyme or ⅛ teaspoon dried thyme

¼ teaspoon chopped fresh rosemary or ⅛ teaspoon dried rosemary

Cut the crusts off the bread and discard. Tear the bread into pieces. In a blender or food processor, combine the pieces of bread, salt and pepper. Process to form coarse crumbs.

Add the thyme and rosemary and pulse a few times, just until well mixed. Use immediately, or store in an airtight container in the freezer for up to 1 year.

Makes about 1 cup (2 oz/60 g)

Apple-Mint Chutney

1 small red bell pepper
(capsicum)

3 large tart apples such as Granny
Smith, McIntosh, or Rome Beauty

³/₄ cup (4 oz/125 g) golden raisins
(sultanas)

1 cup (7 oz/220 g) firmly packed
light brown sugar

¹/₂ cup (4 fl oz/125 ml)
Champagne vinegar or other
white wine vinegar

3 tablespoons minced fresh mint
or 1 tablespoon dried mint

Roast the bell pepper as directed in the glossary, page 324. Pull off the loosened skin and remove the core, seeds, and ribs. Cut the pepper into ¹/₄-inch (6-mm) dice; set aside.

Peel, quarter, and core the apples. Slice each quarter in half again lengthwise and then cut into ¹/₂-inch (12-mm) chunks. Put into a heavy enameled or stainless-steel saucepan. Add the raisins, brown sugar, and vinegar. Bring just to a boil over high heat. Reduce the heat to a simmer and cook slowly, uncovered, stirring several times, until the apples are tender and the juice reduces and thickens, 45–60 minutes.

Add the mint and bell pepper. Stir well and cook for 2–3 minutes longer.

Let cool to room temperature and serve. Or cover tightly and refrigerate for up to 2–3 days; bring to room temperature before serving.

Makes about 2¹/₂ cups (1¹/₂ lb/750 g)

Apple-Orange Cranberry Sauce

This flavorful blend can be made a day in advance and refrigrated in a covered container until ready to use.

¹/₂ orange

1 tart apple such as Granny
Smith, pippin, or McIntosh

3 cups (12 oz/375 g)
fresh cranberries

1¹/₄ cups (10 oz/310 g) sugar

¹/₂ teaspoon ground cinnamon

¹/₄ teaspoon ground cloves

Squeeze the juice from the orange half and set aside. Remove the membrane from the inside of the orange shell and discard. Cut the shell into small dice. Put into a small saucepan with 2 cups (16 fl oz/500 ml) water, bring to a boil, and cook for 10 minutes. Drain and set aside to cool.

Peel, quarter, and core the apple, then chop into small pieces. Place in a saucepan. Sort through the cranberries, discarding any soft ones. Add to the apples along with the reserved diced orange peel, the reserved orange juice, the sugar, cinnamon, and cloves. Bring to a boil, reduce the heat to a simmer, and cover partially.

Simmer gently, stirring occasionally, until the sauce has thickened, the apple is tender, and the cranberries have burst, about 10–15 minutes.

Transfer to a bowl and let cool before serving. Or cover and refrigerate; bring to room temperature before serving.

Makes 3¹/₂–4 cups (2¹/₄–2¹/₂ lb/1–1.25 kg)

Applesauce

This applesauce can be stored in the refrigerator for up to 1 week or for up to 6 months in the freezer.

8–10 large, sweet, flavorful
apples such as Rome Beauty,
Baldwin, or McIntosh, 2–3 lb
(2–2.5 kg) total weight, quartered and cored

1¹/₂ cups (12 fl oz/375 ml)
apple cider or water

¹/₂ teaspoon ground cinnamon

³/₄–1 cup (6–8 oz/185–250 g)
sugar

Fresh lemon juice

Peel the apples (you can leave the peels on if you will be using a food mill). Combine the apples with the cider or water in a deep, heavy-bottomed pot over low heat. Cook, stirring once or twice until the apples are very tender, about 20–30 minutes.

Drain the apples, reserving the liquid. Pass the apples through a food mill, adding the cinnamon, sugar, and lemon juice to taste and ¹/₃–¹/₂ cup (3–4 fl oz/ 80–125 ml) of the cooking liquid, or as needed to acieve a good consistency. Alternatively, purée the apples in a food processor adding the remaining ingredients in batches during processing.

Transfer to a bowl and serve.

Serves 8

Minted Cranberry Sauce

1/3 cup (1/2 oz/15 g) firmly packed fresh mint leaves, coarsely chopped

1/3 cup (3 fl oz/80 ml) boiling water

4 cups (1 lb/500 g) fresh cranberries

1 cup (8 oz/250 g) sugar

finely shredded zest of 1/2 lemon

Place the mint in a small bowl and pour in the boiling water. Let steep for 10–15 minutes. Sort the cranberries, discarding any soft ones.

Combine the sugar and 2/3 cup (5 fl oz/ 160 ml) water in a saucepan. Bring to a boil, stirring to dissolve the sugar. Add the cranberries and lemon zest. Return to a boil, reduce the heat to a simmer, cover partially, and cook until thickened and the cranberries have burst, about 10 minutes.

Using a fine-mesh sieve placed over a glass measuring cup, strain the mint leaves, pressing them with the back of a spoon to release all the flavored water; you should have about 1/4 cup (2 fl oz/60 ml) liquid. Add it to the cranberries, stir well to blend, and cook for 1 minute more.

Pour into a bowl and let cool. Or cover tightly and refrigerate; bring to room temperature before serving.

Makes about 2 1/2 cups (1 1/2 lb/750 g)

Pie or Tart Pastry

This pastry can be prepared in advance, wrapped tightly, and stored for about 4 days in the refrigerator or up to 2 weeks in the freezer.

2 1/3 cups (12 oz/375 g) all-purpose (plain) flour

1 tablespoon sugar

1 teaspoon salt

1/2 teaspoon grated lemon zest

1/2 cup (4 oz/125 g) cold unsalted butter, cut into 8 pieces

1/2 cup (4 oz/125 g) solid vegetable shortening, chilled

2 tablespoons fresh lemon juice

2–3 tablespoons cold water

In a bowl, stir together the flour, sugar, salt, and lemon zest. Add the butter and shortening. Using your fingertips or a pastry blender, blend together until the mixture resembles coarse meal. Using a fork, stir in the lemon juice. Stirring gently with the fork, add enough of the water, 1 tablespoon at a time, for the mixture to come together in moist, rough clumps.

Divide the dough in half. Gather each half into a ball, then flatten into a smooth disk about 5 inches (13 cm) in diameter. Wrap each disk in plastic wrap and refrigerate for 1 hour before rolling out the pastry.

Makes 2 disks, enough dough for two 9-inch (23-cm) pie crusts

Lining a Pie Pan: On a lightly floured work surface, roll out the chilled pastry disk into a round slightly larger in diameter than the pie or tart pan. To transfer the pastry, loosely roll it up around the pin, then unroll it onto the pan and press gently into the bottom and sides. Gently repair any tears by moistening the torn edges with a little water and pressing them together; or use pastry scraps to fill any larger gaps.

Weaving a Lattice Crust: On a lightly floured surface, roll out pastry into a round. Using a pastry wheel, cut into strips. Place a large sheet of waxed paper on the work surface and dust lightly with flour. Weave the strips on top of the waxed paper to form a lattice. lift the paper and slide the lattice onto the pie filling.

Fluting the Pastry Rim: After the lattice or top pastry are in place, trim off overhanging edges. Lightly moisten the edge of the bottom pastry and press gently on the strips or top pastry to seal with the bottom pastry. Using your thumb and forefingers, decoratively flute the edge.

Bittersweet Chocolate Ganache

This ganache has a variety of uses: it's a filling when chilled, an icing when cooled, and a glaze when warm.

1/2 cup (4 fl oz/125 ml) heavy (double) cream

2 tablespoons unsalted butter

1 tablespoon light corn syrup

6 oz (185 g) European bittersweet chocolate, finely chopped

In a small, heavy saucepan over high heat, combine the cream, butter, and corn syrup. Bring to a boil and remove from the heat.

Stir in the chocolate and then place the mixture over low heat. Whisk until the chocolate melts and the mixture is smooth, about 1 minute. Remove from the heat. Use as directed.

Makes about 1 cup (8 fl oz/250 ml)

Buttercream Frosting

To turn this creamy, rich icing into coffee-buttercream frosting, add 2 teaspoons instant espresso powder to the egg yolk mixture before heating. For orange-buttercream frosting, use orange-flavored liqueur in place of the brandy and add 1 teaspoon grated orange zest with the vanilla extract.

4 egg yolks

1/3 cup (3 oz/90 g) sugar

2 tablespoons brandy

3/4 cup (6 oz/185 g) unsalted butter, at room temperature

1/2 teaspoon vanilla extract (essence)

In the top pan of a double boiler or a heatproof bowl placed over (but not touching) simmering water, combine the egg yolks, sugar, and brandy. Whisk until very thick and pale, about 4 minutes. Remove the pan or bowl from over the simmering water and let cool to room temperature.

In a bowl, combine the butter and vanilla. Using an electric mixer set on medium-high speed, beat until very soft and fluffy, about 5 minutes. Gradually beat in the cooled egg yolk mixture. Let the mixture stand at room temperature, stirring occasionally, until spreadable, about 20 minutes.

Use as directed immediately, or cover and refrigerate overnight or freeze for up to 1 month. Before using, let stand at room temperature until softened, then beat with an electric mixer set on high speed until smooth and fluffy.

Makes about 1 1/2 cups (12 fl oz/375 ml)

Lemon Whipped Cream

To make this rich yet refreshing topping, use regular heavy whipping cream with a short expiration date.

1 cup (8 fl oz/250 ml) heavy (double) cream

2 tablespoons sour cream

2 tablespoons confectioners' (icing) sugar

1 tablespoon fresh lemon juice

Finely grated zest of 1 lemon

In a large bowl, combine the heavy cream and sour cream. Using a whisk or electric mixer, beat until the mixture begins to thicken. Add the sugar and lemon juice and zest. Continue beating just until soft folds form. Cover and refrigerate for up to 3 hours. Stir well before using.

Makes about 2 cups (16 fl oz/500 ml)

Ginger or Orange Sabayon Cream

Flavoring this whipped-cream sauce with either ginger or orange produces equally delicious results. Use regular heavy whipping cream, not the ultrapasteurized kind that can be difficult to whip. This sauce is excellent with steamed puddings, gingerbread, fruit breads and poached fruit. It can be made several hours ahead, and leftover sauce can be tightly covered and refrigerated for up to 2 days.

3 egg yolks

1/4 cup (2 oz/60 g) granulated sugar

1 teaspoon finely grated fresh ginger, or the finely grated zest of 1 orange and 1 tablespoon fresh orange juice

1 cup (8 fl oz/250 ml) heavy (double) cream

1 tablespoon confectioners' (icing) sugar

Have ready a large bowl three-fourths full of ice and a small amount of water. In a heatproof bowl placed over (but not touching) barely simmering water in a saucepan, whisk together the egg yolks and granulated sugar. Add the ginger or the orange zest and orange juice. Using a whisk or electric mixer, beat until light colored and thick, about 5–6 minutes. Remove the bowl from the heat and nest it in the ice water. Continue whisking until cold. The mixture will get quite thick. Set aside.

In another bowl, whip the cream until soft folds form. Add the confectioners' sugar and whip until stiff peaks form. Stir the whipped cream into the egg yolk mixture until blended and smooth.

Cover and refrigerate. Stir well before serving, as the sauce may separate slightly upon sitting.

Makes about 2¹/₂–3 cups (20–24 fl oz/ 625–750 ml)

Vanilla Pastry Cream

Use whole milk for this recipe; low-fat or nonfat milk will not produce the desired rich flavor or texture.

²/₃ cup (5 fl oz/160 ml) milk

1 piece vanilla bean, 2 inches (5 cm) long, split in half lengthwise

2 egg yolks

3 tablespoons sugar

1 tablespoon cornstarch (cornflour)

In a small, heavy saucepan over high heat, combine the milk and vanilla bean and bring to a simmer. Meanwhile, in a bowl, whisk together the egg yolks, sugar, and cornstarch until well blended.

When the milk reaches a simmer, remove it from the heat and gradually whisk the hot milk mixture into the yolk mixture. Return the mixture to the saucepan and place it over medium heat. Cook, whisking constantly, until the pastry cream thickens and boils, about 1 minute. Discard the vanilla bean and transfer the pastry cream to a small bowl. Use as directed.

Makes about 1 cup (8 fl oz/250 ml)

White Icing

Add enough milk to achieve the desired consistency; less milk yields a thick frosting for piping or spreading onto cookies, more milk results in a thin glaze perfect for drizzling over cakes and coffee cakes.

1 cup (4 oz/125 g) confectioners' (icing) sugar

¹/₄ teaspoon vanilla extract (essence)

4–5 teaspoons milk

In a bowl, combine the confectioners' sugar and vanilla. Stir in enough of the milk to thin the icing to the desired consistency. Use as directed.

Makes about ¹/₂ cup (4 fl oz/125 ml)

Brandy Butter Sauce

4 egg yolks

¹/₄ cup (2 fl oz/60 ml) good brandy or Cognac

2 teaspoons fresh lemon juice

¹/₂ cup (4 oz/125 g) granulated sugar

¹/₂ cup (4 oz/125 g) unsalted butter, cut into small cubes

¹/₂ cup (4 fl oz/125 ml) heavy (double) cream

1 tablespoon confectioners' (icing) sugar

Have ready a large bowl three-fourths full of ice and a little water. Pour water into a small saucepan to a depth of 1 inch (2.5 cm) and bring to a simmer.

In a heatproof bowl, whisk together the egg yolks, brandy, lemon juice, and granulated sugar. Place over (but not

touching) the saucepan of simmering water and whisk vigorously until thickened and doubled in volume, about 6–7 minutes.

Remove the bowl from the heat and beat in the butter, a little at a time, until dissolved and blended. Immediately nest the bowl in the ice water and continue beating until cold and quite thick, about 6–8 minutes.

In another bowl, whip the cream until soft folds form. Add the confectioners' sugar and whip until stiff peaks form. Using a rubber spatula, fold the cream into the yolk mixture. Cover tightly and refrigerate. Serve cold.

Makes about 2¹/₂ cups (20 fl oz/625 ml)

Poached Orange Slices

1 or 2 small thin-skinned oranges

1 cup (8 oz/250 g) sugar

2 cups (16 fl oz/500 ml) water

Cut each unpeeled orange crosswise into 7 or 8 thin slices, discarding the end pieces and any seeds. Fill a sauté pan or frying pan half full with water and bring to a boil. Add the orange slices and cook for 1 minute. Drain well and set aside.

In the same pan combine the sugar and the water. Bring to a boil, stirring to dissolve the sugar completely. Reduce the heat to medium-low, add the orange slices and gently cook uncovered, turning a couple of times, until tender, about 5 minutes. Set the slices aside to cool in their liquid.

Makes 7 or 8 slices per orange

Trussing

Tying, or trussing, whole turkeys or chickens into a compact shape yields a roast bird that is easier to carve.

There are many different methods for trussing. The method used here is quite simple and requires a single piece of string that is at least long enough to wrap twice lengthwise around the bird; the longer the piece of string you use, the easier it will be to pull tight. Choose a sturdy linen kitchen string, which is less likely to scorch in the heat of the oven.

If you've stuffed the bird, handle it carefully to make sure nothing spills out, holding the neck flap securely shut as you complete the trussing.

First, secure the drumsticks. With the bird breast-side up, slide the center of the string under its tail. Cross the ends above the tail and loop them around the drumsticks; then cross them again and pull them tight to draw together the tail and the ends of the drumsticks.

Next, to secure the wings, turn the bird over and tuck the wing tips securely across the neck flap. Pull one string end along the side, loop it around the nearest wing, pull it tight across the neck flap and loop it around the other wing. Tie the 2 string ends tightly together. Cut off any excess string.

Carving

Carving roast poultry or meat for the holiday table is often regarded as a skill requiring years of practice to master. In fact, provided you have the proper tools and understand the basic shape of the roast at hand, carving turkey, chicken, ham, beef, or lamb can be a simple, even pleasurable task.

A good, sharp slicing knife and a two-pronged fork to steady the roast are essential. While an all-purpose slicing knife may be used for carving any type of roast, different knives are better suited to some roasts than to others. One with a long, flexible but still sturdy blade is best for following the contours of a large turkey. A shorter, sturdier knife makes quicker, smoother work of the smaller chicken. Long, straight blades with serrated edges cut more readily through red meat. Whatever knife you use, make sure it is well sharpened for easier, safer carving.

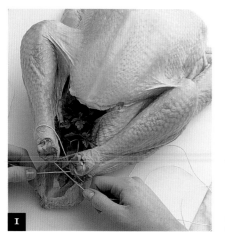

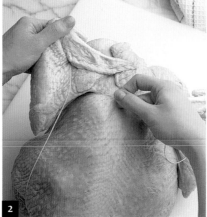

CARVING TURKEY

Carve only as much as is needed to serve at one time, completing one side before starting the next.

1 Remove the leg and wing. With the turkey breast up, cut through the skin between the thigh and breast. Move the leg to locate the thigh joint, then cut

through the joint to sever the leg. In the same way, remove the wing (shown above), cutting through the shoulder joint where it meets the breast.

2 Next, cut through the joint to separate the drumstick and thigh. Serve them whole or carve, cutting the meat into thin slices parallel to their bones.

3 Carve the breast. Slightly above the thigh and shoulder joints, carefully carve a deep horizontal cut toward the bone, creating a base cut on one side of the breast. Starting near the breastbone, carve thin slices vertically, cutting parallel to the rib cage and ending each slice at the base cut.

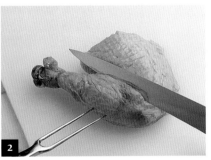

CARVING CHICKEN

Depending on the number of guests, the entire chicken may be carved at once.

1 Begin by removing the leg and wing. With the chicken breast up, cut through the skin between thigh and breast. Move the leg to locate the thigh joint, then cut

through the joint to sever the leg. In the same way, remove the wing, cutting through the shoulder joint where it meets the breast.

2 Separate the drumstick and thigh. If the chicken is small, serve the whole leg as an individual portion. If it is larger, cut

through the joint to separate the drumstick and thigh into two pieces. You can also slice a large thigh into 2 pieces.

3 Carve the breast. Starting near the breastbone, cut downward and parallel to the rib cage, carving the meat into long, thin slices.

CARVING BEEF

A prime rib of beef, also called standing rib roast, can be quite simple to carve, provided you have a large, sharp carving knife for slicing and a sturdy fork to steady the roast, taking care not to poke holes in it. You might wish to leave some slices atttached to the ribs, for guests who prefer the meat on the bone.

Carve only the meat that will be consumed at the meal. The leftover meat will stay juicier if it remains uncarved. Once carved, the meat should be arranged attactively on a platter, usually in evenly overlapping slices, or placed directly on individual plates.

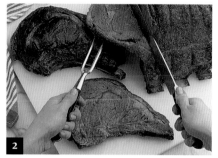

1 Place the roast, ribs down, on a carving surface and steady it by inserting a carving fork. Using a long, sharp, sturdy blade, cut a vertical slice across the grain from one end of the roast down to the rib bone, cutting along the bone to free the slice.

2 Cutting parallel to the first slice, continue to carve slices of the desired thickness. As individual rib bones are exposed, cut between them to remove them; or leave them attached to slices for guests who request them.

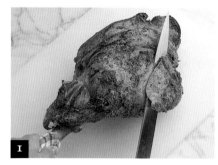

CARVING LAMB

The keys to successfully carving a leg of lamb lie in cutting parallel to the bone and providing guests with slices from both sides of the leg.

1 Slice the rounded side first. Firmly grasp the protruding end of the shank bone with a kitchen towel and tilt it

slightly upward. Using a long, sharp, sturdy knife, carve a first slice from the rounded, meaty side of the leg at its widest point, cutting away from you and roughly parallel to the bone.

2 Cutting parallel to the first slice, continue carving the meat in thin slices until you have cut enough to give each guest a slice.

3 Carve the inner side. Grasping the bone, rotate the leg of lamb to expose its other, flatter side—the inner side of the leg, which is slightly more tender. Still cutting parallel to the bone, carve a slice of this meat for each guest.

Canning Basics

All of the preserves in this book can be made with or without a water bath and stored safely in the refrigerator for up to 3 weeks.

STERILIZING JARS AND LIDS

1 Place washed and rinsed canning jars upright on a metal rack in a large pot. Carefully add hot water to cover by about 1 inch (2.5 cm). Bring to a boil and boil for 10 minutes at altitudes less than 1,000 feet (300 meters), adding 1 minute for each additional 1,000 feet. Leave in hot water until ready to use.

2 Place washed and rinsed lids and screw bands in a small saucepan. Carefully add hot water to cover and bring to a simmer, then remove from the heat. Leave lids and screw bands in hot water until ready to use.

HOT WATER BATH FOR CANNING

1 Remove one jar from hot water, drain, and fill with the food to be canned. Remove one lid from the hot water and seal the jar tightly with a screw band.

2 Place the jars on a metal rack in a large pot. The jars must not be touching. Pour in enough boiling water to cover by at least 1 inch (2.5 cm). Cover the pot, bring to a boil, and boil for 15 minutes.

3 With jar tongs, remove the jars from the pot and put on a metal rack. Let cool.

4 Press down on the center of the lid and then lift your finger. If the lid stays down, the jar is sealed and can be stored in a cool, dry place for up to 1 year. If it pops back up, refrigerate no longer than the time specified in the recipe.

Glossary

Apples Primarily a late-summer to autumn crop, apples are a favorite fruit of the holiday season. Tart green apples, often used in cooking, include Granny Smiths, an Australian variety, and pippins, green to yellow-green apples with a slightly tart taste suited to salads or cooking. Among the large, sweet varieties are slightly tart Rome Beauty apples, ideal for baking or eating raw, and red-and-green McIntoshes, good for eating raw or cooking.

TO CORE AN APPLE
Using a small, sharp knife, cut the apple into quarters through the stem and flower ends. Then, cut out the seeds and fibrous core section from each quarter. Alternatively, using an apple corer, press its sharp edges firmly down through the stem end to cut out the core whole.

Bell Pepper
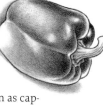
Fresh, sweet-fleshed, bell-shaped member of the pepper family. Also known as capsicum. Most common in the unripe green form, although ripened red or yellow varieties are also widely available. Creamy pale-yellow, orange, and purple-black types also may be found.

TO ROAST PEPPERS
Place the peppers, resting on their sides, directly on the grid of a stove-top gas burner on medium-high or on a heavy wire rack placed over an electric stove-top burner (its feet resting on the stove top). Using metal tongs, turn the peppers over the heat until blackened, 5–6 minutes. Transfer to a colander and place in a sink under cold running water. Using your hands, hold each pepper over the colander and under the running water, rub off the loosened, blackened skin. It will fall off easily. Pat dry with paper towels, cut in half vertically, and remove the core, seeds, and ribs.

Bourbon American form of whiskey made from at least 51 percent corn, plus other grains. Aged for at least two years in new, charred-oak barrels that impart a smoky, slightly sweet flavor and rich caramel color.

Brandy Applies to any spirit distilled from fermented fruit juice. While the term most specifically refers to dry grape brandy, it also covers dry to sweet distillates of such fruits as apples and berries, whose fruity fragrances can also lend themselves as flavorings.

Butter, Unsalted For the recipes in this book, unsalted butter is preferred. Lacking salt, it allows the cook greater leeway in seasoning recipes to taste.

Calvados Dry French brandy distilled from apples and bearing that fruit's distinctive aroma and taste. Dry applejack (apple brandy made in the United States) may be substituted.

Cheese In its many forms, cheese makes an excellent ingredient in or garnish for holiday meals. For the best selection, buy cheese from a well-stocked food store. The commonly available cheeses called for in this book include:

Blue Cheese Blue-veined cheeses of many varieties have rich, tangy flavors and creamy to crumbly textures: Roquefort, a French cheese made from sheep's milk, with a creamy consistency and a rich, sharp taste; Gorgonzola, a semisoft Italian variety; and Maytag blue, an American blue cheese, generally milder than its European counterparts and with a fairly firm consistency, are examples.

Feta White cheese made from sheep's or goat's milk; notable for its salty, sharp flavor and crumbly interior. The consistency ranges from creamy to dry.

Gruyère Variety of Swiss cheese with a firm, smooth texture, small holes, and a strong, tangy flavor.

Mozzarella Rindless white, mild-tasting Italian cheese traditionally made from water buffalo's milk. Look for fresh mozzarella sold immersed in water. Mozzarella is also aged or even smoked, yielding a firmer texture.

Parmesan Hard, thick-crusted Italian cow's milk cheese with a sharp, salty, full flavor resulting from at least 2 years of aging. The finest variety is designated Parmigiano-Reggiano.

Always try to buy Parmesan in block form, to grate fresh as needed.

Chestnuts Whole peeled chestnuts or chestnut pieces are available in specialty-food shops. Remove their glossy brown shells before use. To peel chestnuts, use a sharp knife to score an **X** in the shell on the flat side of each chestnut, then bake or boil.

To bake the chestnuts, place in a baking pan large enough to hold them in a single layer, add $^{1}/_{2}$ cup (4 fl oz/125 ml) water and bake in a preheated 400°F (200°C) oven until the shells begin to turn brittle and peel back at the **X**, about 20 minutes. While the nuts are still warm, peel off the brittle shells and the furry skin directly beneath them. Do not allow the chestnuts to cool or they will be difficult to peel.

To boil the chestnuts, cook in boiling water to cover for about 15 minutes. Turn off the heat but leave the chestnuts in the water to keep warm and facilitate peeling. One at a time, peel the chestnuts.

Coffee, Ground For ground coffee, you'll get the fullest, finest flavor by grinding fresh coffee beans as you need them. An adjustable burr-type grinder, which crushes the beans to a preset particle size, is fairly expensive. If using a common and relatively inexpensive electric blade-type grinder, a medium grind is achieved in about 10 seconds of continual grinding; finely ground coffee results from 15–20 seconds of grinding.

Chocolate

Purchase the best-quality chocolate you can find. Many cooks prefer the quality of European chocolate made in Switzerland, Belgium, France, or Italy.

Bittersweet Chocolate Lightly sweetened eating or baking chocolate. Buy bittersweet chocolate that contains at least 50 percent cocoa butter.

Milk Chocolate Primarily an eating chocolate, enriched with milk powder.

Semisweet Chocolate Eating or baking chocolate that is slightly sweeter than bittersweet chocolate, which may be substituted.

Unsweetened Chocolate Pure cocoa liquor (half cocoa butter and half chocolate solids) ground and solidified in block-shaped molds. Also known as bitter chocolate.

Unsweetened Cocoa Fine-textured powder ground from the solids left after most of the cocoa butter has been extracted from chocolate liquor. Cocoa powder that is specially treated to reduce its natural acidity is known as Dutch-process cocoa.

White Chocolate A chocolate-like product made by combining pure cocoa butter with sugar, powdered milk, and sometimes vanilla. Check labels to be sure that the white chocolate you buy is made exclusively with cocoa butter, without the addition of coconut oil or vegetable shortening.

CHOPPING CHOCOLATE

While a food processor fitted with the metal blade can be used, a sharp, heavy knife offers better control. First, break the chocolate by hand into small chunks, handling it as little as possible to avoid melting. Then, using a heavy knife and a clean, dry, odor-free chopping surface, chop into smaller pieces. Continue chopping across the pieces until the desired consistency is reached.

MELTING CHOCOLATE

Place pieces of chocolate in the top pan of a double boiler over barely simmering water, taking care that the pan doesn't touch the water and that the water does not create steam. Stir gently until the chocolate has melted. Alternatively, create your own double boiler by placing a heatproof bowl on top of a pan of simmering water.

MAKING CHOCOLATE CURLS

Curls of chocolate make an attractive decoration. To make curls, set a large block of good-quality chocolate in a warm place until slightly softened. Then, firmly drag the sharp edge of a large knife across the surface of the block to form long, thin curls.

Herbs

A wide variety of fresh and dried herbs add flavor and variety to festive dishes. Those called for in this book are:

Basil Sweet, spicy herb popular in Italian and French cooking.

Bay Leaf Dried whole leaves of the bay laurel tree. The French variety has a milder, sweeter flavor while bay leaves are stronger in character.

Chives Long, thin green shoot with a mild flavor reminiscent of the onion, to which it is related.

Cilantro Green, leafy herb with a sharp, aromatic, somewhat astringent flavor common in many cuisines. Also called fresh coriander and sometimes referred to as Chinese parsley.

Dill Fine, feathery leaves with a sweet, aromatic flavor. Sold fresh or dried.

Marjoram Pungent, aromatic herb used dried or fresh to season meats (particularly lamb), poultry, seafood, vegetables, and eggs.

Mint Refreshing herb available in many varieties, with spearmint the most common.

Parsley This fresh herb is available in two varieties, the curly-leaf type and a flat-leaf type. The latter, also known as Italian parsley, has a more pronounced flavor and is preferred.

Rosemary  Mediterranean herb, used either fresh or dried, with an aromatic flavor well suited to lamb and veal, as well as poultry, seafood, and vegetables.

Sage Pungent herb, used either fresh or dried, that goes particularly well with fresh or cured pork, lamb, veal, or poultry.

Tarragon Fragrant, distinctively sweet herb used fresh or dried.

Thyme Fragrant, clean-tasting, small-leaved herb popular fresh or dried. A variety called lemon thyme imparts a lemon scent to foods.

CHOPPING FRESH HERBS
Wash the herbs under cold running water and thoroughly shake dry. If the herb has leaves attached along woody stems pull the leaves from the stems; otherwise, as in the case of parsley, hold the stems together. Gather up the leaves into a tight, compact bunch. Using a chef's knife, carefully cut across the bunch to chop the leaves coarsely. Discard the stems.

CRUSHING DRIED HERBS
If using dried herbs, it is best to crush them first in the palm of your hand to release their flavor. Alternatively, warm them in a frying pan and crush the herbs using a mortar and pestle.

Crème de Cacao Sweet chocolate liqueur that is made by percolating or steeping cocoa beans.

Crème Fraîche French-style lightly soured and thickened fresh cream. Increasingly available in well-stocked markets, although a similar product may be prepared at home by stirring 2 teaspoons well-drained sour cream into 1 cup (8 floz/250 ml) lightly whipped heavy (double) cream. Refrigerate until ready to serve.

Espresso Powder, Instant Instant espresso powder, or granules, provides an easily blended source of intense coffee flavor to baked goods. Available in the coffee section of well-stocked food stores, in Italian delicatessens, or in specialty-coffee stores.

Flour Some common types of flours used in this book include:

All-Purpose Flour The most common flour for baking, a blend of hard and soft wheats available in all food markets. Also called plain flour.

Buckwheat Flour Flour ground from the seeds of an herbaceous plant originating in Asia. Popular in the cuisines of both Russia and Eastern Europe, its strong, earthy, slightly sour flavor is usually modulated in commercial products by the addition of a little wheat flour.

Cake Flour Fine-textured bleached flour for use in cakes and baked goods. Also called soft-wheat flour. All-purpose flour is not an acceptable substitute.

Framboise Clear fruit brandy, or eau-de-vie, flavored with the essence of raspberries.

Frangelico Italian sweet liqueur based on wild hazelnuts and herbs.

Grand Marnier A popular brand of orange-flavored liqueur, distinguished by its pure Cognac base.

Indirect Heat In grilling, refers to the method of grilling larger, long-cooking items that would burn if direct-heat cooking were employed. Once the coals are hot, spread them in a compact area away from the portion of the rack on which the food will be placed. If you wish, place a steel pie plate or pan beneath the cooking area to catch drips.

Madeira Sweet, amber-colored dessert wine originating on the Portuguese island of Madeira.

Maple Syrup Syrup made from boiling the sap of the maple tree. Buy maple syrup that is labeled "pure," rather than a blend.

Marsala Dry or sweet amber Italian wine from the area of Marsala, in Sicily.

Mincemeat Old-fashioned pie or tart filling made from raisins and dried currants, apples, candied citron, sweeteners, and spices. Originally, it included finely ground (minced) beef and suet. Prepared mincemeat is available.

Salad Greens

An ever-greater range of salad leaves is available at food stores and green-grocers, offering a wide variety of colors, shapes, tastes, and textures to the salad bowl. Those called for in this book include:

Arugula Green leafy vegetable, Mediterranean in origin, with slender, multiple-lobed leaves that have a peppery, slightly bitter flavor. Often used raw in salads; also known as rocket.

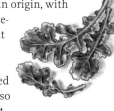

Belgian Endive Slightly bitter spear-shaped leaves, white to pale yellow green—or sometimes red—tightly packed in cylindrical heads 4–6 inches (10–15 cm) long. Also known as chicory or witloof.

Butter Lettuce Relatively small type of round lettuce with soft, loosely packed, tender, mildly flavored leaves. Also known as Boston lettuce. Butter lettuce is a member of the butterhead family, which also includes the Bibb, or limestone, variety.

Chicory A relative of Belgian endive, with loosely packed, curly leaves characterized by their bitter flavor. The paler center leaves, or heart, of a head of chicory are milder-tasting than the dark-green outer leaves. Also called curly endive.

Frisée A close relative of chicory (curly endive) but with a more delicate flavor and slightly tenderer leaves. The pale green leaves with spiky edges form a loose head.

Green Leaf Lettuce Variety of loose-leafed lettuces characterized by their slightly crinkled, medium- to dark-green leaves and by a flavor more pronounced than Bibb or butter lettuces.

Radicchio Leaf vegetable related to Belgian endive. The most common variety has a spherical head, reddish purple leaves with creamy white ribs, and a mildly bitter flavor. Other varieties are slightly tapered and vary a bit in color. Also called red chicory.

Romaine Lettuce Popular variety of lettuce with elongated, pale-green leaves characterized by their crisp texture and slightly pungent flavor.

Savoy Cabbage Flavorful variety of round cabbage with attractive, tightly packed leaves patterned with a lacelike network of veins.

Spinach Choose smaller, more tender spinach leaves for salads. Be sure to wash thoroughly, in several changes of water, to eliminate all dirt and sand.

Watercress Refreshing, slightly peppery, dark-green leaf vegetable sometimes found in freshwater streams.

Molasses Thick, robust-tasting, syrupy by-product of sugarcane refining, a procedure that may or may not include the use of sulfur. Light molasses results from the first boiling of the syrup; dark molasses from the second boiling.

Mustard Pale in color, fairly hot, and sharp tasting, Dijon mustard is made in Dijon, France, from dark brown mustard seeds (unless otherwise marked blanc) and white wine or wine vinegar. Coarse-grained mustards, also referred to as whole-grain mustards, have a granular texture due to roughly ground mustard seeds.

Nuts Rich and mellow in flavor, crisp and crunchy in texture, a wide variety of nuts complements both sweet and savory recipes. For the best selection, look in specialty-food shops, health-food stores, or the food market baking section. Toasting brings out the full flavor and aroma of nuts. To toast nuts, preheat the oven to 325°F (165°C). Spread the nuts in a single layer on a baking sheet and bake until they are fragrant and just beginning to change color, 5–10 minutes. Remove from the oven, transfer immediately to a plate, and let cool to room temperature. Toasting also loosens the skins of nuts such as hazelnuts and walnuts, which may be removed by wrapping the still-warm nuts in a clean kitchen towel and rubbing them with the palms of your hands.

Olive Oil Extra-virgin olive oil, extracted from olives on the first pressing without use of heat or chemicals, is preferred for salads and other dishes in which its fruity taste is desired. The higher-priced extra-virgin olive oils usually are of better quality.

Port Robust fortified wine from Portugal, often sweet. Sipped on its own usually at the end of the meal, Port can also be used to flavor fruit desserts or sauces.

Puff Pastry Form of pastry in which pastry dough and butter or some other solid fat are repeatedly layered to form thin leaves that puff up to flaky lightness when baked. Commercially manufactured frozen puff pastry is available in well-stocked markets.

Rum Any of a wide variety of spirits distilled from sugarcane or molasses, a specialty of the Caribbean. So-called light or white rums are clear, fairly flavorless spirits; dark or Demerara rums carry some of the caramel color and distinctive flavor of their sources.

Salt, Coarse or Kosher Kosher and coarse-grained salts are well suited for use in dry and wet marinades and seasonings. Sea salt, which has a stronger, more pronounced flavor, is an acceptable substitute.

Sherry Fortified, cask-aged wine, ranging in varieties from dry to sweet, enjoyed as an aperitif and used as a flavoring in savory and sweet recipes.

Spices Many different spices add enticing flavors to both savory and sweet dishes:

Allspice Sweet spice of Caribbean origin with a flavor suggesting a blend of cinnamon, cloves, and nutmeg—hence its name. May be purchased as whole dried berries or ground.

Aniseed Sweet licorice-flavored spice of Mediterranean origin. Generally sold as whole seeds, which may be crushed with a mortar and pestle.

Cardamom Sweet, exotic-tasting spice used in Middle Eastern and Indian cooking as well as in European baking. Its small, round seeds are best purchased whole, then ground with a spice grinder or with a mortar and pestle as needed.

Cayenne Very hot ground spice derived from dried cayenne and other chile peppers.

Cinnamon The aromatic bark of a type of evergreen tree, it is sold as whole dried strips—cinnamon sticks—or ground.

Cloves Rich and aromatic East African spice used whole or in its ground form to flavor both sweet and savory recipes.

Cumin Middle Eastern spice with a strong, earthy, aromatic flavor, popular in cuisines of its region of origin along with those of Latin America, India, and parts of Europe. Sold either ground or as whole, small, crescent-shaped seeds.

Curry Powder Blends of spices used to flavor East Indian–style dishes. The most common is Madras curry powder. Buy in small quantities, because flavor diminishes rapidly after opening.

Nutmeg Baking spice that is the hard pit of the fruit of the nutmeg tree. May be bought already ground or, for fresher flavor, whole.

Oregano Aromatic, pungent, and spicy herb—also known as wild marjoram—used fresh or dried as a seasoning for all kinds of savory dishes.

Paprika Powdered spice derived from the dried paprika pepper; available in sweet, mild, and hot forms. Hungarian paprika is the best, but Spanish paprika, which is mild, may also be used. Buy in small quantities to ensure a fresh, flavorful supply.

Peppercorns Pepper, the most common of all savory spices, is best when it is purchased as whole peppercorns, to be ground in a pepper mill as needed, or coarsely crushed.

Saffron Aromatic spice, golden orange in color. Offers a delicate perfume and golden hue to baked goods. Sold either as threads or in powdered form. Look for products labeled "pure saffron."

Turmeric Pungent, earthy-flavored ground spice that, like saffron, adds a vibrant yellow color to any dish.

Sugar Several different forms of sugar may be used in holiday baked goods:

Brown Sugar Rich-tasting combination of granulated sugar and molasses (in varying quantities to yield light or dark brown sugar) with crystals varying from coarse to finely granulated.

Confectioners' Sugar Finely pulverized sugar, also known as powdered or icing sugar, which dissolves quickly and provides a thin white decorative coating. To prevent confectioners' sugar from absorbing moisture in the air and caking, manufacturers often mix a little cornstarch into it.

Granulated Sugar A widely used form of pure white sugar. Do not substitute superfine granulated sugar unless specified. In Britain, caster sugar is a good substitute for American granulated sugar.

Raw Sugar Sugar labeled "raw" is not true raw sugar, which contains too many impurities to be sold. What is labeled as raw sugar is a coarse, brownish, partially refined product that still contains the natural molasses present in sugarcane. Either turbinado sugar—coarse amber crystals that have been treated with steam to remove impurities—or demerera sugar, which is commonly found in Britain and is more highly refined that turbinado sugar, can be used in recipes calling for raw sugar.

Vanilla Bean Vanilla beans are dried aromatic pods of a variety of orchid and provide one of the most popular flavorings in dessert making. Vanilla is most commonly used as an alcohol-based extract (essence). Vanilla extract or beans from Madagascar are the best. To split open a vanilla bean and thus expose its tiny, flavorful seeds, use a small, sharp knife to cut the bean in half lengthwise.

Vermouth Dry or sweet wine commercially enhanced with herbs and barks to give it an aromatic flavor.

Vinegars Literally "sour wine," vinegar results when certain strains of yeast cause wine to ferment for a second time, turning it acidic. Red wine vinegar, like the wine from which it is made, has a more robust flavor than vinegar produced from white wine. Sherry vinegar has its own rich flavor and color reminiscent of the fortified, cask-aged aperitif wine. Balsamic vinegar, a specialty of Modena, Italy, is a vinegar made from reduced grape juice and is aged many years. Flavored vinegars are made by adding herbs such as tarragon and dill or fruits such as raspberries.

Zest The thin, brightly colored, outermost layer of a citrus fruit's peel, containing most of its aromatic essential oils— a lively source of flavor. Zest may be removed with a simple tool known as a zester drawn across the fruit's skin to remove the zest in thin strips; with a fine handheld grater; or in wide strips with a vegetable peeler or a paring knife held almost parallel to the fruit's skin. Zest removed with the latter two tools may then be thinly sliced or chopped on a cutting board.

Index

First published in the USA by Time-Life Custom Publishing.

Originally published as Williams-Sonoma Kitchen Library:
Grilling (© 1992 Weldon Owen Inc.)
Beef (© 1993 Weldon Owen Inc.)
Fish (© 1993 Weldon Owen Inc.)
Potatoes (© 1993 Weldon Owen Inc.)
Thanksgiving & Christmas (©1993 Weldon Owen Inc.)
Gifts from the Kitchen (© 1994 Weldon Owen Inc.)
Holiday Baking (©1995 Weldon Owen Inc.)
Pork & Lamb (©1995 Weldon Owen Inc.)
Shellfish (© 1995 Weldon Owen Inc.)
Cooking Basics (©1996 Weldon Owen Inc.)
Holiday Entertaining (©1996 Weldon Owen Inc.)
Healthy Cooking (© 1997 Weldon Owen Inc.)
Outdoor Cooking (© 1997 Weldon Owen Inc.)
Thanksgiving (© 1997 Weldon Owen Inc.)

In collaboration with Williams-Sonoma Inc.
3250 Van Ness Avenue, San Francisco, CA 94109

Oxmoor
House.

OXMOOR HOUSE INC.
Oxmoor House books are distributed by Sunset Books
80 Willow Road, Menlo Park, CA 94025
Telephone: 650-321-3600 Fax: 650-324-1532
Vice President/General Manager: Rich Smeby
National Accounts Manager/Special Sales: Brad Moses

Oxmoor House and Sunset Books are divisions of
Southern Progress Corporation

WILLIAMS-SONOMA INC.
Founder and Vice-Chairman: Chuck Williams

WELDON OWEN INC.
Chief Executive Officer: John Owen
President and Chief Operating Officer: Terry Newell
Creative Director: Gaye Allen
Publisher: Hannah Rahill
Associate Creative Director: Leslie Harrington
Senior Designer: Charlene Charles
Assistant Editor: Donita Boles
Editorial Assistant: Juli Vendzules
Production Director: Chris Hemesath
Production Coordinator: Libby Temple
Color Manager: Teri Bell

Williams-Sonoma Holiday Favorites was conceived and
produced by Weldon Owen Inc.
814 Montgomery Street, San Francisco, CA 94133
Copyright © 2004 Weldon Owen Inc.
and Williams-Sonoma Inc.

First printed in 2004.
10 9 8 7 6 5 4

ISBN 13: 978-0-8487-2800-7
ISBN 10: 0-8487-2800-9

Printed in China by SNP Leefung Printers Ltd.

CREDITS
Authors: Lora Brody: Pages 50, 90, 154, 196, 225, 316 (Applesauce);
Joyce Goldstein: Pages 61, 62, 89, 92, 314 (Beef Stock); Kristine Kidd:
Pages 17, 19, 20, 23, 29, 38, 44, 45, 47, 52, 58, 67, 75, 82, 107, 112, 123,
124, 125, 127, 143, 146, 152, 153, 166, 168, 177, 178, 189, 202, 220, 235,
254, 266, 270, 272, 275, 277, 279, 280, 283, 285, 286, 289, 298, 301, 302,
303, 304, 307, 308, 309, 311, 312; Norman Kolpas: Pages 24, 64, 120, 140,
159; Jacqueline Mallorca: Page 88; John Phillip Carroll: Pages 30, 68, 71,
79, 97, 314 (Roasted Vegetable Stock); Diane Rossen Worthington:
Pages 14, 51, 95, 136, 142, 150, 162, 244; Jeanne Thiel Kelley: Pages 103,
104, 108, 114, 184, 186, 190, 191, 193, 194, 199, 200, 201, 205, 206, 209,
210, 211, 212, 214, 217, 218, 219, 228, 236, 238, 240, 243, 247, 248, 251,
252, 253, 257, 258, 259, 261, 263, 264, 265, 317 (Tart & Pie Pastry,
Bittersweet Chocolate Ganache), 318 (Buttercream Frosting), 319
(Vanilla Pastry Cream, White Icing); Joanne Weir: Pages 18, 41, 42, 63,
80, 222, 231, 315 (Herbed Bread Crumbs); Chuck Williams: Pages 33,
34, 37, 48, 55, 72, 73, 76, 85, 86, 94, 98, 111, 117, 118, 128, 131, 132, 139,
145, 149, 156, 161, 165, 170, 171, 172, 180, 181, 183, 232, 233, 239, 246,
262, 314 (Chicken or Turkey Stock), 315 (Chicken or Turkey Gravy),
316 (Apple-Orange Cranberry Sauce, Apple-Mint Chutney), 317
(Minted Cranberry Sauce), 318 (Lemon Whipped Cream, Ginger or
Orange Saboyan Cream), 319 (Brandy Butter Sauce, Poached Orange
Slices).

Photographers: Noel Barnhurst (front cover), Allan Rosenberg (recipe
photography), and Chris Shorten (recipe photography for page 88).

ACKNOWLEDGMENTS
Weldon Owen would like to thank Desne Ahlers, Linda
Bouchard, Carrie Bradley, Ken DellaPenta, Jonathan Kauffman,
Karen Kemp, Joan Olson, Kari Ontko, Lorna Strutt, and Sharon
Silva for all their expertise, assistance, and hard work.

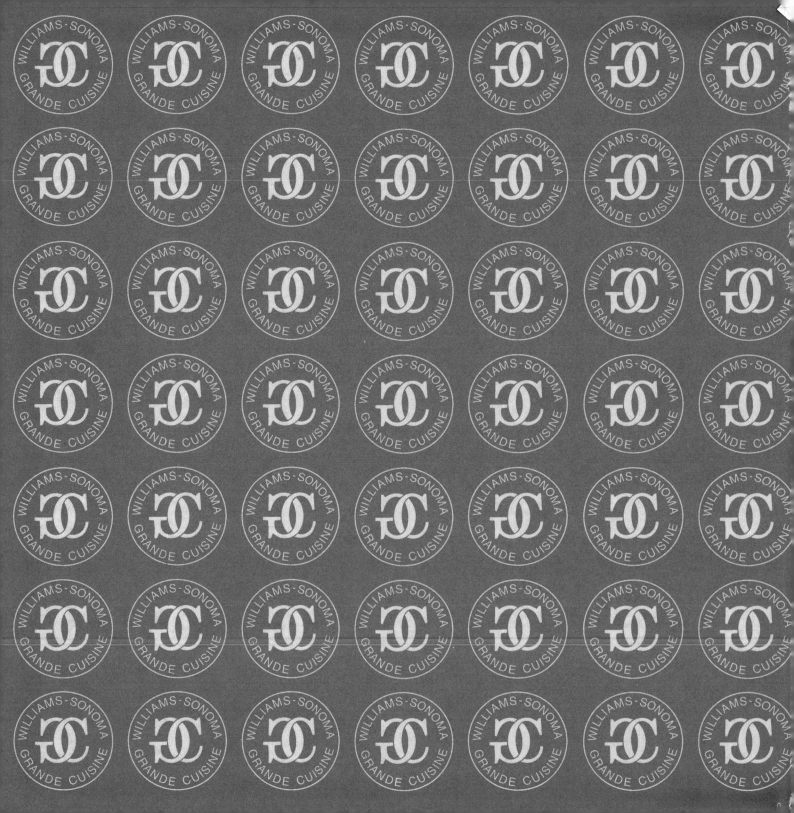